Also by Judy Oppenheimer

Private Demons: The Life of Shirley Jackson

DREAMS OF GLORY

A MOTHER'S SEASON WITH HER SON'S HIGH SCHOOL FOOTBALL TEAM

JUDY OPPENHEIMER

SUMMIT BOOKS

New York London Toronto Sydney Tokyo Singapore

SUMMIT BOOKS
Simon & Schuster Building
Rockefeller Center
1230 Avenue of the Americas
New York, New York, 10020

SUMMIT BOOKS and colophon are trademarks
of Simon & Schuster Inc.

Designed by Irving Perkins Assoc.
Manufactured in the United States of America

1   2   3   4   5   6   7   8   9   10

Library of Congress Cataloging in Publication Data

Oppenheimer, Judy, date.
Dreams of Glory : a mother's season with her son's high school
football team / Judy Oppenheimer.
p.   cm.
1. Bethesda-Chevy Chase High School—Football—Case studies.
2. Football—Social aspects—Maryland—Bethesda—Case studies.
3. Oppenheimer, Judy   I. Title
GV958.B48067   1991
796.332'62'09753—dc20   91-19435
CIP

ISBN 0-671-68754-9

ACKNOWLEDGMENTS

I KNEW FROM THE START that in order to write about a high school football season I would have to be vitally dependent on the time, energy, generosity, and descriptive powers of others. How else to discover exactly what was being said, done, and most important, felt, on the field, in the locker room, on the way to practice? For it was the inner core of the season, the subtle shifts, the inner changes, the emotions, which fascinated me. I wanted, as much as possible, to get inside the minds and hearts of the participants, and for that, I needed their help.

Thankfully I got it, beyond my wildest hopes. Parents, coaches, and boys were overwhelmingly open, willing to share feelings, to pinpoint moments of shift in perception, to recall interchanges on and off the field with amazing clarity—and to spend hours answering my questions. I am eternally grateful to them all, especially to coaches Pete White, Mitch Babashan, and Bob Plante, who willingly gave me long stretches of time, week after week. But the deepest debt by far is owed to the boys themselves. Any value this book has is directly attributable to their honesty, their insight, their courage, their humor, their talent for self-revelation, their unbelievable generosity of spirit. Claims of objectivity are rarely persuasive; it is far wiser, I have always felt, to simply state one's own prejudices up front, simply and honestly. For the record, then—

though I think it's probably obvious from the first paragraph—here are mine: I love all these kids very much.

Inevitably, there are scenes and conversations recorded here that I did not personally witness. Whenever possible, these have been corroborated by more than one source; in the vast majority of cases, several sources. The very nature of the project—I could not, after all, don pads and helmet and insert myself directly into the fray, not without grossly changing the nature of the thing I was trying to study—ensured that I could not be on hand for every exchange. When I could be present, I was; when not, the boys and coaches took me there.

As always, my debts are legion—to the friends and family who not only encouraged me but let me talk about football endlessly for months without screaming; to my sons, Jesse and Toby, for being such good guys; to Jerry, who was enthusiastic about the project from beginning to end; to my pal David Perel, a former sportswriter who indoctrinated me, patiently and painstakingly, into the world of football terminology; to the fantastic pizza at Il Forno, which accompanied many interviews, adding so much to the general atmosphere (at least ten extra pounds at last count).

Thanks are also due to my editor, Dominick Anfuso, whose probing, insightful queries not only pushed me to greater depth but vastly improved the final manuscript. And to Flip Brophy, for being herself—agent, friend, supporter, and all around rare jewel.

For all the boys' parents, but especially
Carole, Matt, Judy L., Judy B., Jo-Ann and Sal—
for our glorious Chevy Chase Lounge roundtables.

1988 BETHESDA/CHEVY CHASE BATTLIN' BARONS

FRONT ROW (*left to right*): M. Bitz, K. Bae, B. Reed, B. Symes, B. Stone, D. Bardach, G. Smith, R. Fiscina, A. Burgess, E. Kraus, J. Everett, M. Gage, D. Thompson

MIDDLE ROW (*left to right*): S. Dempsey, J. McDonald, G. Heintz, M. Dahl, M. Mitchem, B. McPherson, J. Han, D. Duvall, R. DePeralta, T. Oppenheimer, W. Meadows, J. Loretto

BACK ROW (*left to right*): M. Noble, M. Kane, Head Coach P. White, C. Hadas, E. Karlsons, M. Calderone, R. Gutierrez, T. Kim, D. Finley, C. Dade, E. Bachman, T. Seagears, B. McReady, C. Doyle, Assistant Coach M. Babashan, Assistant Coach B. Plante, S. Efantis

PREFACE

IN THE FALL of 1987, I had just completed my first book and was waiting anxiously for critical response. Walking along a suburban street on a warm Saturday afternoon, I fell rather easily into one of those pact-with-the-devil interior dialogues familiar, I imagine, to many first-time authors.

Let's see, said a voice from inside my brain craftily. You've finished the book. You want it to do well. In fact—why lie?—you would prefer that everyone who reads it loves it wildly, that it be received with a blast of critical acclaim, that it bring you fame—not just ordinary fame, but the sort that causes every person in the world who ever bought you a soda in the past to realize, with terrible poignancy, what a jewel they lost. That kind of fame. You want it. The question is, how much?

Would you (the voice pursued) prefer that the book do wonderfully, or that everyone you love has a happy, healthy life? Choose.

Happiness all around, of course, came the prompt response. Much too easy; a ridiculous choice.

Fine, we'll narrow it down, then. The book does well—or everyone in your immediate family has a good year?

Again, reaction was swift—the year, naturally. One good year for everyone was too much to give up.

9

Okay, the voice persisted, a bit testily. The book does well, or your oldest son, away at college for the first time, has an enjoyable first semester. Just that.

Another strikeout. Not even tempting. Hey, I'd spent eighteen years on him; naturally his welfare was going to be more important than my book, right?

By this time my husband and I were walking down the narrow path that led to the high school football stadium. We had gotten close enough to hear the band. ALL RIGHT, said the voice inside, now thoroughly disgusted. We'll make it real easy, okay? The book does well—or they win this game?

And to my amazement—to the complete shock of my entire system—the answer came roaring back, unmistakable. I WANT US TO WIN THIS GAME!

The force of that realization was almost physical; there was no underestimating its validity. What was going on here? Somehow, in some unknown way, a team of high school football players had become so important to me that I was willing to throw away my own success, at least figuratively, to ensure theirs. Not just willing—eager! There was no way to minimize that reaction.

I was not being swept away by the moment. We had not even reached the stadium yet; the band was barely audible. Nor was it mother ego. My own son, a first-year player, would be on the sidelines for the whole game, I knew. No, it was something else that had me in its grip, as fiercely powerful as it was mysterious. What the hell could it be?

And I knew then that I would have to find out.

There are those who grow up in homes where serious attention is given to lobbing, spiking, swinging, and dunking. I wasn't one of them. I had almost nothing to do with the world of sports as a kid; I was insulated by gender, by a largely female family—two sisters, six aunts, a mass of girl cousins—by the bookish atmosphere of my own home, and by the times themselves—the fifties. My mother had fond memories of basketball and tennis games she had played in the thirties; by the late seventies, girls would once again start showing up on the fields. My age group fell between the cracks. Then, too, there was my own physiology: a case of scoliosis that

kicked in at age twelve, a sudden awkward growth spurt at fourteen, that left me with even less grace than before. Which had not
been much.

But there was something more subterranean at work, too, an
attitude I had somehow incorporated, a very real sense that such
matters were not serious, not for real minds, not worthy of true
attention. Or was it just that they were truly foreign, and so not for
me, in the way junior cotillions were not? A lingering mind set,
legacy of my Eastern European immigrant grandparents? For there
were older members of the family, my grandmother, for instance,
who still divvied up the world sharply into Jewish and non-Jewish
sectors, and sports definitely fell in the latter category.

Whatever the reason, no baseball or football games ever poured
out of the console radio in our living room, or later, out of the small
black and white TV. No RBIs or ERAs were discussed at our table.
As long as I lived at home I never once attended a professional
game of any kind. This was a world we did not move in, which
therefore, in the inherent logic of childhood, did not exist.

Right away I think of an exception. My aunt and uncle in Queens
had allowed, even encouraged, their children to catch the baseball
fever rampant in their city. Perhaps surer of their place, Jews who
had not settled in the diaspora of suburban Northern Virginia, as
we had, and perhaps, also, because they had finally produced a son,
they did attend to scores and sports announcers, and one summer
day I even went with my cousin Ellen to the Polo Grounds to
watch the New York Giants. The experience elated me: I was
entranced by the green turf, the bat's crack, the soaring ball, even
while feeling like an impostor. My knowledge of the game was
slight, but the scene itself charged me with emotion, an excitement
similar to the one I would later feel watching Elvis appear on
television. There was a danger, a freedom, a force at work here, and
yes, it did have a sexual—or at any rate, highly male—component.
For a time I even attempted, self-consciously, to attend to scores
and ratings, but this interest withered quickly back home.

Other than that one small frisson, though, the door seemed
permanently closed to a world I never thought I wanted or missed.
I attended a few high school games, rarely even glancing at the
field—for me these were social events only. In college my post-Beat
pre-hippie circle viewed all sports and sportsmen with contempt,

and if any whiff of sour grapes emanated from the intense young men I knew, I was not the one to recognize it. Eventually I did begin to notice that most men seemed to like to watch football games, but this I took as one of those inexplicable quirks of the sex. Actually I did not believe for a minute they really enjoyed them; I was cynically sure this was something they felt they had to do, for peculiar Freudian reasons best left unexplored. Sports remained a mystery—not one I had any interest in piercing, not one I ever expected I would. By the time I reached adulthood, my own opinions were solidly in place: athletes were fools, nonintellectuals, macho jerks. Sports were ridiculous. Parents who cheered themselves hoarse at games, getting vicarious thrills, were especially repulsive.

Then life, as it often does, threw me a curve. I gave birth to boys, not girls. Yes, I raised them in that supremely feminist-conscious decade the seventies, doing my best to introduce them to dolls and peace toys and artistic pursuits. And no, it didn't make any difference. I gave birth to boys; inevitably, sports began to seep into my life. I found myself at hockey arenas, basketball courts, baseball stadiums. It wasn't my idea, of course; it was theirs. Left to my own devices, I would have continued wheeling them through art galleries, as I had when they were tiny and compliant—but what parent is ever left to her own devices?

So we went to games. And the realization began to grow— slowly, slowly—that there might be something to this stuff after all. Standing at one arena or another, the roars of the crowd washing over me, I found myself responding almost despite myself to the pure drama of the thing, the way each event followed a familiar pattern, yet was fraught with endless possibilities—for heroics, for tragedy—like the best theater. Of course, none of this was personal—yet. But that was coming.

Both my boys were active youngsters, but Toby, the younger, seemed to have an especial zest for the physical right from the start. At four months he wore out the springs on his baby jumper; at nine months he was climbing up the table, to the stove, to the top of the refrigerator, regularly and relentlessly. Jesse, my older, loved to listen to me read books aloud. With Toby, I was literally forced to act them out with him strenuously, if I wanted to keep his attention. Both boys enjoyed the tire swing in our backyard, but only Toby spent an entire summer on it—he was three at the time, and accuracy forces me to add, stark naked.

There was no question of hyperactivity—amazingly, since those were the years they were pinning that label on everyone. No, the kid just liked to keep moving. What was most striking though was the amount of control he seemed to have over his body. Even as our hearts jumped to our throats, several times a day, watching or grabbing for him, it finally began to dawn on us that he almost never got hurt. He seemed to go at nearly every physical endeavor with a kind of inherent grace. Not quite two, he grabbed a Frisbee for the first time and, ignoring our instructions, sent it flying in a perfect arc. When, a few months later, he picked up a whiffle-ball bat, we stared at each other in shock. Feet apart, knees bent, he had automatically assumed a perfect batter's stance.

What was going on here? Unlikely as it seemed, impossible as it seemed, had we produced some kind of . . . athlete?

With that realization, my entire prejudice against sports began to crumble. Within a few short years I was standing on a soccer field making an utter fool of myself, screaming my head off in the best tradition. What had happened? It was obvious even to me. Toby had thrown open the door to a world I had never known I missed. All along, it seemed, I had been missing it like crazy.

My husband, it is important to mention, did not react like this, not at all. A sedentary man, he enjoyed throwing an occasional ball to his sons, he watched sports on television with them, he could now and then be persuaded to attend a baseball game. But he regarded my enthusiasm for Toby's personal athletic involvement with distaste—his wife, who had passed herself off for years as a serious, thoughtful person, had apparently been harboring a secret all this time. What she'd really wanted, it turned out, was to be a cheerleader.

Yet this reaction bothered me not at all. For I knew my enthusiasm to be oddly impersonal, in a way. I enjoyed, tremendously, discovering this energetic new world and was grateful to Toby for opening the gate. After all, I had begun to realize by now that this was a major perk of parenthood: children took you places you had never been before. You were a fool, I figured, not to enjoy the ride.

At the same time, though, I knew I had no deep urge to see Toby on the cover of *Sports Illustrated*. I had seen too many parents taken over by their kids' talents to a dangerous degree. A boy down the street was being groomed to be a tennis champion, daily and arduously. Sports were fun in their place, that was enough. Toby was a warm, open, delightful kid; sports were a part of his joy, and I enjoyed sharing it. But serious?

Over the years I cheered his soccer, basketball, and baseball endeavors. Yet I knew he was a team animal, quintessentially—practically the only physical activities he avoided were running, biking, and swimming, activities generally done alone. So perhaps it was not a complete surprise that he finally gravitated, quite late, at age sixteen, to the king of all team sports: football.

Football, however, was another matter. Football terrified me. Everything I had ever felt about sports, pre-motherhood, went triple for football. My revulsion, my distaste, my horror, all ran deeper. I had never taken the kids to football games; I didn't even like to be around when my husband and sons occasionally watched them on TV, venting the horribly coarse, macho noises the game seemed to demand. Football was not an arena for casual enjoyment, for joy. Football was a sport for killers. I had always been glad we lived in a suburb, Chevy Chase, Maryland, where most families steered their kids firmly toward soccer when they were growing up; far fewer played Peewee football, which was viewed by many with suspicion, if not contempt, a sport with a brutish, even blue-collar, cast to it. A person could get hurt doing that. As my *bubbe* would have put it, what does a Jewish person need with football?

Soccer and baseball were fun; football had always struck me as a grim and joyless business. All that bulky equipment, all those tense bodies smashing into each other with such lethal purpose. What would playing such a game do to my child? What would happen to that warm and joyous spirit out there on that killing field?

But at sixteen, already six feet two inches tall, Toby was no longer a child—that was obvious. When he announced his intention to try out for the team at Bethesda–Chevy Chase High School, urged on by one of his closest friends, Billy Stone, a veteran player, we were faced, yet again, with one of parenthood's most difficult and constant balancing acts: the eternal seesaw between protective urges (we'd always had more than our share) and the desire to see one's child emerge as an independent being. In the end, teeth clenched, we voted for independence.

Nervous, edgy, I showed up each week that first season to see the games, getting my first close look at the sport I'd despised for forty-five years. And in the process, of course—human perversity being what it is—discovered what I really felt. No way to dodge it—I was insane about football. More than soccer, more than basketball, more than any sport I had ever come in contact with, I purely adored the entire wild, maddened, electric, power-pumping totality of this game. Football unleashed something primitive buried deep inside me, something that had obviously always been there, waiting to spring to life. A coach would later tell me at length about the need to unearth the buried animal when training players, the animal that lies dormant in our soul. Well, football released my animal, too. Even that epiphany should have come as no surprise, really—I had known from the start that this game exerted a powerful pull on my heart.

I had no illusions that this was the same force that had fueled my pleasure standing on soccer sidelines for so many years. No, there was something darker and infinitely more powerful about this enthusiasm; it swept you up, took you over completely. And yet my reaction did not come as a total surprise. More than midway through the journey of our life, years into the humbling thicket of parenthood, I suppose I had finally come to acknowledge the terrible truism: while what you despise may not *always* be what you secretly love, it is invariably a big mistake not to cover the bet.

And the truth was, Toby's first year on the team made it easy on us. Yes, us, because to my amazement, my husband too seemed suddenly interested; no one had to beg him to go to games anymore. As a first-year player, our son was rarely on the field; his safety seemed insured. I could yell and scream for harder hits, rougher play, to my heart's content—hey, it wasn't my kid out there.

But all the time, throughout the 1987 season and the rest of the school year, I could hear the muffled drums drawing closer. His time, I knew, was coming. The next season, my son, too, would be on the line.

And I wanted him there! That was the most shocking part. I wanted to see him big, looming, triumphant—the warrior. What scared me was that God was going to punish me for taking pleasure in his risks, but what chilled me even more was something else. If this was how I was about football, how would it be if one of my sons were marching into combat? Along with the icy horror, would I also feel a heart-leaping thrill? Good God, would it turn out after all this time that I loved war too? The famous scene from *Patton* swam in my head—the one where the general kisses a fallen soldier on the battlefield, saying huskily, "I love it more than life." Repulsive, I had thought at the time—or at least, had *thought* I thought. Was Patton, of all people, going to turn out to be *mon semblable, mon frère*? If so, I was in real trouble.

My embrace of sports, but particularly football, and most particularly this coming season, had led me finally to this pass . . . murky waters, indeed. I found myself feeling deeply jealous of other parents of team players—both those who were frankly opposed to their sons' playing and those who were frankly, unapologetically, excited and happy. Only I, it seemed, was caught up in the barbed wire of ambivalence, twisting slowly in the wind.

I needed to examine more closely both my own feelings about the game and its effect on all involved—coaches, parents, and boys.

Particularly the boys. For over the years I had been raising my own sons, I had come to realize something—that sports, in some bone-deep, almost mythic, way, has much to do with what forms a man. True, only a handful of boys play football, basketball, or baseball, even in high school—but this does not matter. The sports ethic is in the language they speak, the air they breathe, the business and professional arenas they enter. Aware or not, players or not, their views of themselves and the world are formed by sports.

And I wanted to know how that worked, to know more about this process, and the ways it changed and affected men. For it had, I had come to realize, affected them all.

Shortly before the football season began, my father told me a story. As a young teenager in the late twenties, he had lived with his older sister in the Bronx for a year, attending Yeshiva classes. The schedule was grueling, with a school day that ended at nightfall, too late for play. But every morning, my father and a few of his friends gathered early, before six o'clock, to play baseball in a neighborhood sandlot. Once and only once, up at bat, he hit the ball with the pure, total impact of a perfect slice. It rose high in the air, cleared the fence, and dropped to the gray dawn streets far below.

That was over sixty years ago. Yet sometimes still even now, when he is drifting off to sleep, he has a sharp vision. He sees the ball coming toward him again, he swings, he hears the crack of that connection, sees the ball arc high in the air, out of sight. Peace falls over him. He sleeps.

My father has never in his adult life participated in a sport. He has rarely attended a professional game. He is a learned man who nurtured learning in his daughters, imprinting each of us with a deep respect for the life of the mind, in part because we knew this was his world, and we loved him. It was his world, true enough. But it was not, as it turns out, the whole story.

Yet my father never told me about that one moment until I was middle-aged—and the mother of a football player. Maybe he thought that would help me understand certain things—why he never missed one of his grandson's games, why he took such pleasure watching him play. Or maybe not. He simply handed me the story without comment; another piece of the puzzle. A piece I had not known was missing.

For it had never been just sports that was a mystery to me growing up . . . it was men as well. And in an odd way, I had always been loath to pierce that veil, too. Mystery can fuel romance, even passion; mystery lends itself to endless Heathcliff-Cathy scenarios, and I had certainly done my share of howling on the moors. But the time had come. My sons had been babies, then little boys, but the years had passed, their bodies had lengthened and hardened, childhood had ebbed. They were landing on another shore now, one I still, after all the years of marriage and motherhood, knew little about. They were becoming men. It was time, past time, to learn something about that world.

I was determined to start. I would spend the next season, the season of 1988, with my son's team, the B-CC Barons, watching carefully, a visitor to a foreign land, talking to coaches, parents, but most of all to the boys. Attending, noting, recording the changes they went through on the way to becoming football players—and the changes I went through myself. I would listen, learn, and then write about all of it. Only by writing, I knew, could I come to any real understanding.

Once the idea had seized me, I became obsessed, talking about it to everyone. There was only one negative reaction, but unfortunately, it came from Toby. "Mom, the locker room? You'll be in the locker room?" he groaned. He had a point, and I knew it; how could I do that to him? Liberation or no, freedom of the press or not, what seventeen-year-old wants his mother hanging around a locker room? Years ago his brother, then ten, saw a piece I had written in *The Village Voice,* liberally sprinkled with his quotes; he was enraged. "You do that again and you pay me—that's me in there, not you," he said with icy dignity. And I knew he was right. Using your kids in your writing could be a form of betrayal . . . could be, well, using your kids. No writer can completely avoid using the people she knows and loves in her work, but it's a fine line, always. When does use become abuse? If Toby felt that strongly, I would respect his wishes.

Months went by; the season got under way, with myself in close attendance, working for the Booster Club, getting to know the parents, coaches, and boys, hanging around the field with elaborate casualness, even—I couldn't help it—taking notes, a little furtively. I was, I had to admit, consumed by this idea still, despite Toby's opposition. Who knew? Perhaps when he was forty, he would change his mind.

It happened long before that, however. "If you're still interested in doing that book, it's okay now," he said casually one day. Still interested? It was, in fact, the only thing I wanted to do.

Certainly it was a challenge—one that made me feel anxious, fearful, and thrilled. I was going to chart the progress of a season, of boys becoming players. I had a quick vision of myself being lowered, in a Jacques Cousteau sort of bubble, to the bottom of the sea. It was unknown territory I was descending into, without question. But it was a voyage I had been moving toward for years.

It was not until I was well on my way that I realized that the boys themselves had a name for this process I was trying to learn about so avidly, a name for the entire alchemy involved in becoming a football player—and more. A name so fitting there was no way I could ever have improved on it. They call it "being the man."

CHAPTER ONE

THE AIR in the high school weight room hung heavy as glue, as if the entire August heat wave plaguing the area had been balled up and stuffed into a tight space the size of a holding cell. Walking in it hit you like a fist, solid, dense, unwieldy as a weight mat. Yet no one complained. When you walked over that threshold, you left your complaints outside. It was as simple as that, and every boy knew it.

This was the first day of football practice, August 18, 1988, and the boys entering that room were prepared to take a great deal of discomfort. They were ready to suck up bad air, to work out long hours, push their bodies to the limit. Whatever it took. They were about to begin the training that would turn them into the 1988 varsity football team of Bethesda–Chevy Chase High School—the B-CC Barons. They squared their shoulders and entered the room.

On the face of it, their school and its environs made an unlikely backdrop for a football season. Located two miles over the Washington, D.C., line, in the heart of downtown Bethesda, Maryland, B-CC was all but lost in a jumbled terrain of towering office buildings, apartment complexes, fast-food joints, frenetic traffic jams, and endless building construction—the tortured landscape of runaway development.

All this was relatively new. Not long before, downtown Bethesda had been a modest collection of small stores running along a strip of Wisconsin Avenue, many of them unchanged for decades: an ancient Woolworth's that boasted one of the last remaining soda fountains in the entire area, a 100-year-old hardware store still run by the descendants of the original owners. But the prospect, and eventual reality, of a subway station right at the center of town—Wisconsin Avenue and East West Highway—had knocked Bethesda on its ear. Developers cooed seductively, were given the go-ahead by a starry-eyed planning council, and promptly ran amok, totaling the town. There was barely an inch of downtown Bethesda that had not been leveled, dug out, and built on. In Washington, no structure could be built higher than the Monument. Bethesda had no such rules. You could not have seen the Monument, had it been nearby; you could barely, at this point, make out the sky.

Not football country, this, not by a long shot. Football country was far away, out there in the small, dusty towns of Florida, Texas, Pennsylvania, towns scarcely changed from the fifties, where entire populations turned out religiously for Friday night games at the local high school stadiums.

Bethesda had never been such a town, even before its metamorphosis into concrete jungle. Hearts here did not automatically beat faster on Friday nights during high school football season. Whole segments of the population were untouched by it—high school football made no difference in their lives. A town of white-collar professionals, this one—career junkies, men and women who dashed out the door at 6:30 A.M. and headed into the city, leaving the suburban streets to kids and maids and retirees. Maybe if anyone had stuck around during the day to object, the developers wouldn't have gotten such a free ride.

The boys now entering the weight room were not slated to be the pro players of tomorrow, either. They were hothouse flowers, sprung from the most affluent, overeducated soil in the country; some said the world: Montgomery County, Maryland, a place where the average adult education level included at least a year of graduate school. These boys had options; they were headed for professions, headed for power—high school football was a minor byroad on their route.

Or by all rights should have been. There was no reason, logically, for them to have spent time preparing, longing, dreaming for this day, the official start of the season. No point at all for them to yearn for it—impatient, tense, eager—as the most important, anxiously awaited event in their lives. Logically, it made no sense. But then, logic had nothing to do with it.

The boys were having the dubious honor of starting their season in the midst of one of the worst summers in many years. August in Washington was always hellish; August 1988 approached the Machiavellian. It was times like these that you remembered the city had originally been built on a swamp. The unbroken daily string of temperatures over 90 degrees, the constant 98 percent humidity rate, all contributed to the inescapable sense that the swamp had risen like a live thing to throw a stranglehold over the city, reclaiming it in a thick, sodden, choking embrace.

Yet, bad as it was, the weather was not the worst problem facing the area that summer. Washington was a city under siege in August 1988—in the past few months it had made a jump from a city of moderately stable criminal statistics to the murder capital of the world. The body count rose daily in a terrifying spiral—four slayings over a seven-hour period on July 20; six murders on August 12. Statistically, so far, there had been more murders than days in the year.

Crack was the reason, overwhelmingly; the vast majority of the murder victims were either direct or crossfire casualties of shootouts between drug dealers. Once word had gotten out that crack could be sold for a higher price here than in New York, rival gangs had swarmed into town to divvy up the market. Only no one wanted to divvy—they wanted it all, and the free-enterprise system had rarely been so lethal. Arguments raged. Why was D.C. getting hit so much harder than everywhere else? One answer seemed to be that since government had always been the major industry here, organized crime had never gotten much of a foothold—without such a structure to hold free agents in check, the violence had spun out of control. Even the police had come to the dismal point of hoping that, sooner or later, one gang would overcome the rest and order would be restored.

Nearly all the murders took place in what was known as the

Other Washington, east of Rock Creek Park, "the place that tourists don't see," as Mayor Barry pointed out. That didn't stop anyone from feeling uneasy, though. Washington is a small city; Bethesda is barely twenty minutes from the White House—and even closer to some of the city's worst blocks. "Hang out on them corners," late local talk show host Petey Greene had warned once, "and tomorrow isn't promised to you."

In August 1988 in Washington, dangerous corners suddenly seemed to stretch everywhere.

Heat, crack, rising homicide rates, plagued many East Coast cities that August. But Washingtonians knew they had it worse. More heat, more murder, more nerves at the breaking point. Then, midway through the month, a series of swift, brutal thunderstorms tore explosively into the area, bringing no relief from the heat but leaving some 100,000 homes without power for days.

The majority of those homes were in the Bethesda–Chevy Chase area. Most of their owners could well afford to be away from the area during this time of year, and many of them were. But not all—a number of families had been forced back to town in the middle of the worst month of the worst Washington summer in years, and there they stayed.

These were the families of the prospective Baron team members. In their homes, the date of August 18 had a preternatural significance. Preseason football training began on this date. Since no slack was given to latecomers, it was imperative that the boys be there. The rule was iron-clad; there was no excuse. And so their families stayed in town. Grim, whining, miserable, and, since the storms, without even the modern-day balm of air-conditioning. But stuck.

Every varsity football training program starts in August. For two weeks before the beginning of school, at a time when the rest of the world, it often seems, is lolling on beaches, football players begin the grueling process known as two-a-days—two practices daily, morning and afternoon; a fiendish combination of training, orientation, indoctrination, drill, discipline, and plain physical punishment. No other high school activity demands anything like this sort of commitment from male adolescents; wisely, perhaps, since it is unlikely any other activity would be able to get it. Football demands it; football gets it. Football is different.

The boys entering the weight room knew, by and large, what they were getting into. There are rarely any novices on varsity teams. The next two weeks would involve pain: headaches, muscle cramps, nausea. There was a good chance they would involve actual injury as well; the vast majority of football injuries take place during practice, not games. No one expected to get hurt—injuries were for other guys—but the pain, that was a certainty. Yet they were ready. They would suck it up, just like the air, and be—the coaches would say so, anyway—the better for it.

Only a handful of boys, all seniors, entered the door with the unique swagger that denoted their awareness they had reached the rarest of all high school football strata—an insured starting position. Two boys made their entries with a special flourish—Rick Fiscina, the returning quarterback and the leading passer in the county last year; and Geoff Smith, the gangling wide receiver. These were the team's two full-fledged, acknowledged stars, responsible for more than one explosion of magic on the field last season. Everyone assumed this would be their year, but these expectations were mild next to those of Rick and Geoff themselves. Confidence and energy radiated off both of them in giant waves; they bestrode the crowd like adolescent colossi, greeting other boys, working the room like a pair of seasoned politicos. Both had prepared for this day by having the letters B-CC etched clearly in their scalps. Rick had taken it one step further, emptying a bottle of peroxide over his dark hair.

Alex Burgess, another returning veteran, who would be heading up the offensive line, watched them from the side, his green eyes amused. Alex was a more contemplative type, a student of military strategy who took his leadership role seriously. He would be the one imposing discipline on the new offensive line this year, a difficult task, but the prospect pleased him. Alex knew he was good at imposing discipline, at least on others. For himself—Alex shifted his six-foot-three-inch body uncomfortably. His weight, always a problem, had shot up past 300 pounds over the summer. All that fat wasn't making the air in the room any easier to take.

Others waited in the room more tensely. They knew the next few weeks would be the proving ground. This would be their only opportunity to show the coaches they could do the job. If they were not able to earn a position by the end of the month, the chances that they would do much playing during the ten-week season were slim to none. Seniors knew they had a better chance at making it, simply by dint of being seniors, yet this in itself was not enough to make them relax completely—several of the juniors had already developed reputations on the junior varsity team, and how much more humiliating to lose your position to a younger man. Seniors eyed juniors warily that first day: How much do I have to worry about these guys?

Toby Oppenheimer, in particular, was feeling some trepidation. A tall kid, almost as tall as Alex, his black hair closely cropped, he looked the image of the vigorous high school jock, the kind of guy who made a coach's eyes light up. At the moment, though, he was feeling about as vigorous as a beached jellyfish. He had barely recovered from the mononucleosis that had flattened him over the summer. He hadn't even been able to take it easy—he'd had to pull himself out of bed every morning to go to summer school; either that or kiss football good-bye. Well, he'd done it, gotten up every day, hardest thing he'd ever done, and now he was here. A little shaky still, sure, but, hey, he'd made it, hadn't he? Things could only get better.

James McDonald, on the other hand, was feeling nothing but self-assurance. And why not? He'd earned it. Once a scrawny kid, he'd spent his summer systematically working out with weights, for hours every day. The result was undeniable, particularly from the waist up. James had turned himself into a Black Mr. America poster. Ebony muscles bulged impressively from his T-shirt. Sure, he didn't have an insured position yet, but what coach could resist? He flexed himself happily, basking in some of the other guys' reactions. "Good God, James, you're a machine!" one hooted over to him. James just grinned.

Nervous, eager, and sweaty, the boys gathered. All were young, sixteen or seventeen; most were fairly fit; every face was charged with anticipation. Other than that, there were few clear-cut similarities between them. They were a motley crew of adolescents, this group, a grab bag of sizes, shapes, and complexions. Most teams in the area and, in fact, throughout the country were made up of either all white, all black, or an even-handed black-white mix of players. Often, too, the boys were of a similar height and weight, lending the sort of geometric precision to their lineup that warmed coaches' hearts.

A B-CC Barons lineup, however, would have looked like a zig-zag, from a low of five-six up to Alex Burgess's strapping six-three and right back down again—there just weren't that many big kids on the team. A true international flavor pervaded the group as well. At least five of the boys had foreign accents; the team included Jamaican, Hungarian, Chinese, and Korean natives. Two more had immigrant parents, from France and Yugoslavia; one was the grandson of a Holocaust survivor. There were even a few pedigreed Wasp types, to round it out—one boy was the direct descendant of a signer of the Declaration of Independence, another the grandson of a genuine World War II hero who had received the ultimate accolade: immortalization in a comic strip.

The boys' coloring reflected the variety of their roots. They were a crazy quilt of hues, an adolescent Rainbow Coalition come to life. Skin, hair, and eyes ranged from deepest black to lightest pale, with every variation in between. With one exception—there was no redhead on the team. It seemed almost an oversight.

Over time their very diversity would give them a certain unity— eventually they would come to revel in it. "It's more American this way," one boy told me seriously—a boy who, in point of fact, had been born in Taiwan, and had not set foot in this country until he was seven. "We're all weird, we're different, we're queer!" another would chortle gleefully. "We're individuals!"

They would come to speak contemptuously of "cookie-cutter" teams in the county, like Gaithersburg and Churchill, with their overabundance of square-jawed, blond players, teams "where you think every player is the same person," as one boy said, and to draw deep satisfaction from some of the shocked looks they got when they played against them. "Hey, look, Ma—Koreans," they mimicked.

Yet in other, less visible, ways, the boys shared a vast similarity. With the exception of a few, they had grown up in solidly middle-class homes. Security was not the only given in this area—perks, too, were often assumed: large homes, two or more cars, compact-disc players, exotic vacations, generous allowances, even, in some cases, country-club membership. Most of the boys had held jobs during the summer, or the preceding school year (not, of course, during football season), but it was rare for the money earned at those jobs to go toward anything more basic than an off-meal pizza, a movie, a tank of gas. Materially almost no one was hurting—or could ever remember hurting.

Not that they were the sons of inherited wealth, not at all. Many of their parents had grown up in radically different settings—the South Boston projects; a tiny row home just off the railroad tracks in a bleak upstate New York town. No, these boys were the children of achievers—professional men and women. Both parents, in almost every case, were college graduates (our home was one of the few exceptions), and many had racked up several graduate degrees as well. A striking number, in fact, were hyphenates, East Coast style—doctor-lawyer, lawyer-accountant, architect-consultant. They were professionals, educated, achieving, articulate.

Their sons, now moving around the weight room, were not, of course—at least, not yet. They had barely begun their educations, and though every one of them, without exception, intended to go on to college, there were few honor-roll students among the group. Eligibility requirements at B-CC were simple. You were allowed the leeway of one failed course in the semester preceding football season; more than that and you needed to make it up, before you could play. The only catch was that this rule applied to quarter grades—even if you had managed to pass a course for the semester, you still needed to make up any failed quarter mark. A stumbling block that had tripped up more than one player, including Toby, my own son.

Yet academic superstars or not—and most were certainly not—the boys were nonetheless their parents' sons. Almost all saw themselves as headed toward white-collar goals, as yet undefined; each one had at least a certain respect for education, even though most believed this was something that would start in college. And all of them, every single one, were talkers.

It was not surprising. The art of communication had been taken in with mother's milk. These kids had been read to, talked to, listened to; spent their childhood swimming in a sea of words. To a man, these guys could talk; the stuff rolled off them. Furthermore, they were prime appreciators of each other in this field—

special verbal skills which developed during the season, such as one boy's dry wit, another's perceptive flashes, were honored, it often seemed, as much as a wild leap or a bone-shattering tackle. It was at least as important to Alex Burgess, for instance, to describe to me the time Rick Fiscina took "a nothing subject, public vs. private school, and did twenty minutes on it," reaching such heights of eloquence that he and another player "had actual tears in our eyes." Such things mattered to these kids, sons of their parents, children of the word.

The boys who gathered to launch the 1988 season had been born to expect a reasonable quota of comfort. Their parents had done their best to build safety nets around them. But no net can filter out every evil. Many had already been forced to deal with difficult, even harsh realities, in their lives.

A sizable number had faced the pain of their parents' divorce; others had coped with such problems as learning disabilities, a substance-abusing parent, a disturbed sibling, child abuse, or the death or desertion of a parent. Two boys, both black, had been adopted into white families; six had been ripped away from everything familiar at an early age, forced to cope with a new language, new country, new mores.

No one was to blame for most of these difficulties. They just *were*, immutable as the suffocating August heat. The fact was that over half the team members had already learned for themselves President Kennedy's famous dictum: life is unfair. They had been forced at an early age to play a difficult hand.

But there was also a group who—almost miraculously, it seemed—had so far managed to live their lives untouched by any of these problems. Boys from stable, intact families, homes in which no tragedy had ever occurred. Curiously, there was an air of innocence, almost childishness, about these boys. They were untried, they had not yet weathered any storm, and in some unconscious way the other boys sensed their vulnerability and reacted almost protectively. There was something these kids did not yet know about the world. And oddly—or was it so odd?—both Geoff and Rick, the team superstars, fell into this group.

Most of the boys knew the city of Washington well—its galleries, monuments, college bars, music clubs, Georgetown, Adams Morgan. They knew, too, that there was another part of the city, where you did not go: the war zone.

They had all done their share of silly, dangerous activities, naturally—shinnied up the six-story rock sheet next to the Georgetown steps made famous in *The Exorcist*; dived into the Potomac River from the railroad trestle near Chain Bridge; made reckless use of a golf cart lying fallow at the Columbia Country Club. Risk was appealing. But death was not, and they stayed out of the war zone.

But the fears that had risen in the wake of D.C.'s crime surge had reached out indirectly to touch them nonetheless. One of the area's oldest teenage customs was pool hopping—splashing your way, uninvited, through a series of private pools. Even in my day, thirty years ago, pool hopping had been a tradition; most considered it innocent mischief.

But when journalist Carl Rowan discovered a group of former B-CC students in his pool early this past summer, he had reacted with something more than mild annoyance. Marching out on the lawn, he confronted the kids, firing a gun at one boy, hitting his hand. The boy and a girl—sister of one of the players—were arrested. The others escaped.

"Guess what just happened?" we said to Toby when he got in that night. He paled. "Guess what I was just doing," he said (not, thankfully, at Rowan's house). Grimly, we told him his pool-hopping days were over. Innocent mischief, it seemed, could be dangerous to your health.

The boys had spent the summer preparing for the upcoming season in various ways. A number, including Rick and Geoff, had attended a week-long football camp in Lebanon Springs, Pennsylvania, with B-CC's head coach. Others, like James, had spent a good deal of time right here in the weight room, working out. James had wrought the most radical change on his body, though another kid, Kong Bae, a Korean boy, had probably done more lifting. Everyone knew Kong was the most dedicated player on the whole team; he was short, even slight, but try shoving him—the guy was like a metallic coil. The Master of the Orient, they called him.

It was the time of year, the last moments before two-a-days

officially began, when, as their head coach liked to say, optimism runs especially high.

In fact, it had never run higher, not in the past thirty years. It had been almost that long since B-CC had had a championship football team. One of the boys knew that fact especially well—his stepfather had been a star player on that team, the 1959 B-CC Barons, and had told him the tale many times. "We were undefeated, scored on twice all year," he liked to remember fondly.

No Barons team had come anywhere near that record since. No one knew exactly why, though everyone had a theory. Some parents and coaches blamed the social disruptions that had swept the school in the sixties and seventies—the drugs, the dropouts, the lax discipline. Certainly those years had seen plenty of changes. Why, for a time there, it was suddenly, amazingly, more socially prestigious to strum a guitar, wear a headband, and smoke a joint than to run down a field and smash people. School athletes, for so long at the top of the heap in any high school social strata, had been relegated to a lower position for quite a while. It was only recently that this had begun to reverse itself.

Others pointed to the so-called "soccer mentality" so rampant in lower Montgomery County. The Montgomery Soccer Institute, MSI, started in 1971, the year the seniors were born, had swiftly become the most popular channel for grade-school athletics in the area. Boys grew up playing soccer, not football. "I think the higher up you get in the socioeconomic level, the more inclination there is for parents to push kids to soccer. Fewer injuries," one father of a player explained it.

For myself, it had always seemed no accident that the rise of soccer so closely paralleled the rise of women's liberation—soccer was seen as a distinctly less macho sport. Even baseball had been somewhat eclipsed in the county. Though not so rough as football, baseball was seen as dangerous for another reason: there were too many moments in the game when an individual boy was on the line. Feelings could be hurt.

And the truth was that the parents in the area worried about things like that; we worried, many of us, about everything. Well meaning, compulsive, militantly on the job, we pushed our young sons to organized soccer, and to a lesser extent, basketball and baseball, swimming, ice skating, tennis, and golf lessons. But in the free moments in between, the precious few free moments, when the boys gathered at a field alone, they played what they wanted to play. And inevitably, that meant football.

There were boys who had escaped the MSI deadlock, boys with fathers who had played football themselves, or wanted to a great deal, boys who had strapped on the pads before high school. But there were many others who had not escaped, and now mourned their misspent youth—all of that energy thrown into what they now knew had been the wrong sport.

"I see these little kids, out there, kicking the soccer ball," said one, shaking his head helplessly. "And I want to say to them— PLAY FOOTBALL."

Yet both soccer and social change had affected other schools in the county too. So perhaps B-CC's dismal record had something to do with its own history—specifically, its setting. No other county school existed in such an urban setting, or had gone through anything like B-CC's change in atmosphere.

The high school still sat far back on its lawn, just as it had when it first opened its doors back in 1926, a small country outpost of a school. But the recent explosion of downtown Bethesda had left the school looking as out of place as a squatter's dwelling. Wide lawn or not, B-CC was now for all intents a city school.

There were advantages, of course—you could pop on the subway two blocks away and be downtown in minutes; you could skate at the Hyatt Hotel's tiny ice rink; you could gorge yourself on fast food. (The school had finally given up and allowed students to lunch off campus; what cafeteria could compete with the Golden Arches, Shakey's Pizza, Jerry's Subs, Roy Rogers fried chicken—all within a one-block radius?)

But urbanization had its price, and a more fractured school community was part of it. Not that the urban flavor came from the new skyline alone. Perhaps because of a number of nearby apartment complexes, possibly, too, because the school's boundaries extended into the less affluent Silver Spring area, B-CC had a more diverse mix of students—black, white, Hispanic, Asian—than any other school in the county. "Good God, it looks like Brooklyn," my sister said on her first visit.

Perhaps all these factors had had some effect on the school's football record, perhaps not. But for the coaches, boys, and parents, analysis of the past was less important than contemplation of the future—the possibility, slim but tantalizing, that things might be about to change, that B-CC's star, lost behind the clouds so long ago, might be ready to surface once again.

The weight room was posted with signs: WIN 8 IN '88 AND GO TO THE STATE! Even a year ago, such a sign would have seemed ludicrous, a joke in the worst possible taste. But last year something had happened. The Barons had had their first, intoxicating taste of success.

No one had expected it. The team had in fact just lost their coach of several years, a tough, fire-breathing top-sergeant type, famous for ball-breaking drills and locker-room tantrums. On one memorable night he had paced the length of the line, spitting in the face of every player. He was a man who had no patience with injury: "It don't hurt, boy! It don't hurt unless you let it! Suck up that pain," he would yell. "You want to be a man, mister?" He inspired loyalty in some, affection in a few, anxiety in all.

He had seemed to fill the role to almost mythic perfection: the macho, demanding, irascible, hard-as-nails coach. He reminded a few old-timers, in fact, of the very coach who had led the 1959 Barons to glory (a crusty son of a bitch who had once grabbed a passing bee with one swipe of his paw and crushed it to death). Yet, for all the bullying, the team's winning percentage had been markedly low. Still, it was a shock to many when the new varsity coach was announced for the 1987 season—Pete White.

Pete White had been the junior varsity coach for two years, and a more completely different entity from his predecessor would have been hard to find in a nationwide search. Physically Coach White was soft where the old coach had been hard—a pudgy bear of a man who walked with a springy, upbeat gait. It was symbolic, that gait; he was a man of almost unquenchable good spirits, funny, cheerful, rarely ruffled.

For years he had coached Boys' Club football in nearby Silver Spring, dealing with youngsters—and it showed. He had the mild forbearance of a man accustomed to the uneven skills of ten-year-olds. He also coached baseball at Georgetown Prep, the tony Jesuit private school a few miles away, and often refereed basketball games in the area, and this too showed. His patience was close to inexhaustible, his serenity all but unassailable. In his off-hours, those not involved with sports, he was the local distributor for Pepperidge Farm products—Goldfish, cinnamon cookies, wholesome snacks. That, too, seemed fitting.

Some of the fathers who had played football themselves were shocked at the appointment. How could a man this genial, this pleasant, Mr. Pepperidge Farm, for Christ's sake, coach varsity football? Their sons reacted differently, very differently. The boys, without exception, loved Pete White. They would have done almost anything for him, because of the kind of person he was, because for the first time, for many, they were with a coach who "made football fun." And because, as one boy put it, with careful precision, "We wanted to show we could succeed under a more positive system."

And amazingly, considering that it was Pete White's first season with the varsity team and that he still had a lot to learn about the sport (coaching Jayvee, so much less serious a business, required only minimal knowledge of the complexities of the game), the boys managed to do just that, racking up the best record the school had seen in years: five wins, five losses. Even better, they had managed to shock the entire county by staging a number of substantial upsets—against Whitman, against Einstein, and finally, under the lights, in front of a crowd of eight thousand, smack in the enemy's camp, on the eve of the enemy's homecoming, they had managed to pull off the impossible: scruffy, no-account B-CC had stomped over mighty, undefeated Churchill—one of the best teams in the entire area—for a wild, delirious win.

What happened then was probably predictable—like the cartoon character who dashes over the cliff, stands stock-still, suddenly realizes where he is, and drops like a stone. In the wake of that unimaginable win, the boys had clutched, faltered, and gone down for good. They suffered a humiliating defeat at the hands of Wheaton—a good team, but no Churchill—and never regrouped.

But the boys had gotten a taste for it. And they weren't the only ones. Last year's season, with its abundance of heart-stopping moments, had been the kind tailor-made to turn even suspicious first-time viewers into raging fans.

Certainly it had worked that way with me. I had started the year fearful, unsettled, not at all sure I wasn't a terrible parent for even letting my son play. I had searched the eyes of other parents carefully, guiltily—I'm like you now, I'd thought, we're all allowing our sons to go out on that field, ignoring the possibly terrible consequences. I'm no better.

Then the season unfolded, driving straight under my radar, pulling me into a whirlwind of heady emotion, strong as a drug rush. Had something been lacking in my life all these years? Had I missed out on my fair share of risk-taking activities as an adolescent? Or was I just thoroughly sick of the bland landscape of middle age and hungry for a taste of excitement and turmoil, however vicarious? Whatever, long before the end of the Churchill game, the season's pinnacle, when I ran down to the field to throw my arms around boys wildly, screaming my joy that we had done it, we had won, I knew—the lines separating myself from the team had dissolved completely, and I was hooked. And now, as the 1988 season approached, despite my anxiety about my own son, which continued to throb through my veins, unrelenting, like a slightly raised pulse, my hopes were as high as those of any of the boys.

Why not? Why shouldn't we take it all? Dreams of glory, the looming possibility of grandeur, seemed easily within the far range of reality. Win 8 in '88 and go to the state! It could be, it just could be.

There were obstacles, of course. Everyone knew certain key players had moved on. The entire offensive line, with the exception of Alex, was gone, and that had been the kind of line that made legends. The wide receiver who had done the impossible—grabbed a wild last-ditch Hail Mary pass out of the sky in the last two seconds of the '87 Whitman game, leapt for it, arcing crazily, coming down, against all odds, in the right place, for the win—while the crowd went insane and Pete White just stood stock-still, shaking his head—gone too.

Yet looking around—see who was left! Some of the toughest linebackers on the whole team were still here. Brendan Symes, the Jamaican kid, who was surely the fastest running back they'd ever had. And this junior, Eric Bachman, who was supposed to be the best kicker on county turf—all that soccer had been good for something, after all. And what about Kong Bae, terrible Kong, whose eyes alone, they said, were enough to freeze an opponent at ten paces, since in the heat of a game, through some Oriental alchemy, they turned bright red and glittered demonically through his face mask.

And most important of all, the dynamite duo who had more than once snatched victory out of clear air—Rick Fiscina, quarterback for his entire high school career, and the unbelievable, the unstoppable Geoff Smith. In the Einstein game last year, down 18–0, three times—three times!—Rick had thrown a giant looping pass to Geoff, who had plucked it out of the air, glorious day, for a touchdown.

Oh, there was reason enough to dream, all right, plenty of reason. No one had to say it, it was on everyone's mind. Win 8 in '88 and go to the state! This could be the season they would take it all.

The boys jostled each other in the room; small groups formed, dispersed, re-formed. There were a number of distinct subgroups in the bunch, some predictable, some not.

There was, of course, what almost everyone referred to as the Oriental Connection—Kong Bae and Tae Uk Kim, who were Korean and first cousins, and John Han, who was Taiwanese.

A few years back, on the junior varsity squad, Pete White had been able to get some real mileage out of the Oriental Connection. That was when he had two Taiwanese kids on the offensive line who could speak Chinese to each other out on the field. Nothing very complex, of course—more along the lines of "Hey, what're we supposed to be doing, huh? Oh yeah, you're supposed to cover that guy"—but it was enough to disconcert the opposition and delight Pete, who had a fondness for little tricks. But one of the kids had quit football, so that was that. The Korean boys, Kong and Tae Uk (pronounced Tie-Youk) were rarely on the line together.

Actually, the three Asian boys were very different. Kong, a senior, went at football with intense, grim-faced dedication; Tae Uk, a year younger, could be hyper, even giddy; and John Han was a rather breezy, amiable sort of guy. Yet Pete saw similarities. He met a lot of Asians through his job. They were impressed with him because he took care of his 93-year-old grandmother; he was impressed with them for other reasons.

"They've got that work ethic, you can't beat it," he said. "We got to get more of the team eating rice."

The three boys lived near each other and hung out together, along with another boy, Eric Knaus, who was fair-haired, sweet-faced, and widely considered to be the nicest kid on the team. Too nice, many thought—no compliment for a football player. James swore he had once heard Eric say "God bless you!" during an assembly when someone had sneezed on the other side of the auditorium. Tae Uk, though, took his part loyally. "I've known Eric eight years, and he is NOT too nice," he would argue.

Toby stood with his closest friends on the team, among them Billy Stone, who had been the one to convince him to play last season, and Mark Dahl, known to everyone as Lunkhead, a name his fiendish older brother had affixed when he was small. Toby himself had a nickname, Farney, whose origins were obscure, although a few thought it might have derived from Foghorn—he'd had a deep, resounding voice since childhood.

Toby's group included many non–football players, not a few of whom had been cut from the team because of academic ineligibility. They were widely reputed to be a nonserious, party-mongering bunch who liked their beer. This was not, in my view, a totally undeserved reputation.

Rick and Geoff, the superstars, formed another core group, along with a couple of others—a much more competitive one than Toby's. The boys in this group had all played football before high school, all had wrestled, and all—particularly Rick and Geoff—seemed to go at nearly everything competitively. Including friendship. Rick and Geoff had known each other for years, and depended on each other; most of the team assumed they were best friends. And they were, in a way—yet there was an ongoing tension between them, almost unconscious, a perpetual jockeying for position, a constant search for the upper edge.

Rick was strikingly handsome, with the look of a rugged Rob Lowe. "Typical quarterback, the kind of kid who never had a pimple in his life," one coach dubbed him; hyperbolically—Rick had known a zit or two in his time. But his popularity in the school was unquestioned. "He is God, you know," one kid had told a teacher, only half sardonically. The subgroup known as "Rick, Geoff, and them" was widely understood to be the topmost rung on the B-CC ladder.

Yet he'd dealt with his share of resentment, too—a sign posted out front of the school a few years back hailing his exploits had needed several coats of paint, since person or persons unknown could not resist adding a "P" to the poster, resulting in a large homage to "PRICK FISCINA." Although he was well on his way to being a twelve-letter man, in football, baseball, and wrestling, it nevertheless was clear to many boys that it wasn't always that easy to be Rick. "It's lonely at the top," one put it.

Geoff—well, Geoff was different. Popular, cocky as hell, a wild guy, an undeniable team star, Geoff somehow never attracted the same resentment as Rick—except, perhaps, from Rick himself. Skinny, with a crop of blond hair sticking up on his head, crowning his wide-eyed baby face, Geoff had something so wholehearted and open about him, it was hard to be annoyed at him for long. "Rick's sort of like, I'm great and you suck. Geoff's like, I'm great and you're great and life's great," one boy tried to explain.

Seeing him now, bouncing around the room, obviously on top of the world, it was hard not to catch some of that enthusiasm. For no one in the room was happier than Geoff Smith right now; no one had spent the summer waiting for this moment more eagerly. His senior year football season was about to begin; the best year, his favorite sport. Geoff was flying high.

Dave Bardach was not. Black, sturdily built, with heavy, athletic legs, Dave had a stern, handsome face with a touch of Indian about the cheekbones—the sort of face that knew how to glower. Dave felt himself to be something of a loner on the team this year; most of his closest friends had graduated. Many players would come to see Dave and Rick as mirror images of each other. Dave was black, Rick white; Rick was the quarterback, Dave would be the quarterback of the defense. Both boys were exceptionally bright, opinionated, and handsome, well built, with hardy, sizable egos. Dave's own group, none of them here today, was a small clique of boys who considered themselves the black male elite of the school, with some reason: all were successful academically, socially, and athletically (several played basketball). "We are THE men," said Dave. One girl had told him recently that many black girls considered them out of reach, untouchable, and it was true that many mostly dated white girls.

Dave was eyeing the room with some misgivings at the moment. He wasn't that thrilled with what he saw. Last year's team had been a strong one—mature, disciplined, hardworking, serious. It looked to him like there were a lot of premier party animals in this group, and as far as he was concerned, that boded no good. As one of the five team captains (Rick, Geoff, Alex, and Billy Stone were the others), he was going to have to handle these people on the field, he knew it; not exactly cause for rejoicing. The sight of James McDonald strutting around with his new muscles did nothing to improve his mood. What an ego that guy had—unbelievable. James, noticing his baleful eye, smiled benignly.

Some of the boys stayed near their closest friends, others moved easily from one group to another, and there were those who stood alone.

As the season unfolded, though, there would be fewer and fewer sharp boundaries between the separate groups, between all the boys. "The lines are coming down," Toby reported with satisfaction. And this would please everyone. It meant they were becoming a team.

Coach White stood at the front of the room with two younger men. He eyed the congregating boys happily, greeting most of them by name. They were good kids. He knew he had a reputation around school, with some teachers, even with the athletic director, for being a bit of an optimist where adolescent boys were concerned— sometimes he even forgot to lock the equipment away, which was something you just didn't do these days, not if you wanted to see it again—but he couldn't help it. It was his nature to trust, to believe the best of the boys. He knew this year's seniors weren't quite as—well, call it mature—as last year's. They were a social bunch, these guys, they had a tendency to get a little too enthralled, let's say, with every skirt they saw walking down the halls, they partied a little too hard now and then, but hell—he'd known most of them three years now, through Jayvee and varsity, and he was comfortable with all of them. Good kids. It was hard to believe, no matter what you heard, that kids today were basically any different from the way they'd been back in the fifties.

Of course, it surprised him that some of these boys hadn't ended up at Georgetown Prep, instead of B-CC—a private school, all male, a good, strong Jesuit education, you couldn't do better than that. Not for all of them, of course, but a kid like Rick Fiscina, or Billy Stone, why, their dads had even told him they had considered it—they could certainly afford it. Rick's father, Sal, he knew, had taken Rick up for a walk-through; he'd had some concern that Rick was such a social guy, those gals were going to make him crazy. Maybe he should go to a good Catholic school where he could concentrate. And Billy's father was a Georgetown Prep alumni himself. Yet both boys had ended up here. Pete couldn't figure it out.

B-CC—well, it had taken some getting used to, he admitted it. When he had gone to school, back in the fifties, down in Southeast Washington, integration was just starting. Now you saw black and white kids dating. And the girls here—they drank as much as the boys, they were aggressive, they weren't like the 17-year-old girls he had known. Things had changed, all right.

But some things hadn't; this he knew. Sports were important to these boys, as important as they had been to him, and that had been very important indeed. Pete knew as well as anyone that life was not always fair. He was the son of an alcoholic father, and his mother had been almost the sole support of the family; an older brother had lost a leg, fooling around with some friends on a freight train. Not always fair, no. Yet on the playing field, it seemed to come closer to being so than anywhere else. No matter who you were, or where you came from, if you worked hard enough, you improved. There was an evenness there that appealed to him. He'd played coming up, gone on to play both football and baseball at Gettysburg College. A small place, but if you played there, you were someone—people knew you. Sports could do that for you.

He had gravitated into coaching naturally when he got back from the service. Been an MP in Okinawa; managed to miss Nam;

it was early in the war. He hadn't had any idea what was going on over there until he'd come back, started meeting some of the guys who'd been in it. At first, he'd been totally behind it, couldn't understand the people who weren't—but after a while, you listened, you learned a little more; maybe they had a point at that. Of course, he still had some friends, like one buddy who was an ex-Marine. Boy, you didn't mention Jane Fonda's name around that guy, even today. Just didn't say it.

He had first started coaching back in his old neighborhood in D.C., then with the Silver Spring Boys' Club, after he'd moved out to the suburbs. He'd come to B-CC as an assistant—it wasn't something he needed. He had his Georgetown Prep job coaching baseball; he didn't even think he'd like it that much; he'd had to take all kinds of courses, too, to qualify—that was Montgomery County for you, always making you take some kind of course. He hadn't expected to stay long, but hell . . . you got fond of the kids, that was what happened, and then you didn't want to leave.

A football coach got respect—respect and a certain amount of power. What could a teacher do except threaten a kid with a bad grade? A coach could hold out a real threat: keep your nose clean or you don't play. Now that was real power.

But you had to be careful not to abuse it. Especially in a school like B-CC, where your pool of players wasn't that large. Churchill, only a couple of miles away, had a thriving football program, had had it for years; parents held steak dinners and big breakfasts every week during the season; every year at least ninety guys showed up to try out for the team. At B-CC, you were lucky to get forty, so you had to handle things differently.

For instance, smoking and drinking were strictly forbidden during the season—Pete let them know that right away. "If you do it, I'll find out, and you'll be sorry," he told them. Of course, if a kid drank a beer at home, Pete wasn't going to be out there looking in the window, but if he made any kind of fool of himself, tried to drive, or slapped some girl around, it wouldn't take thirty seconds before Pete would know about it. It was that kind of school, B-CC; people told you things. Especially the girls—they couldn't wait to let you know.

"You'll be sorry," he told them. But he didn't tell them exactly how they'd be sorry, that was the thing. He wasn't about to paint himself into a corner like that. Did sorry mean the kid was off the team? Did it mean he missed a game? Maybe it meant a whole day of hill drills, which everyone hated like poison. Anyway, Pete wasn't telling. You knew damn well that if someone did smoke a cigarette during the season, it was never going to be the worst player on the team. So you had to handle that sort of thing one case at a time. Inflexibility didn't do anyone any good.

Last season had been exciting, and this one could be even better. Sure, they'd lost the offensive line—a hell of a line that'd been— and a couple of good guys had been knocked out by academic ineligibility, which was a damn shame. But they still had the skill people—Rick, Geoff, Brendan Symes. And this year he was bringing in a couple of young assistants to help out, guys who were really serious about football, Mitch Babashan and Bob Plante. These guys could really make a difference.

Those two men were, in fact, now standing next to Pete, also eyeing the crowd of boys, but not warmly, not warmly at all. In fact, their faces bore almost identical expressions of icy, disdainful contempt. There were other similarities between them as well— while Pete White slouched casually, his round body spilling comfortably out of his Bermuda shorts and shirt, these two stood firmly at attention, feet slightly splayed, muscles tensed. It was hard to ignore those muscles. Sharply defined, they showed signs of steady, loving, long-term cultivation. You could bounce a dime off any one of those pecs.

Mitch Babashan was the larger, a hulking oak of a young man, still the very picture of the all-Met all-County linebacker he had been at Springbrook High, in upper Montgomery County, eleven years before. But it was his eyes you noticed first, behind glasses, such an odd color, the faintest, most delicate shade of robin's-egg blue. Looking into them was like looking into an ice chamber, one boy thought.

With Bob Plante it was the mouth more than the eyes that drew attention—that ever so slight upward curve of one side of the lip that gave every word an edge, a small sarcastic charge. Other than that, his face still bore signs of the freckle-faced kid he must have been not long ago: wavy, reddish-brown hair, brown eyes, regular features. But the lip changed the whole picture, giving it a slightly sinister cast.

Standing next to Pete White, the two formed a dark counterpoint to his sunny affability. More than one boy, glancing over, felt a slight unease, which would have pleased both of them mightily had they known.

They wanted to provoke unease. They wanted, in fact, to scare the boys shitless. It was part of their game plan.

They were best friends who worked together in Bethesda selling commercial insurance, which was about as much fun as getting stung by a thousand bees, Mitch thought, but still, something you needed to do. The work earned the bankroll, the wardrobe, the health-club membership, the cars, and the two spanking-new Harley motorcycles they liked to drive. So the work was necessary; it just wasn't important. What was important was football.

This had always been true. Mitch had come of age in upper Montgomery County, a rural, blue-collar area wholly unlike Bethesda, where cows still grazed and football was king—no soccer mentality there, by God. He had grown up playing, blossomed into a star linebacker, and been headed directly for a fully paid athletic scholarship.

Then disaster had struck. In preseason practice at Virginia Tech, before his freshman year had even started, Mitch took a bad hit. It hadn't seemed that bad at first, he wasn't even knocked out . . . but it was that bad; a few blood vessels had been crushed, and the year before a player had died on the field, so the college wasn't taking any chances. Mitch was out. He had worked all his life to get to this point, to play college football. One hit and it was all over. As a matter of fact, he still got migraines from that blow.

He'd gone through college anyway, and later worked for a time as an assistant coach at a small Pennsylvania school. He thought maybe he'd be able to stay around football that way, but while attending a college coach convention, he saw a sight that chilled him—a 45-year-old man lying on the floor in front of a hotel room, waiting for an interview with the guy inside. Like a dog waiting for a bone—a 45-year-old man! If this was his future, Mitch wanted nothing to do with it. He got out of college coaching fast.

He'd done some high school coaching since then, and last year had even helped Pete out a little with the defense at B-CC. He'd known Pete White for years; in fact, Pete had coached him once on a Boys' Club team. This year would be his first as assistant coach, and the first time he would be working with Bob, his closest friend.

Bob Plante had come up a little differently from Mitch—he'd been raised in a more affluent milieu, slightly down-county, though he, too, had played football all the way through. He'd never, though, been the first-team all-Met natural athlete Mitch had been; he'd always had to work a little harder for that extra edge. And that was what had led to his disaster.

"What are you doing to keep in shape off-season?" a coach had asked him on a recruiting trip during his senior year in high school. "Why don't you wrestle? That'll keep your edge up."

So Bob wrestled. Briefly. At the end of his first match—a match he'd been winning, nine to three—he was thrown to the mat forever: his ankle was broken in five places, rendering him essentially unfit for any sport for all time. The University of Richmond had been willing to give him a chance, saying he'd get a ride if he made the team, but the first day he went out on the field for drill, he fell flat on his face. Done. Finished. He just couldn't run. Even after several operations, the damn thing still bothered him.

Bob and Mitch had hated each other cordially on sight; each thought the other a cocky asshole. "Two egos don't fit in the same room," Bob explained it. But one night a few years back, down in Ocean City, they'd run into each other, shared a few drinks, a few women, a few spots of trouble; then, driving back (they'd had to get out of there fast), had discovered they shared the most important thing of all: football. Their friendship was solid from that point on.

Both were looking forward eagerly to this season, their first high school coaching gig. It meant plenty of time and effort, all of it unpaid; it meant both would be giving up their vacation time this year in order to spend the first two weeks with the team. But it would be worth it. They would be putting into effect all the strategies and philosophies they had been talking about together for so long, all the theories they loved to discuss, late into the night.

Some things they disagreed on, of course, but on one point they were in total accord. It was absolutely necessary—philosophically necessary, if you liked—to start out the season being the nastiest, meanest son of a bitch you could be. Muscles tensed, loins girded, they were prepared to give it their best shot.

Pete smiled beneficently; Mitch and Bob glowered; the boys milled around, nervous, eager, tautly expectant. Pete blew the whistle that hung on a chain around his neck. The 1988 football season had officially begun.

CHAPTER TWO

PETE WHITE SEATED HIMSELF in a metal chair behind a table; the boys slid quickly into chairs themselves. With the sound of the whistle the room had fallen abruptly, totally silent. Pete introduced the two brooding assistants: "Mitch Babashan is going to give us a hand on defense; Bobby Plante here will handle the offensive line." Mitch, he told the boys, had coached in college. He knew things that were really going to help the team. Both men continued to stare coldly at the room, muscles still tensed.

In rapid-fire staccato, Pete read off several points he had written earlier on the chalkboard to his right: rules for the season. "No smoking, no alcohol—none" was the first ("And don't worry, I'll know," he assured them). "Ten-thirty curfew weekdays, twelve-thirty weekends" was the second. "Late you hurt the team" the third. "Means just what it says, and it means extra work—climbing hills, we'll think of something," he added. The last two were attitude reminders: "Team—no 'I' in that word" and "Sure, Coach, whatever it takes to win."

"That's what I want to hear whenever I tell you to do anything," Pete said.

At the bottom of the board was a brief description of what every player should be: "One, a gentleman; two, a student; three, an athlete."

"In that order," Pete said.

There was barely a scuffling of feet in the room as he talked. The boys wore identical expressions of serious concentration. "No watches, no rings, no jewelry of any kind," the coach continued. "No diamond-crusted jockstraps on the field. You want to wear an earring, I don't have any problem with that. But not on the field." A faint noise from the back riveted him at once. "I hope you're not talking when I'm talking," he snapped crisply; paused for one beat; then continued.

He spoke calmly and evenly, accepting the scene before him as if it were a common one—though it was, in fact, one that few teachers or parents had ever been privileged to witness: a roomful of male adolescents utterly attentive, focused on every word. There was no need for tricks—repetition, raised voice, the occasional hard rap on the table—and he used none. It was enough to say something once, for the simple, miraculous reason that everyone was listening.

There were boys in the room whose attention span had been derided in the classroom; boys who seemed to have difficulty understanding math, science, languages. Yet within a few days, these same boys would be learning a variety of plays as complex as any geometric formula; study codes as impenetrable as any language; and do it all while pushing themselves to the maximum degree of physical effort. They would not complain and they would not quit.

Nobody, not the coaches or the boys, found anything strange or inconsistent in this. After all, this was football. Football was something each boy in the room cared about deeply—school, frequently, was not. Even with the boys who generally did do well in the classroom, there was often that faint sense that maybe, just maybe, you were doing it partly for your parents.

Football, though, was different—football you did for yourself. Some of the boys had athletically inclined fathers, sure, but no one in the room felt he was there because a parent had urged him to be: this was their choice. They had decided on their own to do this thing, play varsity football, and that made a difference . . . made, in fact, all the difference in the world.

The focus of that first day was just as notable on the field, where the boys underwent several hours of conditioning drills. "Nothing much, we're not going to kill anyone the first day," Pete promised.

First came the stretching exercises, for which the boys lined up in perfect rows. "And keep that same spot every day, so I can see if you're here . . . if you're not there, I figure you're not playing football." Each exercise (jumping jacks, push-ups, leg lifts) was done to a slow count of five; after which the boys chorused, "six-seven-eight," and clapped in unison.

Intermittently coaches and boys exchanged a chant: "How you feel?" "JUST GREAT." "How you feel?" "JUST GREAT." "Are you ready?" "YOU BET."

The synchronization was impressively smooth, almost from the start. Any variation was caught at once ("Six inches up on those leg lifts"; "Bitz, get your butt UP on those bicycles") and corrected. The boys still wore their own shorts and T-shirts, of varying shades and logos. "If it smells like fish, eat it," said one. Practice jerseys would not be given out till the second day. But already, differences were blurring.

. The assistant coaches hovered nearby, helping out with drills, saying little; it was Pete who set the tone that first day. They would have their chance a few days later, when uniforms and pads were issued, and the team was ready to go all out. For today, it was Pete who dominated the arena.

The coach's amiability and mild demeanor tended off the field to mask to a degree his sharp brain and shrewd awareness of human behavior—but on the field there could be no doubt. By the end of practice, even the first-timers on the team had realized the coach knew exactly what each boy was doing at each moment; and knew a great deal about that boy in general, too. It was no lie, apparently—as he said, he really did know what everyone was up to.

Pete's swift reflexes flashed out midway through one fiendishly complicated exercise, in which each boy ran in place double time—"chop-chop"—between laid-out tackling dummies, then, at Pete's direction, jumped over one, then another, continuing to run, while the coach held up his hand—"How many fingers?"—forcing them to keep their heads up. The drill demanded complete concentration from boy and coach, yet when one boy stumbled, and another, waiting in line, snickered, Pete was on it instantly. "None of you have cause to be laughing," he snapped, without interrupting the drill. "A guy who locks himself out of his own car don't have the right to laugh at anyone else. How many fingers?" Without shifting his eyes he had identified the chuckler from one snort and nailed him with a personalized zinger.

He could be caustic. Directing all the players to jog twenty yards, using a high-stepping bandleader gait, he quickly called them back and made them do five push-ups before trying again—one player had not followed directions. "You'll figure out who the jackass is." Yet his barbs, too, were even-handed. "At least he went for it," he tempered, after yelling at a player's misfired grab at a tackling dummy. "He had the spirit—just not too bright, that's his damn problem."

The coach set the tone, that first day, too, vis-à-vis the delicate problem of ethnic differences—and set it in a way that delighted the boys. Because to Pete White it was no problem at all. He was going to say what he wanted, poke fun at everyone. Evenly.

"Hey, Brendan," he yelled at Jamaican running back Brendan Symes, whose dark, soulful good looks made him a favorite with the girls, "what is that, some kind of go-go step?"

"Oh, man, a black entourage"—wading through one group of players on the field—"am I gonna get mugged here or what?"

"Great, Tae Uk's not doing anything, just supervising—" as the boys struggled to set up a tackling rack. "That's what I need, a Korean supervisor, right?"

"Dirkey"—to another black player—"you gonna move faster or we gonna have to get out that watermelon?"

No one on the team escaped; that was the key. "Toby, I don't care what you bring to that potluck lunch," he would say later that week to my son. "Just make sure it's kosher." No matter who the kid was, even if he didn't have an ethnic characteristic readily available for needling, there was always something, some sensitive nerve to be probed—weight, background, hairstyle, something. "Billy, I've seen that house of yours," he jibed at Billy Stone, whose home in ritzy Kenwood was lovely. "Some reason you go around in torn pants all the time? You trying to hide something?" "I swear to God, Christo, if we didn't need your mother to make up those programs, no way we'd let you hang around." "Jesus, Alex, move back, big fellow, you're blocking out the sky."

He was hardly ever at a loss, although the first sight of the

B-CC-etched scalps of his star players, Rick and Geoff, had given him a moment's pause. "What the holy hell is THAT?" he had finally said.

The wisecracks leveled everyone indiscriminately. They were rough, direct, and the boys loved them. Not a teacher in Montgomery County would have dared to talk like that to any of them, and they knew it. Teachers in the county had been trained intensively, in all-day awareness seminars, to be careful and sensitive about ethnic differences to such a high degree that they would just as soon have shot themselves in the foot as talk like Pete White. They were well meaning to a fault, only all that heightened sensitivity could be a real burden at times; sometimes it led to ridiculous, unnatural extremes.

Dave Bardach had experienced this himself, when a visiting teacher at a B-CC honors class had assigned a paper on the importance of peace. Dave, feeling testy and not particularly pacific, had responded with a treatise railing at white-supremacist society, quoting liberally from Malcolm X, one of his heroes. A day later the teacher had called him over, tentatively: "Uh, excuse me," he said, clearing his throat embarrassedly, "but are you, uh, Dave Bardach?"

"I'm the only black student in class—who the hell else is going to write a paper like that?" Dave said later, shaking his head. "No, I'm not Dave Bardach, right?"

The fact that the man was a respected teacher as well as a journalist made no difference—to Dave's mind, he had just been revealed as a fool. Pete White was no fool; he had never attended an awareness seminar; Pete White had no problem yelling at Dirkey, who was extremely dark, during one late practice, to "open those eyes, for God's sake, or smile or something, we can't hardly see you on that field," and to the boys, all the boys, that was not just funny, it was a giant relief. "Sure, Coach *White*," Dave had yelled happily.

There was no question that his brand of teasing—rough, blunt, male—could initially be shocking to an onlooker. Certainly it was to me. Frankly, at first I was a little horrified, and never entirely at ease. But a conversation with an old friend one day—totally unrelated—helped me to understand. He was discussing how uncomfortable he felt at times around a colleague whose husband headed a Judaic studies institute. "They're Orthodox; I'm always afraid I'll say something that sounds anti-Semitic," he admitted.

I stared at him. "You haven't been afraid to say anything anti-Semitic in front of me for over thirty years," I told him. "You've never been afraid to say anything in front of me, ever."

"Well, of course not," he snorted. "Why would I care with you? You're—I *know* you, you're you," he said. What he meant was he didn't have to censor himself with me, he could be himself; I was his friend, not a walking Minority Representative. I might scream bloody murder, but I sure as hell wasn't going to stop being his friend. And, by God, the guy had a point.

No one on the field, least of all Pete White, spent time analyzing any of this, of course—but the truth was he could have talked himself blue in the face about equality, brotherhood, and fairness to all and the kids would have shrugged it off like a bad smell. But by meeting all the taboos and stereotypes head on, going straight through them, with humor, instead of tiptoeing nervously around the edges, he dissolved them. Yeah, the message went—you're black, you're Jewish, you're fat. We've all got something, and so what. Now let's get out on that field and see what you've really got. Differences don't matter out here; only the game. Not everyone could have pulled it off the way Pete did, of course. But like all adolescents, the kids had the kind of real awareness no seminar has ever been able to convey—they knew who their friends were. What they knew in their gut, consciously or not, was that Pete wouldn't talk that way if he didn't care about them. And they were right.

But on the surface, all that mattered was that "Coach White is so funny." They waited for his cracks, loved them all, and were especially proud when he'd gotten off a good one at their expense.

And I myself knew for the first time that Pete had begun to relax with me when after months of interviews, he introduced me to someone, saying, "She says she's a writer. I haven't seen anything yet, of course, but that's what she says. Her son played last season— well, you know, 'played.'" And he rocked his hand from side to side, deprecatingly, and I suddenly knew exactly how the boys had felt. Because I was not just pleased. I was, I realized, almost idiotically flattered.

The heat and humidity were unrelenting that first day of practice; after three hours on the field nearly everyone looked close to collapse. "I know it's hot, I know you're tired, we're all tired," yelled Pete, lining them up for a final drill. "But suck it up, suck it up, you'll be the better for it."

"Of course," he added, after sending them off for a water break—they drank directly from faucets set up on the edge of the field—"this first day we took it pretty easy; tomorrow we're gonna start running you." Two girls walked slowly by the field, and a number of adolescent eyes automatically shifted. Pete was on it at once: "Get those eyes off those britches," he snapped. "We're gonna try to concentrate on football for a couple of weeks here." He paused for his characteristic one beat, then continued. The Barons would have their first scrimmage against a tough up-county team, Friendly, "where they milk the cows by day and play football all night"; those guys were going to "come on the field smelling of horseshit from stepping in those cow patties" and the boys had better be ready. "Okay, okay," he said, and waved them off to the locker room.

Standing in the small gym—the large gym was for everyone else—forced inside by the rain, viewing the players lined up in front of him, Bob Plante grimaced, his lip curling upward automatically. If these were the prospective offensive linemen, he had his work cut out for him.

The first three days of two-a-days had been a chaotic, bureaucratic blur—making sure everyone's medical forms were in, issuing uniforms and helmets, taking the kids through conditioning drills. No hitting—that was the rule, in the county. You had to spend a few days getting the guys in shape before you let them loose. Didn't want any of the little babies passing out on you in the heat. Of course, a few of them had started sneaking in an occasional solid whack or two by the second day—when they were supposed to be just walking through plays—and by the third day, nearly all of them had smashed into someone at least once. Couldn't stop kids from hitting completely. But still, that was the rule.

Today was the first day they could legally go all-out, and none too soon, either. It was also the first time Bob had had a chance to isolate the offensive linemen and take a good, hard look at them. It wasn't exactly a cause for joy. Most of them weren't even that big, and the ones who were—Erik Karlson, only a junior, barely out of nursery school; Alex Burgess, center, the only veteran, huge, but so badly out of shape he could hardly squat—Christ, the kid must be carrying 320 pounds! And then there were the lightweights, like Tae Uk Kim. Good God, how were these kids supposed to do anything on a line? Toby Oppenheimer—the kid was big enough, but Jesus, he looked so knocked out he could barely stand straight; it was obvious, too, that he knew absolutely nothing about the game.

They were a sorry bunch, that was for sure. Bob had spent the last forty-five minutes stalking up and down, observing them, as they struggled to stay in one of three football stances—two point, three point, four point—knees bent, helmet UP—five minutes at a time. It was a good way to see who was in shape and who wasn't, and he had his answer—no one. Christ, Burgess had barely lasted thirty minutes before he stumbled out of the room, retching, his overstuffed buddy Dimarlo Duvall, a black kid, following close behind.

The thing about the offensive line—Bob knew this well—it wasn't a glory position. Important, yes; as the old saw had it, the game was won in the trenches; or, as Pete put it, the horses pull the plow. Glorious, no. The glory went to the skill men, the quarterbacks, running backs, wide receivers.

Defense was another matter—that was where you had your fucking lunatics, guys who ripped heads off. A player could really let it all out in defense. Most football players who wanted to be real men wanted to play defense, and Bob could hardly blame them. Hell, he loved defense himself.

For the offensive line, you needed more control—it was the one place on the team, the way Bob saw it, where a dorky, slow-moving guy could do well. Your lesser athlete. Linemen were clumsy, they lacked that special grace that made a quarterback or a wide receiver; these were your meat-and-potatoes guys. Quieter, too—you could be in a room with one and not know it. Not your best-looking guys, either, usually; more the back-of-the-rack type. "Take a look around you, men," he would tell them in a few days. "These are all the guys who won't be going to homecoming this year."

He knew what he wanted in a lineman, what he looked for. "I'd prefer him to be ugly, spend a lot of time in the weight room, be quiet, shy, and just have murderous tendencies. That's what makes a great offensive lineman. The kind of guy who's quiet, doesn't say much, but if you really got him mad he might pull an M-60 on you." Once you got one, of course, it was up to the coach to motivate him.

And how did you motivate an offensive lineman? Ah, that was where it got interesting—at least to Bob Plante, who was a keen student of management techniques. The offensive lineman wasn't going to hear the crowd roaring for one of his blocks; he wasn't going to get his name announced over the loudspeaker; he wasn't going to have his picture in the local newspaper, the *Montgomery County Journal*. So what did you do?

What you did first was isolate them. The offensive line was a team within a team, operating on its own, pretty much independent from everybody else. Anything you could do to underscore that was a boost. That's why he had them back here, in the small gym, even though it was at least 20 degrees hotter than the main gym, which was no picnic either. It was also why he'd urge them in the coming days to stay together as much as possible. "I want you guys to hang out together, eat together, drink together." "If he'd had his choice, I think we would have slept together," said one kid. The idea was to forge a unit—strong, tight, impenetrable. More than a unit: an identity.

It boiled down to one thing, basically—the lineman was going to have to do it for the line itself, for pride, for his sense of himself as a man, and for his coach. Especially for his coach. So it was extremely important to be the right kind of coach.

The way Bob saw it, there were three different types. There was the camp counselor, the buddy-buddy, let-me-help-you, I-want-you-to-love-me coach—a coach like Pete White, to tell the truth. Then there were the nuts-and-bolts guys—the eggheads, all numbers and chalk talk, Tom Landry types, the kind players never really loved.

Then there was the third kind, his kind—the romantics, the warrior types, the Pattons. Guys were scared to death of them, but they respected them, too. Like the coach he'd had in high school, Tom George. The guy was incredible; Bob still remembered the greatest speech he'd ever made. It had been two words long.

"We were in a 7–7 tie. And he didn't come in the locker room at half time. We were waiting and waiting. What's going on, where is he? Finally the ref came in and said, 'Let's go, boys, you got to get out on the field.' And just before we all left he walked in and just said, 'We *will*.' That was it: 'We *will*.' And he walked out.

"We charged out. We were so pumped, we ended up winning, 21–7."

A true romantic, Tom George. All football players were romantics at heart, and so were the best coaches, Bob thought. "I guarantee you, if we went back to Renaissance days, the Knights of the Round Table, those knights would be the best football players . . . in the arena, with the women in the stand waving handkerchiefs, the men on the field with their gear going into combat."

That was the kind of coach he wanted to be. Of course, you had to keep a certain distance from the kids in order to pull it off, but that was okay. Bob believed there should be clear lines between coaches and players; that was how you got true leadership. "I'm Mr. Enigma, I don't want you to know me," he would tell his troops in the coming days. You let the lines down, you left the gate open for mutiny, and Bob wanted none of that. "A player does it my way or highway. When Coach Plante says jump, all he wants to hear is how high?"

Drama, theatrics, control, that was the ticket. Well, it was up to him now to assume the mantle.

Bob stalked down the length of the room one more time while the boys sat on the floor, recovering. He was ready to start the process. "Gentlemen," he said in clear, cold tones, "I want to talk to you about something important for each of you to know—what makes a pussy. Are you a pussy? Are all of you pussies? Do you want to be a pussy? That's what we gotta know right now.

"A man is born a fucking pussy. You either are a pussy or you're not; there's no other way. Now, we saw that in wartime. In Nam. In wartime the pussies came out—they showed themselves. Non-pussies kicked ass; they killed some gooks. They were men. Pussies were pussies.

"In football, gentlemen, you're either a fucking pussy or you're not. It's as simple as that. You think about that right now. Any of you want to be pussies? Do you?"

His eyes moved up and down the group; they were listening, all right. Burgess, Oppenheimer, all of them. Motivation—that was the key. And he was going to make it work.

Alex Burgess was listening intently. The way Bob Plante was stalking up and down the line—arrogant, assured, totally in control—reminded him of his favorite scene from his favorite movie, *Patton*. Taking charge—leadership—a man who could lead other men, that was what fascinated Alex about football; about the line—and about the military, too. He had been reading books on military strategy since he was a kid; he wanted to be a career military officer. His father had been a career officer in the Navy. The funny thing was, his father had almost no use for football, though he came to the games. He thought sports were silly; men acting macho. Alex guessed that maybe when you'd seen the real thing—watched enough of your friends get blown to bits—you lost patience with games. It was his mother who loved it—she'd come to the games and scream like a banshee. You could always hear her, too, since she had such a powerful voice, she was a singer. Even before he'd played, she used to watch football on TV. His father would drive her nuts by asking her what inning it was. Different types, all right; divorced now, several years.

What his father couldn't see was that football could be a good training ground for someone like himself, who was interested in leadership. He wasn't one of those guys who had always had a burning need to play the game, like Geoff, who lived for it. Actually, he'd gotten into it for one reason only: to lose weight. But it wasn't long before he'd realized that football was a damn good leadership-training arena. And this year, when he'd be the head guy on the line, should be very interesting indeed.

Alex listened carefully, taking mental notes. The guy was good; he was going at it the right way. Alex approved. He might be able to use some of this speech himself sometime.

Toby was listening too. He had already been the target of Bob's scorn. It was sad but true, as Coach White said, that if you're bigger, more is expected of you. And Toby was big, nearly six-three. But so far he hadn't shown much strength.

On the inside, he'd made a decision that day to take an enormous risk, but nobody knew about that.

He'd gone to school all summer long, straight through: two sessions, advanced algebra and chemistry, six full weeks. There wasn't any choice, not if he wanted to play football. He had to bring up his grades. He had done the crime, spent the spring quarter having fun and letting his grades go to hell, so he would do the time, even if it meant missing any vacation at all, sticking around when his family cleared out to go to the beach. Not that he'd been happy about it—when he first learned he'd have to go, he'd grabbed an old guitar, gone outside, and swung it against the brick wall until it exploded in a thousand chips. When his mom yelled at him to stop, he'd been firm. "I just need to smash something, then I'll be okay." And of course, he was, as he had known he'd be—once he'd gotten out his anger, he was ready to do what he had to do.

Last year had been his first season ever; his friends had talked him into going out. Then, on the night before two-a-days started he had broken his toe in a pickup softball game. He had spent almost the entire season on the sidelines; it wasn't until a late-season scrimmage that they saw he might be able to do them some good. Coach White had said it at the football banquet, when he announced his name to the audience: "We think this big guy might be able to help us out next season."

So he'd pushed himself with summer school, getting more and more exhausted, until he found out about the mono. Even after that, he'd kept pushing, getting up, going to school, barely conscious. You had to—one day's absence from summer school meant an automatic fail. Then a few weeks before two-a-days started, he'd gone to the doctor he'd known all his life, a doctor who had played football himself, someone he'd thought would understand. The guy wouldn't budge an inch. No playing for another five weeks. Even his mom had felt bad about that, tried to intervene. She knew the kind of summer he'd spent.

"He has an enlarged spleen; it could burst," the doctor told me when I called, seeking leniency for my son. His voice rose. "I am not performing an emergency splenectomy on this kid! No way—five weeks is the absolute minimum."

"At least you'll be able to play during the season. It's just training you'll miss," I told Toby comfortingly, I thought.

Just training—the proving ground, the make-your-bones arena. Just training, with hungry juniors eyeing any free position, straining for a chance to jump into the breach. Some comfort. What did I know?

The doctor's warning ringing in his ears ("He didn't just tell me, he gave me a half-hour lecture"), Toby went to practice and sat out. For two days. It felt awful. "I was getting glimpses of the previous year, with my toe, and watching people run around and hit, sitting there like an asshole again—I had heard rumors I was up for a position on the defense or offense line, and now I was watching eleventh-graders trying to take my spot. . . ."

And so he made his decision. "I just said to myself, it's my spleen—it's *my* spleen. It's not my mother's spleen, it's not the doctor's spleen, it's my spleen and I'll do what I want with it."

With cold purpose, he strapped on his shoulder pads, strapped on his leg pads, and entered the fray. He had made his choice (one I would not know about until most of the season was over). Good or bad, crazy or sane, it was his; he was taking responsibility for his own body. In a way, it felt like he was taking over the reins of his own life for the first time.

But barely recovered mono victims make lousy football players, so Toby was not impressing anyone right now. "Bag of pus," Bob Plante had snarled at him outside earlier, the first time he saw him try to block. Along with pussies, it was his favorite expression, the boys would learn, soon to be abbreviated to "bopper."

"We thought we'd seen signs of goodness in Toby, back there at the end of last season, but Bob wasn't around then," Pete said. Well, he was now, and what he was seeing wasn't exactly the sort of thing that made him jump up and down. Alex, Dimarlo, Toby—all of them looked ready to croak any minute. But they were listening, all right.

"Gentlemen, it's as simple as this—there ain't no place in football for a fucking pussy." He glared at them all. Yeah, he had 'em;

he was going to take this sorry bunch and turn them into his own little hit squad, sure enough. "Now tell me, all of you—are you pussies?" he roared.

In the main gym, Mitch Babashan was having his own face-off with the defensive players. Only Mitch handled it all a bit differently. This was where his approach and Bob's diverged.

Mitch was an emotional guy, he admitted it. He knew there should be boundaries between a coach and player, but it wasn't always easy to keep from slipping over. Thing was, he got so involved. He was intense, always had been.

Mitch couldn't play it cool; he couldn't keep himself removed from the boys. He couldn't play Patton, aloof, sneering slightly, giving the charge to the troops. He just cared too damn much, that was the problem.

Even last year, when he had just helped out on the defensive line a little, he'd gotten caught up with the kids. This one kid, Tyrone Jenkins, one game, he'd been holding on to this other kid's jersey while the guy was running down the field! Running straight down the field, with Tyrone hanging on to him for dear life! Jesus, he couldn't believe it—the heart of the kid. He loved it, he loved him. Here he was, not stopping the guy for a minute, but he wasn't going to let go. Mitch had run all the way down the field with him, on the sidelines, cheering him on. How did you stay aloof from a kid like that? A few weeks ago, he'd run into Tyrone on the street—the kid had stopped his car in the middle of the street, jumped out, run over, and given him a big hug. That was the sort of thing that stuck with you. The feelings that developed between you and the kids. The bond.

The truth was, Mitch was a sensitive guy and knew it. It had given him trouble before. His high school coach, for instance, had never been able to understand the kind of guy Mitch was. An athlete, sure, but not a rah-rah type; Mitch just didn't fit that mold. Before every game, back then, he liked to go into a corner, sit down, and concentrate, by himself—getting himself prepared, focusing on what he was going to do, seeing it through to completion in his mind. A kind of Zen approach. He didn't do a lot of yelling and screaming to get himself ready; a lot of guys did, that was fine, but it wasn't his way. Also, he liked to be the last one out of the locker room—another one of his little quirks. It drove the coach nuts. "He thought it had an air to it that I wasn't being one of the team."

Yet wasn't that true about a lot of great athletes? People like that weren't conformist, they made their own paths. They weren't just all-American great guys, they were different. Unique. Individuals.

But his coach had never understood that; he'd resented him, resented his differences. Had almost seemed, in a way, to have a vendetta against him. One time in practice, when he'd messed up a play, the coach had yelled at him, "You're nothing but yesterday's newspaper!" Because Mitch was always getting his name in the papers, he was such a star, and the coach resented that. It had been so humiliating . . . not the words so much, but the way he'd said it. The tone. Everybody had just froze on the field. Mitch had never forgotten that moment; it still bothered him all these years later. You didn't get over something like that.

He knew he was sensitive. And knowing that, his way was clear— he needed to be at least twice the bastard Bob was being right now. It was the only way to make it work.

You had to break them down to the point that they all hated your guts. That was Mitch's philosophy. "You break 'em down so they bond together, against you. That's how you get unity on the team. Then, bit by bit, you bring them back up." That was the only way to go, with defense players, and as far as Mitch was concerned, defense was the only thing that mattered.

"You know what offense guys are?" he barked at them. "Donkey dicks. Yeah. Defense—that's where the men hang out. You want to play defense, you gotta be a man—and you sorry scumbags have a long way to go."

Actually, they didn't look all that bad—there were some kids he could see already might really have the stuff. Not that he was going to tell any of them that, not for a long time.

For one thing, Mitch liked the fact that there were a lot of black players out there on that gym floor, at least nine or ten. Maybe it sounded racist, hell, maybe it even *was* racist, but he couldn't help it—he just believed black kids made better athletes. They ran faster, hit harder. They stomped over other players; they were more arrogant, tougher, meaner.

"They've got some instinctive aggressiveness to them a lot of white kids don't have. Maybe it's from growing up in a more hostile environment. I don't know. There's always white kids who like to play dirty. I did myself. You'll find a few white guys who are mean cats, and that's what you want. But you line up a hundred black and a hundred white, there's gonna be a lot more mean black kids than mean white kids."

And for Mitch, mean was what counted. "This is a vicious game, gentlemen," he bawled at the players, a line he would repeat almost daily throughout the season. "A vicious, vicious game."

Black guys had the right attitude. Mitch identified more with them than with white guys, especially these B-CC white guys, who looked like a bunch of pampered pussies who'd never done a bit of hard work in their lives.

Take a white guy like Billy Stone, for instance, a guy who thought he was set to play both ways—tight end and linebacker—and didn't look to Mitch like he was ready to play either. One of Pete's favorites, too, Mitch could tell; Pete had coached him since freshman year, with the Jayvee. He was full of praise for him. Blond, blue-eyed, all-American kid. "Stone, where did you ever get the idea you could play?" Mitch had screamed at him earlier, out on the field. "You suck, you know that?" The kid was showing nothing.

The reason was simple: Billy Stone was sick as a dog. Not recovering, either, like Toby was; right in the thick of it. He had a raging peritonsillar infection that was barely being held in check with heavy antibiotics. He'd had a fever and a terrible sore throat for weeks; only a tonsillectomy would bail him out. He had begged his mom to let him put off the operation till after the season—she was a nurse practitioner down at Georgetown University Hospital—but there was no way. So he'd taken the next best route and let her schedule the operation before two-a-days even began.

It had gone smoothly up to the point when they were about to wheel him into the operating room. A nurse had drawn some blood and noticed it looked a little thin. You weren't supposed to take anything, no aspirin, nothing, before an operation, but his mom—

his nurse mom!—had insisted he take an Advil or Motrin, one of those pills. One pill—he could have done without it, it didn't hurt that much—and they couldn't do the operation. He was wheeled out and they had to reschedule the operation for just before the first game. He would have blown up right there—Billy had a temper, he could go off—but his mom started crying, she felt so bad, and she looked so cute standing there, he just couldn't get mad. So he didn't.

But now, of course, he felt rotten; his throat hurt, his head hurt, and he wasn't about to take anything for it and run the risk of having the operation postponed again. As it was, he'd have to miss at least one game. And here was this asshole, Mitch Babashan, dressed in Spandex head to toe, flexing his muscles like some kind of macho wanna-be, telling him he sucked. He and his buddy Bob Plante swaggering around, yelling, like walking stereotypes, the kind of guys who are so afraid of ever being called gay they have to overdo the macho bit to a ludicrous extreme.

At least, that was how Billy had figured them out. He enjoyed studying people, always had. One of the main reasons he liked B-CC was that there were so many different types around to study. He'd come up through private schools, went to a small Catholic school for junior high, but when it was time for high school, his dad had said the decision was up to him—if he wanted to go to public school, he could. Billy had thought about it—all his friends were going on to Catholic high schools, after all—but finally he decided to cast his lot with B-CC. There was just something about that progression, one private school to another, that bothered him—it was too narrow a world, too protected, too . . . white-supremacist elite, maybe.

So he'd gone to B-CC, and early the first week of school, when he showed up for junior-varsity tryouts, he opened the door to the gym and saw what looked like a solid sea of black kids lining the bleachers. He never forgot that moment—it was almost as if there were a sign hanging over them: "Welcome to the real world, Billy Stone." He'd taken a big gulp and walked into his new life, knowing no one, a real nerd. Yet even that had been interesting. When you knew no one, you had so much more time to study people, watch how they behaved.

By now, three years later, there was no question Billy was one of the most popular kids in school; yet "I also know what it's like to be a nerd, and it's no different, really, you don't enjoy life any more. You're still the same person." In fact, he was almost looking forward to having the experience again, next year, at college—knowing no one, able to observe.

A longtime football and baseball player, Billy had known many coaches, heard plenty of harangues in his time. But this guy was different; he was over the top. A real asshole. Were they going to be stuck with him all season? He swallowed painfully—God, his throat hurt!—kept his eyes expressionless, and tried to pay attention.

Brendan Reed though, next to him, was listening intently. A medium-sized kid, with a high forehead, round, trusting brown eyes, an almost babyish face, Brendan might not have had the glossy reputation around school of a Rick or a Geoff, but on the team itself, no one doubted it for a minute: this was a true athlete, a guy who would tackle anyone, anywhere, a guy who just did not know how to quit. In the coming weeks, in fact, the only time Toby would have qualms about his vulnerable spleen was when he went up against Brendan one-on-one in a hitting drill. Plenty of other guys were bigger; Toby himself had several inches on Brendan. It didn't matter. The Panther—that was his nickname—was lethal.

No one knew exactly where his tenacity had come from, unless it had something to do with his childhood. He'd been learning-disabled and had had to attend special classes for many years, thrown in with kids who were retarded, disturbed—the whole gamut. The only time he'd been able to hang around with regular kids had been during recess; playing sports. It was his avenue to the mainstream and had quickly become vitally important. Of course, he had been in regular classes now for years; even a couple of honors classes, in history, which he loved. But he'd stayed with the sports, his first love, his first experience of success.

When his stepfather, Mike Reese, had first appeared on the scene, years before (Brendan's parents had been divorced when he was ten months old), he sized it up quickly: this was a kid made for football. His own son had been a great baseball player, but as for football, he hadn't had it, he was afraid. Lots of kids were; they shrank back. Nothing wrong with it, but you couldn't play football if you were scared to get hit. Brendan wasn't scared of anything. Mike had named the kid Panther himself, when he was in the third grade and had owned a T-shirt with a panther on it. But the reason the name stuck—hell, the kid *was* a panther, he'd take on anyone, he was so crazy.

Brendan had heard all of Mike Reese's stories about his own football days on B-CC's last championship team, thirty years back. He loved Coach White, but he could be pretty laid back. This Mitch—he looked like the real thing.

Mitch glanced around the gym to gauge the effect he was having on the boys. Did they look scared enough? Upset? Angry? Billy Stone sure didn't look happy. Good. Let the kid feel anxious, let them all feel nervous; it got the adrenaline up. If they hated his guts, so much the better—they'd take it out on the field, throw it into the game.

Mitch had plans for this crew, big plans. True, you couldn't make chicken salad out of chicken shit, but there was raw material out there on that gym floor. A decent coach, Mitch believed, could always coach 'em up, like the saying went. Besides, he had coached college football; there was no reason not to try to put some of that expertise to work with this team. These were bright kids, supposedly, white-collar types, all headed to college—not like his old high school. At Springbrook, for a lot of the kids, football was the last moment of glory, the last chance at the gold ring. At Springbrook they yelled, "scoreboard, scoreboard!" when they were beating the pants off a team. B-CC, they said, used to come back with their own cheer: "That's all right, that's okay, you're gonna work for us anyway."

"Springbrook is blue-collar, it's down and dirty, you yell, you scream and that's what produces good football." B-CC was a whole different atmosphere. Why, just yesterday, on the field, one of the kids had run up to him and Bobby and asked them to hold his watch for him. A Rolex watch!

Some of the kids here drove better cars to practice than he and Bobby had. And that was fine, nothing wrong with it. Their parents had worked hard and wanted to give their kids the best . . . but sometimes, when you had things given to you, you didn't have to work that hard for it, you didn't have the hunger.

Mitch wanted to arouse that hunger, but he wanted more, too—
he wanted to take this bunch of kids, if possible, and turn every one
of them into a roaring, screaming maniac. As he saw it, that was a
defensive coach's first priority.

"The defense coach's job is to pull out that animal that is hidden
down in our souls. Buried years ago. You have to pull that out, and
turn them into fighters. It's your job to do that. There's no room to
be a nice guy—you gotta be nasty, rule the world."

Offense was different. Offense meant control, thought, cooperation. That's why the offensive-line guys were encouraged to hang
out together, be family; they needed to be able to communicate.
Defensive players—the best ones—weren't out for anyone but
themselves. They walked alone, they made their own paths—they
were nasty, mean, intimidating bastards.

And how did you turn a bunch of well-mannered suburban boys
into nasty, rotten S.O.B.s? Well, for starters, you didn't waste time
checking out stances, like Bob was doing. That was offense, that
was control. With defense, you went right to the hitting drills—
lined them up, sent them roaring out against each other. Then you
screamed at them, berated them, undercut them, and embarrassed
them. Just like he was doing now.

There was no other way. You had to knock them all down, right
from the start; this was the only way to do it.

Bob, he knew, didn't see it quite that black and white. Bob
thought you had to hold out a few crumbs. You might smack a
puppy, but you patted his head, too; otherwise you could defeat
him for good. Their egos were so fragile at this age. But Bob was
working with the offensive line, not defense; things were cooler on
the O-line. Defense ran on emotion, just as Mitch did himself.

"You goddamn bunch of pussies, what the fuck are you trying to
do? Do something right for once, will you?" he blasted them.

As far as Mitch was concerned, he was off to a good start.

CHAPTER THREE

SOMEWHERE AROUND the fourth day of preseason training, Mother Nature decided to give the boys a break: there was a slight dip of several degrees, and even the humidity eased up a little. Everyone was grateful.

By now most of the boys were aching most of the time; everyone except Billy Stone was popping painkillers—Advil, Excedrin, you name it. Most spent the hour between morning and afternoon practices lying motionless on a couch in their air-conditioned living rooms; few were able to eat. "We'd just lie down in a dark room and cry for an hour," one boy said.

Three of the junior players spent one break swimming in the luxurious indoor pool at one boy's house, but the change in atmosphere was too much to take—floating in the cool water, yet knowing within thirty minutes they would be back on the field, in uniform, sweating like pigs. After that, they saved the pool for the end of the day.

Yet some of the veterans, who had trained under the old coach a couple of years back, found this season's two-a-days too easy. "I knew what a hard two-a-day was like, and these weren't that hard," said Brendan Reed. "Sometimes Rick and I would even go running after practice. You're supposed to be dead tired." He, for one, would have liked to see more sprinting. To Dave Bardach, two-a-days were hard, but nothing like the old coach's—compared to him, Coach White's training was a walk in the park, he thought.

But others found the training quite enough as it was. "It was so hot, I was like dying out there, feeling so sick, dizzy; everybody was out of shape," said Toby's friend Lunkhead, who was tall, skinny, and had allergies that tended to turn into bronchitis—"the only player," cracked Pete, "who brings his own Kleenex to practice."

"That first day, I wanted to die," said Brendan Symes; in the previous season he had racked up enough injuries to earn Pete's description as "NIH's answer to B-CC football." (The National Institute of Health was a Bethesda landmark.) "My head was spinning, my heart going really fast. Alex and I had to run hills, up and down. Alex couldn't go anymore, and if he didn't, we all had to keep doing them. I was grabbing him, pushing him up the hill. You have to do that." For Alex Burgess, the rigors of two-a-days were having a dramatic effect: within less than a week, he had lost fifteen pounds.

"They're hell days. Torture," said John Han. "You go in, everybody's out of shape. Nobody except Kong has been preparing.

"At the beginning, they were just teaching us the moves. But then we got into hitting—it was constant, all this contact. People would walk in the next day, ohhh, I can't move my neck, who's got the Advil? It was so painful.

"You go in there, start playing, and keep playing until you can't breathe anymore. You play to a point that you feel like you're gonna throw up. The pads and helmet add 30 degrees to your body heat. All we'd look forward to was water breaks—hey, coach, when we gonna get water? Shut up. They worked us so hard, 'cause if we didn't get in shape, we couldn't compete. But it was torture. It seemed like it would never end."

Then there were the boys like Toby and Billy—boys who felt bad to begin with. For them, two-a-days were even grimmer. Whether by accident or design, both Mitch and Bob seemed to save their nastiest jibes for those players who were not in peak physical condition, as a result of illness or injury. The ankle fracture that had ended Bob's football career still bothered him; he often brought a bucket of ice out onto the field to stick his leg in. Mitch still battled the headaches his concussion had caused. Yet the sight of illness or injury in these young boys seemed to trigger in both of them an almost brutal, knee-jerk contempt.

"When you have an injury, something like that, you're just the lowest," said Toby. "They'd say, you fucking pussy—they'd joke, but it still made you feel bad." His exhaustion this first week was almost overwhelming, but he knew he couldn't complain—what good would it do? What did they care about the effects of mono? All they cared about was whether or not you could do the job.

"I could barely walk," said Shane Dempsey, who had pulled a groin muscle early on, "and I'd be sitting, watching practice, and the two of them would walk by—you're a pussy! To me it was like, Jesus Christ—was I supposed to go out there and get more injured?"

Again, to those who had known the old coach, this was nothing new. Geoff Smith remembered the former coach standing over him after a bad tackle had come dangerously close to breaking his neck. "It don't hurt, boy! It don't hurt unless you let it! Suck up that pain!" And at the time, he had believed the coach was completely right; he'd been furious at his parents, who'd reacted with such anger, especially his mother. It had been months before he'd begun to see their side. That was what happened with football: you placed your coach above everyone, even family.

Of course, playing through pain was part of the tradition. Since football hurts—and it does—concerned attention cannot be given to every ache and bruise; if it were, few players would still be on the field by the end of the day. And it's all too easy to make the jump from there to ignoring all pain, assuming every player's complaint is bogus. Mitch and Bob were hardly the first high school coaches to take the tack "unless I see bone coming out of the skin, you ain't injured, pal—get the hell back out there." They just happened to take it with unusual relish.

Sure, it was dangerous, ignoring pain. Sure, it was chancy. Of course no mother would have tolerated it for a minute, had they known. They rarely did, however. "I tell them, if you do get hurt, for God's sake, don't tell your mother and don't go to your family physician," Pete White said. There were sports doctors for that sort of thing, doctors who understood, who could be relied on to tape you up and get you back out there. Unless, of course, you really were seriously injured, which was, of course—knock wood—impossible.

The idea was to show the boys they could take it. Suck it up, ignore it, play through it, emerge on the other side a better man. At last year's banquet, Pete White had saved his highest praise for the players who "were injured, but that didn't stop them!" Not a boy in the audience missed that message.

The possibility of injury looms over every high school football field every day of the season—as huge, as unavoidable, as a bear in the bedroom. No parent is completely immune from fear. "I cringe. My fingers are crossed always. I worry big time. That's my baby," one Montgomery County football parent admitted recently, without shame, and nobody thought any the worse of him for it, even though the parent happened to be world-famous boxing champion Sugar Ray Leonard.

It is true, of course, that injuries happen in every sport; that walking across a street can be dangerous; that probably the only foolproof method of raising an active child without injury would involve eighteen years of confinement in a padded cell; true, too, that my older son once broke his leg falling out of a hammock. And mercifully, it is true as well that grisly injuries, the neck-snapping kind that haunt parents' nightmares, are rare—although they do happen, inevitably, once or twice every year on a high school field somewhere in the country.

But garden-variety injuries are not rare at all in football; how could they be? What other team sport demands that young bodies repeatedly smash themselves into other young bodies, time after time? According to the National Athletic Trainers' Association, 37 percent of U.S. high school football players had been injured during the previous year at least badly enough to be sidelined for the rest of the day. For basketball, the next most injury-prone team sport, the number was 23 percent, a sizable drop.

Injuries are brutally common on the football field. The bear is with you always. What you do—coaches, players, and parents—is pretend the bear does not exist, or that he is harmless, stuffed. Perhaps then he will leave you alone. Magical thinking, of course, but no football team can get too far without it.

In an odd way, the coaches' attitude wasn't that far removed from the mother who carefully keeps her face expressionless when her two-year-old stumbles, then glances toward her to see if he's seriously hurt. Mothers do not typically tell toddlers to "suck up that pain, you goddamn pussy"—yet, in essence, they are employing the same technique.

The boys sucked it up as well as they could. Complaints were useless; whining was unthinkable. Two-a-days were the basic training for football, traditionally detested by every player, but necessary.

"You guys are going to be in the best shape of your lives after this," Coach White promised them, and that was heartening. But no football player truly loved preseason training. Still, you had to do it—without it, you didn't play. And nothing was more important than that.

"Better than sex." That was what many of them said, often adding the quick assurance, "I've had both, and I know." The pumping, the hitting, the giant, overpowering rush—the boys' descriptions of playing football often tallied word for word with those of junkies describing their favorite drug experience. And they were quite aware of this. "I am a football addict," many avowed. "It must be what cocaine is like," said one.

"Nothing could get me away from playing football—the feeling you get," said Mark Bitz, the junior who was backing up Alex as center. "When you put on the pads and you're hitting people, it's literally a feeling of immortality. You feel like you've got a shield around you that nothing can penetrate. You also feel you've got more outgoing force. Like you've got a destructive power inside you."

Many of the boys found football a sufficient form of intoxication, at least during the season. "There's something about working with your body, it sounds corny and all, but you don't feel like drinking," said junior linebacker Christo Doyle. "When you're drinking you're like trying to lose touch with reality, and when you play football, that's exactly what we're doing—and that's enough. You don't need any more.

"You have a game every weekend, you totally lose touch with everything. You don't need anything."

For the most part, that included steady girlfriends as well—

although a certain number of players continued with relationships that had started before the season. Significantly, however, few high-profile players did.

"When football comes, I can't have a girlfriend. Don't have time," one boy put it.

"Shit, I'm satisfied with just football," said Geoff Smith. "I think if you have football as a love, you don't need . . . it does everything. You don't feel a need for a girlfriend. Wrestling now, I hate the damn thing. You need a girlfriend when you wrestle."

It was not that the boys did not continue to socialize—all were matter-of-factly aware that football itself could be a powerful magnet to the opposite sex. Jocks got the girls; an old-fashioned truism, perhaps, but, hey, if it worked . . . "If I wasn't a football player, I'd resent it," said Kong. "But as long as I am, I guess it comes with the territory."

But for the most part they avoided any steady alliances during the season. In the crude but descriptive B-CC vernacular, they "got on" girls—they just didn't get involved with them.

"Maybe there's some connection between football and wanting to not actually have a girlfriend," said Billy Stone thoughtfully. "That you just get on different girls, there's got to be some connection between football and that . . . football makes you feel you're so awesome, you feel too good for any one girl, maybe.

"It couldn't happen in baseball . . . football is a much bigger commitment. It's like you don't have a life outside of football, it's so big it just consumes you.

"But it makes you the man. Like no other sport can. It makes you feel like the man."

Baseball cap pulled down over his head, his lugubrious hound's face set in its stock expression, which fell somewhere in the stretch between mournful and grim, Sal Fiscina stood watching practice from the side of the field. A viewer would have said he looked like a onetime athlete down on his luck, but he would have been only half right. Sal was a former athlete, true enough, but there had never been anything wrong with his luck.

He had come up hard—well, not hard urban, but not middle

class, either. Italian family, overloaded with women: two sisters, several aunts. His father had worked on the railroad that was barely a stone's throw from their row home in Hornell, New York; a former Brooklyn boy, he had been a barber once, and still cut Sal's hair, all the years he was growing up, in the old barber's chair he kept downstairs. Actually, Sal had lost most of his hair as a young man. You could probably make something Freudian out of that, if you wanted to.

Neither parent had gone to high school, although his mother, who had finished eighth grade, two grades more than his father, was big on education. And for some reason, it had all come easy to Sal—high school salutatorian, full scholarship to Harvard—no one in his neighborhood had even gone to college, much less Harvard. And after that he'd just kept on going—the University of Rochester School of Medicine—why not, after all, doctors were God, who wouldn't want to be God? Then a law degree at George Washington University. The degrees had enabled him pretty much to forge his own career, a very successful, lucrative one. He had his own law firm, which dealt with medical malpractice, he gave lectures and seminars around the country, he'd written a few texts. And all this was good, because it allowed him to make his own hours, giving him the time to do what he wanted to do most in life, which was watch his son play football. So it had all worked out. A lot better than you might have thought it had, seeing that face.

Because none of it meant as much to him as sports did—none of it. Oh, it was nice to have the degrees, let's be honest, people's faces changed when they found out they were talking to a doctor-lawyer–Harvard grad. It meant respect; respect was important. It meant a comfortable life, too; a spacious split-level just off Rock Creek Park in North Chevy Chase, where the closets were about the same size his old room at home had been.

But none of it meant as much as sports. Sports were paramount.

If you asked him what the absolute peak of his life was, the very apex, he'd have to say it didn't have anything to do with academic triumphs at all. No degree, no honor, had ever come close to matching the first varsity football game he'd ever played in high school.

He was fourteen, just a first-year Jayvee player standing on the sidelines. Late in the game, the best varsity player was injured. They put him in as tailback; back then, at his school, that was the key position, the guy who passed the ball, made it happen. He was numb, terrified; a wiry 145-pound kid, barely five-seven, under the lights for the first time. The ball came back, he threw it—and the pass was good. Again and again, four or five times, he threw beautiful, long, perfect passes to the roaring approval of the crowd. He won the game for them; they carried him out, the hero of the night.

It meant everything—instant glory, instant acceptance. It meant he could bury, finally, that memory of having gone home crying from kindergarten, like a little wimp. He'd gone on to play, to huge success, all through high school; all through Harvard, too. But nothing else ever felt quite that good—until the moment nearly thirty years later when he stood behind a fence at the B-CC stadium and watched his son, Rick, do almost exactly the same thing. As a ninth-grader, age fourteen, almost precisely the same height and weight that Sal had been at that age, Rick was put in as varsity quarterback late in a losing game against powerful Springbrook. With forty-two seconds left on the clock, he rolled out and threw a long, perfect, ringingly accurate touchdown pass.

"They say don't live through your kid, but what am I supposed to do, ignore it?" Sal said. For he knew exactly what it meant right away—the glory, the acceptance, the insurance of a golden high school experience. How could he not? He'd had the same shining moment himself.

Of course, he'd had something to do with it, helped set the stage a bit, maybe. Rick was the third child, the first son, born after two girls, wonderful girls; but Sal's wife, Jo-Ann, had never had any doubt: "I knew we weren't going to stop until we'd had that boy." Sal had encouraged sports early and often. "It wasn't really pushing," Rick remembered. "Just—let's go throw the ball. And it was fun, so you did it." The odd thing was, for all his identification with his son, Sal really wasn't a pusher, particularly. "I came to the conclusion long ago, partly because I'm lazy, that I can't control my kids . . . they are themselves, their own persons." Of course he was very much aware that part of the reason he was able to be that way was his wife. Jo-Ann Fiscina had a real flair for administration and no-nonsense discipline, both in and out of the home; as long as she kept everything running smoothly, he was free to play as loose a hand as he liked.

But there had never been any doubt about his interest in sports. By age ten, Rick was playing Boys' Club football; Sal pitched in, doing some coaching. He loved it, he loved being around kids—all kinds of kids. From then on his work schedule revolved around Rick's games.

And it had worked—in a growing crescendo, like one of those soaring spirals both he and his son had each thrown at exactly the right moment, Rick's football game had gotten better and better. Last year had been the best; this year, his senior year, Sal was hoping for even more, even though he was painfully aware last year's line was gone. It had all worked pretty well, so far, even though you might not have known it, seeing Sal, with that tough, grim, Italian streetwise mug. His face was his camouflage, just another way, like sports had been, of burying the wimp inside— "After all, we're all wimps, we all hide it."

The boys had stopped practice and were lining up now for the individual pictures that would run in the program; I stood with Sal Fiscina behind the fence, watching. They were in full armor— helmet, uniform, pads, cleats; each was doing his best to assume a tough, warriorlike grimace for the camera. Yet somehow this only served to underline their youth. Watching them, you were suddenly struck with what you often forgot when they were underfoot around the house—how painfully young they were, how infinitely breakable.

At least, I was; Sal seemed unmoved. "Look mean," he called to Brendan Reed. "Look angry. Pretend someone took away your beer."

For myself, the various ambivalent feelings I had been harboring for weeks about the season, the game, and my role as a football parent were now churning inside me like an emotional Cuisinart. For one thing, I knew the scrimmages were coming, and I had told Toby he could shave a few days off the doctor's directive and play. (I did not, of course, know he had been playing from the beginning.) This had added yet another fillip of guilt to my overloaded psyche.

At the same time, I was annoyed—why couldn't I be like Sal at this point, calm, relaxed, looking forward to the season? Why was I always trying to ferret out deep-seated motives, which invariably turned out to be either unpalatable or downright nasty? Digging under the skin, probing for the nerve . . . it was this examined-life business, I figured. Heartily recommended in theory, sure, but almost always a royal pain in the ass in practice. I took a deep breath and shoved my anxieties into the far corner of my brain, determined to enjoy the day. Zen and the art of football parenthood. It was worth a try.

Even before the team's first scrimmage, Mitch was well on the way to his first goal—breaking the boys down to the point that they hated his guts. In the case of a few players, he might have even overshot the mark.

He told lineman Rene Grave de Peralta that Mike Mitchem could take him any day of the week in one-on-one combat; he told Mitchem that Alex Burgess would leave him in the dust; he told Csaba Hadas, who was Hungarian, and still having trouble with English, let alone football lingo, that no Commie could ever understand an all-American game like football.

A number of boys were bothered by Mitch's fondness for spurring competition by pitting one player against another (a technique dear to the heart of many gruff coach-manager types, and not a few newspaper editors). "He said, 'You better start shaping up 'cause someone's behind your position that's probably better than you,' " said Rene. Rather than pushing him to greater effort, Mitch's strategy left him feeling "like I'm the pits, really bad."

"I saw where he was coming from," said Mike Mitchem, who was an analytic sort. "But it backfired . . . it didn't incite competition and work ethic, it demoralized, it caused resentment, it made relationships between players more tense. He'd use me to spite Rene—Rene was my buddy. I told him not to worry about it, but I resented it."

Mitch continued to yell at everyone, and his temper was a formidable one. Bob Plante's roaring had a planned, almost theatrical quality to it—what's more, he was much more likely to yell at the entire offensive line rather than one individual player. Pete's zingers broke everyone up. But Mitch's ravings struck more than one of the players as being at times seriously out of control "Like someone you'd really worry about," said one.

Billy Stone, for instance, knew all about bad tempers—he had one, and so did his father, his brother, and his grandfather, who was certainly one of the few eighty-year-olds to ever be hauled into court on assault charges. (Ordered to stop hunting for crabs near a private marina, he had given the other man's boat such a solid whack with his oar that charges had been brought; the judge, after one incredulous look at the miscreant and his 89-year-old lawyer, had thrown the case out.) But even Billy found Mitch at times a bit scary. The things he said to people! No one should have the right to talk like that to anyone.

Yet no one could fault his dedication. He showed up every day with sheets of intricate plays, defensive strategies so complicated they had rarely been seen on any high school field; plays that left many of the boys moaning in confusion. Early on Mitch began to depend heavily on Dave Bardach, who played middle linebacker. Dave, he saw, could be relied on to understand the play, then to direct the action on the field.

Dave responded well to this special position, and a real bond began to grow between him and the coach. Mitch's snarling was actually not much worse than the old coach's had been, Dave thought. Of course, at first, that guy had upset him pretty bad— Dave was a sensitive kind of guy. "I'd come home, Mom, I'm not going back. I just died through the whole season." But something wouldn't allow him to quit, and eventually he'd figured it out—you had to listen to what he said, not how he said it.

Also, he'd learned something else. No matter how the guy reamed you out, once you were his friend, you were his friend for good. He'd even told Dave once that if he ever had problems, he'd be welcome to stay at his place. That's the kind of guy he was, off the field at least. Once the face mask was on, though, it was a different story—"we weren't people." Mitch, he thought, was a lot like that coach.

Dave, in fact, was starting to feel better about the season in general. Maybe this year wouldn't be a washout after all, maybe a guy like Mitch could actually shape up some of these soft kids. To his way of thinking, they could use a little rough handling. Coach White was almost too nice, sometimes—a lot of these players didn't even know what hard work was. Maybe now they'd find out. That was fine with him; these guys needed it.

Kong, like Dave, was reminded of the old coach—Mitch even looked a little like him, he thought. Of course, no one had really liked that guy, he was so into winning, but you had to admit he had intensity. Maybe the team needed some of that. Last year Kong had had the feeling for the first time, after the Churchill game—"our destiny was in our hands." He'd give anything to feel like that again. If this guy could help . . .

Mitch did seem to have favorites—not so much favorite players, necessarily, as favorite positions. A former linebacker himself, he had a definite leaning toward linebacker-oriented defense. A number of the linemen bristled at this.

"I remember one time in my junior year he had said, you guys are just like shit—you're here to keep the offensive linemen off the linebackers, so just listen to them; you do nothing, you're mindless, sit there, keep 'em off and shut up," said Mike Mitchem, a lineman. "His attitude toward us was, you're a big dumb brute, take the space up, hold the man in front of you, let the smart intelligent athletes behind you do their thing, if you just hold your man, then, hey, we'll win. But it doesn't work like that."

The linebackers, though—James, Dave, Brendan Reed, Kong— were, unsurprisingly, not at all put off by this attitude. Junior linebacker Christo Doyle, whom Mitch dubbed Goose because of his long neck, decided fairly early that the coach was "really harsh and really caring" at the same time.

And Geoff Smith was thrilled. Sure, Coach White was wonderful, but this guy was different—he really felt for the game. Geoff could tell. The way he screamed at them, so intense; yeah, he came on a little strong, maybe, but at least you knew he cared; he wasn't just fooling around, this was important to him. That was the main thing, as far as Geoff was concerned: he cared. You had to care.

The insults, the nasty cracks, the curses—none of that mattered, not really. Of course, Geoff knew Mitch wasn't talking about *him*: how could he be? The star wide receiver? Geoff knew his worth. He loved playing wide receiver, loved being in the spotlight out there—the ball floating into his hands, the stands exploding. But he loved defense even more, loved playing free safety, tackling, smashing, letting it all out. No holds barred.

All Geoff wanted was for everyone else on the team to feel the way he did—totally committed, totally involved. If they did, the Barons could go to the top this year; nothing would stop them. And Mitch wanted the same thing, he knew it. He wanted them to be the best they could be. Geoff felt he understood the guy.

James McDonald, too, was not bothered in the slightest by the yelling. James came from a family of five boys; he'd heard yelling in his time. The name-calling was no big deal either. He knew how he talked to his younger brothers, especially the eleven-year-old, who thought he was such a hot shot at basketball. It didn't mean anything. What was important was that Mitch was into it. The man knew football.

But many of the others continued to feel wary. And there were some who had already come to look upon the young coach as an enemy.

Shane Dempsey was one of the few boys who would not have looked out of place in a Churchill or Gaithersburg lineup. Tall, blond, blue-eyed, with a wide neck, large arms, and powerful muscularity (he did construction work in the summer), he was readily identifiable in any crowd as a football player. An observer would have pointed him out instantly, while perhaps failing even to notice scrawny, underdeveloped Geoff Smith.

Shane had already played varsity football for two years in Florida before moving to Montgomery County last year. He'd started out playing offense down there, but one day had a small epiphany on the field. "A little fat kid was in front of me"—Shane had been a fat kid himself at one time, and had hated it profoundly—"and he came charging at me and I knocked him off his feet. . . . It was the best feeling in the world. I loved that. I think that's when I realized I wanted to be able to really level someone." Not stand there and block, like on offense—run up and smash.

So Shane now wanted to play defense a lot. But since last year had been his first at B-CC, he had gone with the flow, let them work him in where they needed him most. He and James had played linebacker on the bird-dog team—traditionally the grunts of any team, the bottom of the totem pole, the human tackling dummies used to hone the first string players to steely perfection. Both of them, being juniors, were willing to do the scut work—after all, senior year was coming. They'd even made a game of it, developing special little howls to use. "After all, when you're bird dog, you have to have something."

Only now that senior year had arrived, there were two new coaches, and both of them had decided, apparently, that Shane was a natural for the offensive line. He'd had the experience, he knew how to block, and God knows the offensive line needed expertise.

"I'm like, but I don't want to play offensive line," said Shane, plaintively. "So I'd go over to where the linebackers were practicing—Coach White would send me over—and Mitch would send me back. I'm, should I listen to the head coach, which I should, or should I listen to this bully? He did not like me and I did not like him.

"Coach White was like, get over there, and Mitch was like, get the hell out of here. I was like, I want to hit you so bad." Shane continued to show up for defense drill doggedly, but it was becoming obvious Mitch was not about to give an inch. "He saw it as I had an attitude problem." Even Coach White, when Shane finally went in to talk to him about it, was somewhat noncommittal. Shane, he implied, should probably have agreed to play offense, if that's what they wanted. Things did not seem to be shaping up well for the season.

Mike Mitchem, too, was locked in a power struggle with the coach. Theoretically, Mike fit Mitch's profile for a defensive player almost to the letter—a light-skinned black boy, the product of a biracial marriage, he was strong, tough, powerful, and a lunatic on the field. No one could accuse him of not being individualistic, either. Extremely bright, he had a reputation for being at times a bit spacey, lost in his own world. Once, when practice had been called for nine in the morning, he showed up on the field at nine that night; another time he hitched a ride home, forgetting he had brought his car. "Brilliant in the classroom," said one boy, "but no common sense." But there was no denying he had a real flair—and an unbridled enthusiasm—for knocking people down.

"It's sadistic or something," he said. "If I can just crush someone and make them hurt . . . I really try to hurt them. I'm the kind of player, one of the things I like to do is cause pain to the other player. That's part of my fun, my enjoyment, as much as getting to the ball, I want to hurt the guy in front of me. It's a primordial instinct."

And Mike Mitchem knew more than a little about that instinct—he had come face to face with his own personal capacity for violence long ago. As a kid growing up in Milwaukee, he had been sent to an inner-city public school. "We lived in an all-white neighborhood in a really affluent area. My mom is white, my dad is black. I had no friends around there; the kids were older; they called me nigger; they all chased me and tried to beat me up.

"So all my friends were from this school, from the ghetto, and that's where I started to hang out." And the group he hung out with was a rough one. "All sorts of really bad stuff—fighting, stealing. I saw all sorts of stuff—you'd see people stabbed—and you became really desensitized, totally." Once he cut a white kid in his neighborhood who called him names. "For me to pull out a knife was second nature.

"I'd seen people killed, and then seen it on the news—and you'd be thinking to yourself, I was there, in your mind—and it was exciting. When I see stuff on the news now, a 12-year-old kid robbed and stabbed someone, people say, how could they do this? I'm like, ah, it can happen—you become socialized. Totally desensitized."

Mike's family, which included three sisters, was a stable professional one. His father was a lobbyist who ran a nonprofit organization that aided low-income and minority students; his mother was an administrator who worked with programs for the homeless. "A good family, no drinking, no drug addicts." He had other interests at the time, including a passion for cycling; there was no lack of discipline in the home. Yet he feels sure, even today, that this alone would not have been enough to change him, snap him out of the dangerous whirlpool he had somehow been pulled into. A good friend from a very similar sort of family who had run with the same group never came back; he died, a suicide, a few years ago.

"You have to have something that will bring you out. Something to shock you out of it," he believed. For Mike, it took the form of three separate incidents, all involving friends. In the first, he started to choke a boy—a friend—in a fight, "and he became unconscious and I wanted to kill him and that scared me the most. 'Cause I was like, yeah, you're gonna die—and first I was happy and then I was scared shitless."

Then in a fight with another boy, "there was a car bumper and I had his head and was about to smash it on the bumper . . . and I let him go. I just realized."

But the third incident was the one that changed him forever. "It was my best friend, we consider each other brothers . . . he's white . . . we'd never been in a fight, and I did something that pissed him off and he came at me and cornered me. I thought he was going to punch me. He got close and before I thought about it I just—pow—kicked him in the nuts."

Instantly he was filled with horror. "He was on the ground. I was like, oh my God, are you okay? I'd never do that, I love him so much, to kick him like that, he might not be able to have kids . . . but I did do it." And with that realization, everything changed—he began to avoid fights; he stopped hanging around with the gang at school; the direction of his life shifted, backing away from the abyss. It was years before he told his parents how close he had been to it. "You don't feel comfortable telling until you get to a point where you can look back and not be threatened by it."

He still enjoyed fighting, intimidation, venting his aggression, causing pain—urges like that don't magically dissolve, no matter how many moments of self-knowledge are vouchsafed. But he confined it to the field. That was the place for it. Off the field, he stayed away from fights—away, too, from drugs and alcohol.

Supposedly when Indian tribes gathered around the campfire years ago, no one ever prevented a baby from crawling toward the flames. He would only do it once, they knew, and he would learn a lesson more graphic than any they could teach. Today's cities hold too many complicated dangers to make any real analogy possible. Still, in some sense it was true—Mike had crawled toward the fire, reached his hand out to touch the flame—and pulled back. For him, it had worked. He was immunized. He was also—and he knew this—extremely lucky.

In theory, then, Mike Mitchem was all but Mitch's ideal. Even his idiosyncrasies should have worked for him. "Great athletes make their own paths," Mitch said. But theory was one thing; reality, something else. Mike, who had come to B-CC a year ago, had enjoyed his junior year, mainly because coaches "let me play my own game." He did his best work, he felt, as an "instinctual player."

"I have a really unorthodox way of playing . . . but really successful, no one can deny it—highly successful in sacking the quarterback and stopping plays. And Mitch is the type of coach—he wanted you to strictly adhere to the plays he had worked out. He told me, no more of this wild-man stuff where you go off and do what you want this year—you're gonna listen to exactly what I tell you or you're not gonna play."

Mitch saw the boy as raw talent, fresh for remolding. "He wanted to reform my forearm technique; he wanted to change my stance. He just totally tried to change the way I play football, and that's where the conflict started." Mike felt it was "ludicrous" to try to change a player's technique in his senior year. And while, at first, he actually felt Mitch favored him over the other linemen "when I started not doing what he said, 'cause it didn't work for me," this changed abruptly; by the end of two-a-days, there was a distinct coolness, almost an animosity, between the two.

Both Mitch and Bob had a saying they evoked continually: "What is said on the field means nothing personal, just business." They realized quite early that some of the kids had a hard time understanding that all the yelling and screaming and berating they did was because of the game, the effort. Yeah, they called them fucking pussies, losers—sure, they screamed that they sucked, that they were bags of pus. But it was just business, couldn't they see that? Nothing personal at all.

Pete White himself took both of them aside after about a week, to encourage them to go a little easier. After all, these were B-CC kids, not Springbrook farm boys—they weren't used to being treated harshly. In truth, Pete was feeling a few qualms already about his trigger-happy assistants. He had wanted to introduce new blood, to give the boys a chance to learn more about the sport, but he was beginning to wonder if he hadn't unleashed something unmanageable. Still, it wasn't his nature to come down hard on anyone, especially colleagues; he preferred to handle the problem diplomatically, with suggestions.

He could have saved his breath. Both young coaches were disgusted and roundly indignant. Just what kind of hothouse flowers were they dealing with here? Just how delicately did you have to handle them—and how, please explain, did delicate handling create fierce, steamroller football players?

"When I first came, it was like, these guys, what the hell's the matter with them?" said Bob Plante. "It's like they've never played football before. Overly sensitive, I thought. So I yelled at them worse. My first impression was they weren't used to someone who cared enough to kick 'em in the backside.

"Pete said to take it a little easier on them—they're not used to this, it's a different class of kids. I'm not a poor kid myself. I grew up in a nice neighborhood, belonged to a country club, my friends are wealthy people. And nobody sat around and said, his father makes a lot of money, so be nice, take it easy on him. And I said to Pete, what do you think they do at Churchill? Don't tell me there's not wealthy people over there, and I'll tell you Coach Shepherd kicks them in the backside when they need it. But he said take it slow until they get used to it."

Bob tried to tone himself down for a few days, then gave it up—"I said, the hell with you guys. I don't care if you're sensitive or what your problem is, I'm gonna coach like I want to. I'm gonna yell at you, you guys are gonna cuss me, and we're gonna win games.

"I don't think they want a football coach who's like, why don't you block this way? Do you have a headache? They want a drill sergeant, I think. But you walk that thin line. You can't just browbeat them. I'll be the first one to kick them in the backside, the first one to pat them on the head."

It bothered Mitch, too, that the boys felt he was being hard on them. "Sometimes you have to hurt feelings," he said. "I yell and scream, I call them every name. I'd be thrown out of Montgomery County if they heard . . . but I'm not doing it because it's a macho thing. I get upset when they don't play to their potential." He himself felt warm toward every player, he said—the cursing, the browbeating, the blow-ups meant nothing personal, nothing personal at all; just business.

Only a number of the boys had trouble buying that.

"When Mitch hurled those insults, that destroyed morale," said one boy who in fact was rarely the target himself. "He was throwing grenades that landed hard." There was an old saying: " 'The best player never made the best coach,' " he added significantly.

"Just business," said John Han, with weary amusement. "Yeah. Right." He, for one, was convinced the two coaches were dead serious.

"If they could have, they would have followed us into the school. They took it personally, all right, really personally."

The Barons scrimmaged against several teams during two-a-days. Traditionally, preseason scrimmages not only test a team's mettle but give everyone an idea of what to expect from the coming season. This year, though, the results were resoundingly inconclusive. The boys played with such widely fluctuating success that no coach, no player, no onlooker could extract from their performance any lesson—or even any reasonable expectation—as to the weeks ahead. In fact, no one had a clue. Their ability to play the game was either great, lousy, or fair—depending on which scrimmage you were talking about.

The first, against up-county, rural Friendly, shocked everyone. Friendly had been runner-up for the state championship the year before, losing only to all-powerful Springbrook in the playoffs, in the last play of the game. By all rights, even in a low-key scrimmage, Friendly should have kicked B-CC all over the field. Instead, they barely—just barely—edged out ahead.

Every asset, every skill that B-CC possessed was on display that day. Brendan Symes ran like greased lightning, and in all the right paths (fast as he was, Brendan had a reputation for making crucial directional errors on the field—mistaking holes for piles, piles for holes). Dave assumed the mantle of defensive quarterback with quiet ease—directing, interpreting Mitch's signals smoothly. Rick threw sixteen for eighteen passes to completion, his aim unerring, his control unassailable. Sal Fiscina, the only parent who made the long drive out with the team, was thrilled. Even the line, the brand-new line, looked good, he thought.

It is a truism in football that a powerful, effective offensive line can make a quarterback look awfully good—but perhaps the reverse, too, is true on occasion. An outstanding quarterback, playing at the top of his game, can make an entire line look better than it is. And perhaps that truism was working that day to a degree. For certainly, if the line looked good at the Friendly scrimmage, it was almost pure happenstance. It was the first time the five boys who had been picked as tentative starters—Toby, Marc Gage, Tae Uk Kim, Alex Burgess, John Han—had faced up against another team. Any success had to owe a great deal to blind, dumb luck.

Toby, for one, was completely out to lunch.

"I was so scared. I didn't know what to do, I didn't have a clue," he said. "I've never felt worse in my life—this was the first time I'd ever really played." When the play called for cup blocking—basically, forming a protective cup around the quarterback—he was totally confused. "Hey, Gage, what *is* that?" he hissed desperately.

"Just do what I do," the kid hissed back. But it didn't help much. Defensive players moved by him with consummate ease; he had no idea how to stop them. "I felt so bad, so helpless."

Then came the worst moment—his lowest point. B-CC was seconds away from scoring. Brendan Symes, running with the ball, was headed straight for the gold, only inches away from the end zone. Toby, utterly at sea, following him, came up from behind—and clipped an opposing player. The coaches, all of them, exploded in a chorus of horror: "WHAT ARE YOU DOING? HE'S IN THE END ZONE, WHAT THE FUCK ARE YOU DOING?" Clipping—when an offense player blocks a defense player from behind—is an automatic 15-yard penalty. He had cost the team a touchdown.

"It was pitiful, pitiful," he said. He'd pushed himself to practice, to drill, to hit, despite the mono, despite his exhaustion, and this was the result. "Do something right for once!" screamed someone from the sidelines.

It was a moment of complete humiliation; no one had missed it. In all his years of playing sports, he had never known such a moment. Yet standing there, with the shame washing over him, his failure on display for everyone, he was still conscious of a tiny, fierce nugget of resolve within himself, made up of nothing but belief. He knew nothing, he was terrible—but this was going to change. He was going to make it change. He wasn't showing any ability on the outside; so they had decided he didn't have what it took. But he knew—he *knew* they were wrong. Their screaming neither destroyed him nor galvanized him into determination—the screaming was beside the point. The point was what he knew about himself.

"I didn't care what anyone else said. I just wanted to do it right—and I knew I could. I knew it. I knew I was fucking destined to do it right."

Despite's Toby's poor showing, though, and despite the boys' lack of experience, Bob Plante too was encouraged by the offensive line's performance that day. Marc Gage and Tae Uk—certainly two of the smallest offensive linemen in the county—showed real grit; Bob was elated to see Marc, barely five-six, square off determinedly against a six-foot-three, 250-pound player—and actually cream the guy. It proved his theory: "You can motivate anybody to do anything. If you get him in the right position, balance, low center of gravity, a 150-pound guy can knock the hell out of you. He just nailed the guy." And Tae Uk was so tenacious—knock him down, step on him, he'd still be gnawing at your ankle. The kid had the greatest heart in the world. Bob saw plenty of reason for optimism.

The Friendly scrimmage surpassed everyone's wildest hopes. On the bus ride home the players were in ecstatic, roaring high gear, with Geoff, as always, leading the cheers. So this was the best a bunch of tough farm boys could do? Hey, they were no match at all against urban know-how—the Barons had crawled right under their radar! Win 8 in '88 and go to the state! By God, this was going to be the year after all! They had it, they had it, the potential to be B-CC's greatest team yet.

Then, a scant three days later, they went up against another team and were completely demolished. With swift dispatch, St. John's, a Washington, D.C., Catholic school primarily known for its basketball prowess, chewed them up and spit them out all over the lot.

No one knew what to make of that either. It was a hot, muggy day—but it had been just as hot three days before. St. John's had a lot of huge players—but so had Friendly. And this time, the Barons were even playing on their own field. "Maybe they were overconfident, after Friendly," Sal theorized. "But we just looked horrible. Horrible. So ill prepared. They have a much better team, but we looked bad." Sal was concerned. For the first time he began to have serious fears about the capabilities of the new offensive line, which was looking frankly terrible today. How much could a quarterback do, how much could his son do, with a lousy line?

Diplomatically, he refrained from mentioning this to me—after all, my son was a part of the problem. To me, it just seemed that the whole team was being pummeled equally. A friend's comment rang in my ears: "It's funny, in football. They talk and plan, they scout, they adjust plays, they devise intricate strategies. Then they go out on the field and one team kicks the shit out of the other team."

Over simplistic, I had thought then, primly. But on the day B-CC scrimmaged St. John's, the crack was all too relevant. Everything had gone like clockwork at the Friendly scrimmage; today nothing went. St. John's rolled over B-CC's defense like a set of tenpins; the offensive line was blown away like dandelion seeds. A cloud of gloom seemed to descend on the field, stretching out to the sidelines.

I felt it in the stands intensely: a grim atmosphere boding nothing good for the season ahead. "What conclusion do you draw from this?" I asked a coach friend of Pete White's nervously; he had dropped by to watch the action and sat stolidly on the bleachers.

He turned toward me, expressionless. "The conclusion that it's a damn good thing they're not playing St. John's this year," he muttered.

Scrimmaging St. John's was no pleasure for anyone that day, but worse, perhaps, for Corey Dade, a junior player who had transferred to B-CC after two years at St. John's. He'd had his problems with the school. It had bothered him that a player with potential for success in a varsity sport was treated better than other students, allowed to get away with more; even though, or maybe because, he himself was that sort of player—a running back capable of impressive bursts of speed. He had also felt that the school tended to treat black students like him differently.

Not that Corey was happy with the black situation at B-CC either, but that was different. At B-CC, he felt too many of the black kids had fallen into a bad pattern . . . nonacademic, ultrasocial, with lots of drug-taking around the fringes. He'd always heard it was like this at public school, and it was. To adapt, he felt it was necessary to "separate yourself from the social norms—that's how you protect yourself." Dave's group—the black elite—had the right idea, he felt, even if they did look to some like an isolated, even snobby, bunch. "When you think about it, those are the only seniors, black, who are not the nerds, the only seniors, black, who are going to college, the only seniors, black, who are not going to sell drugs when they get out. People are starting to realize—hey, these guys are the only ones who are going to make it."

He already had plenty of friends both on and off the team. Corey had been playing sports since he was nine; he knew Rick and Dirkey from Boys' Club football, Toby from soccer. Sports were big in Corey's family—his brother, a basketball star, now played at college; his father, a school counselor, had been a baseball and football star; his mother, who worked at IBM, had run track as a girl, and was still running. ("She lives on popcorn, apples, and diet soda.") Corey had inherited athletic talent from both sides. In addition, he was funny and quick, with a mind as swift as his body, an automatic favorite with everyone.

The St. John's team all knew Corey and missed him; they made strident attempts throughout the afternoon to convince him he had made a bad mistake in leaving. "They're all bums, Corey, they're bums!" they yelled from the sidelines. "Can't you see it?" At the same time, he did feel a certain reassurance when he was running on the field. "They're all my boys—they're huge, but they would never hit me hard."

Not that it was necessary. St. John's tromped over B-CC, wiped them off the field, then left in a whirl of ecstatic catcalls—they were no more known for modesty in the face of victory than any other high school team in the area. The boys were downcast, but Pete was as calm as ever. A scrimmage was just a scrimmage; it was meant to show you where your weaknesses were; you had to take highs and lows with a grain of salt; tomorrow they would get back to work—practice, drills, basics. This was still pre-season, after all.

The third scrimmage—which was, in fact, a tri-scrimmage, involving three other teams from up-county—was utterly inconclusive. Nowhere near as bad as the St. John's fiasco, but hardly the triumph that Friendly had been. Basically, it was a day of undistinguished football, occasionally competent, occasionally slipshod. Nothing very memorable happened on the field. With two notable, unfortunate exceptions.

The first was an unusual occurrence on any football field, but particularly a high school one—an open blowout between coach and player. Mike Mitchem and Mitch Babashan had been edging toward a serious confrontation for days—now, suddenly, in the heat of the game, both let go.

Mike had been messing up on the line that day and knew it. It made him nervous; as a good player, who took pride in his ability, he more than anyone was well aware when he was playing poorly. Unfortunately, being aware only made the problem worse—he tensed up even more.

"On this particular play, it was my own personal mess-up. I got the guy and didn't wrap him up and he got away. I quickly got up and made the tackle myself, but it was five yards down the field," he said.

He felt crummy—he *knew* he had loused up. "I was like in my mind so disgusted with myself." And as he was standing there, feeling sick, berating himself, Mitch chose that exact moment to run up and figuratively—though it felt more like literally—kick him in the balls.

"He came running up and cussing me out—WHAT THE HELL ARE YOU DOING? And I just broke, I was like, what the fuck, you asshole, what are you talking about?"

Mitch turned white. "Get off the field!" he screamed. "Get off the field! Get out of here!"

Mike may have done some wild things in his younger days, but he had never in his entire life spoken like that to a coach; no one spoke like that to a coach. He knew it was a bad slip. But Mitch's timing had been so acute, so knife-twisting . . . to run up and jump on him like that, at the very moment he was chastising himself so severely. To Mike, it was as if "he thought I didn't know what I did was messed up—like I thought I was *supposed* to let the guy run for another five or ten yards. I'm a lineman; I have no knowledge; I didn't know what I did was dumb."

He knew, though, that he had made a bad mistake the minute the words were out of his mouth. Every player out there that day knew, and a shocked silence fell on the field. It was a given—bite your tongue, grit your teeth, punch a buddy, but never, never talk back to a coach. Many parents of players and more than a few teachers would have been amazed to see just how capable their feisty sons and students were of holding their tongues when they chose to, often in the face of considerable abuse. Even teachers were taught these days, I was informed by a friend once, not to overreact to a kid's mouth—an occasional muttered "shit" or two, even thrown in their direction, was understandable, "a human thing."

But not to a coach. No one swore at a coach. What Mike had just done, in the minds of many, was nothing less than suicidal.

"He's a young coach; it had slipped out, what I said, in front of the whole team, in direct conflict with his ego and authority." There was no way to take it back. In one brief heated stroke, his conflict with the coach had escalated to the point of a major— possibly irreparable—rift. And the repercussions would reverberate through the season.

The other incident that day was quieter; in fact, almost silent—a tearing ligament in an ankle makes very little sound. It does have an effect, though, and since the ankle in question belonged to Dave Bardach, so recently anointed by Mitch as the on-field chief of defense, that effect had the potential of being considerable.

He knew it right away. "I felt it tear, I wanted to get up so bad, but I looked down and said, there's no way I can even move. The pain started and worked all the way up to my knee." Resigned, he hobbled off the field.

Dave's mother had worked for several years as business manager of the cardiology department at Children's Hospital, so it was natural for him to go there first. The doctor put on a heavy cast, which was obviously unacceptable. A few days later he pressed his mother to take him to a sports clinic. Sports doctors, like Coach White said, understood this sort of thing.

"I don't think he was aware I had torn a ligament; X-rays don't show ligaments. I think he just thought I'd pulled it. He was, it's not broken. So he's like, all right, we'll take off your cast and as soon as you can stand up on one foot and have it balance you can play—and he gave me an air cast to wear.

"It hurt like anything," Dave admitted. "But I'm a man." The season was about to open—Dave had no intention of missing any of it.

CHAPTER FOUR

PETE WAS ALWAYS on the lookout for an edge, a twist, a rallying ploy—something to get the guys all facing in the right direction, as he put it.

Last year it had been easy. No one in the county had expected anything out of the Barons; all Pete had to do to get the team revved up was to underline that fact. This he did gustily, every week of the season. "They're not even *thinking* about you," he'd jeer. "You think Churchill's even thinking about B-CC? Hell no, they're planning their homecoming, they're thinking about the game they're gonna play the following week. Easy win, that's what they're saying, easy win. Got it all penciled in and everything. Well, how about it, guys—are you an easy win?"

And the ploy had worked perfectly—partly, of course, because it was the simple truth; no one *was* expecting much of a fight from B-CC. Practically every game they won last year was dubbed an upset—the Whitman upset, the Einstein upset, the unbelievable, giant Churchill upset. Montgomery Marty of the *Montgomery County Journal,* who had been predicting high school football games in the county for fifteen years, was caught flatfooted week after week. And that too Pete used to his advantage—he'd bring the *Journal* to practice, and read Marty's latest predictions to the team. "He still don't think you have a chance!" he'd goad them. "Okay, this week is this guy gonna be right or wrong?"

This year Pete knew he had to change tactics. B-CC had lost its dark horse status for good—even the *Washington Post* had dropped a small bouquet in its preseason roundup. ("Fiscina, last year's leading passer in the county for yardage, returns along with Smith, Bardach and Stone, leaving the Barons talented in the skill positions.")

And Montgomery Marty, last year's nemesis, had come around completely. "Get the Ben-Gay ready for quarterback Rick Fiscina," he teased, almost affectionately. "His arm is gonna be sore after almost every game because Coach Pete White still loves to throw it. B-CC made great strides last season before tailing off at the end."

"We knew we weren't gonna sneak up on anybody this year," Pete admitted. "People would have to prepare. Even a Churchill, a Gaithersburg."

He needed a new gambit, and fast—especially for the all-important first game of the season, against the Wooten Patriots. Not only had the Barons blown their cover, but Wooten had had a terrible season last year, ending up with a dismal two and eight. This time Wooten was the underdog—they were the ones, according to the *Journal,* trying to "climb out of the cellar." Montgomery Marty gave B-CC the win by a wide margin, 20–9.

A new edge was needed, and for this first game, Pete thought he had it—Tony Riggs.

Riggs was Wooten's star athlete—a sometime quarterback, sometime wide receiver, sometime safety, one of those kids who was so good you couldn't keep him off the field. He was enough to scare anyone. So for Pete, the rallying cry the week before the first game wasn't "Stop Wooten"; it was "Stop Riggs!"

School was now in full swing; the boys attended only one practice a day, from 3:00 to 6:00 P.M.—a piece of cake, after two-a-days. They felt loose, limber, expectant—basic training was over. Friday night the war would begin in earnest. Under Pete's direction, they focused on plays that would stop Tony Riggs dead in his tracks. Stop Riggs and you stopped Wooten.

It bothered Mitch, singling out one player like that. It was like

turning the kid into a god. "All Pete wanted to do was devise
something to stop this one guy. The way I think is, don't let the kid
know that he's that great. If he starts to kill you, yeah—but if you
go out with that kind of defense, you're automatically saying he can
beat you. Then your kids already know this kid is better than
anybody you got. Okay, the coaches might know, this kid is dangerous, better watch him—but you don't let the kids know."

Mitch had his own idea of how to stop Tony Riggs, and it didn't
involve a specially designed defense either. What it involved was
intimidation—specifically, the phenomenon known as "talking
trash."

"As much as football is a physical game, it's a mental game. If
you can dominate somebody, if you can win the game of intimidation, you're halfway there." Mitch knew plenty about intimidation. "I was a very dirty ball player—grab hands, try to break
thumbs. And when you get in a pile, you say things."

It was time, Mitch felt, to let these kids in on the facts of life. In
the week of practice before the opening game, he took a few of his
most intense players aside and explained exactly what he wanted
them to do with Tony Riggs. "Get in his face, say things to piss him
off," he told them. "Whenever Riggs is on the field, I want you to
make some kind of remark. I don't care if it's racial [Riggs is black]
but I want him very upset. Do what you can. But don't get caught—
if you get caught by a ref, I'm going to deny everything," he
warned.

"It's a mean game! You have to play it like a mean SOB! Football is a vicious game, gentlemen," Mitch crooned at them, revert-
ing to his favorite theme. "A vicious, vicious game. You gotta just
walk around like you're arrogant, like no one can touch you. If you
don't have that mentality, you're really not there—football is a
controlled street fight. When you play the game, you have to take
yourself out of the way common society is—it's a different world
out there on the field."

Mitch's advice made sense to Kong. "You don't want to be
intimidated by anybody—and if you talk nasty to a person, it tells
that you're not intimidated. You might *be,* but it shows them that
you're not."

Bob Plante also used the week to try and infuse his linemen with a little more fiber. It was attitude they needed, he felt, something sadly lacking at B-CC—but without it, you didn't win. Attitude was all. "You gotta think you're the nastiest SOBs to come down the pike!" he urged them, fiercely. "If somebody touches you, punch him right in the head—don't take anything from anybody! That's how you develop a psyche."

Off the field, you had to tone it down a little, of course. Then you were back in reality. But on the field—"I call it no mental recognition—you don't recognize the other player as a human being. I don't recognize you as another player on this field—you're nothing. So if the guy bumps you—who're you?"

Sure, it could go too far, this stuff, Bob realized that. A kid walking around thinking he was the toughest dude on the street could get into fights pretty easily. With some teams, the last thing you'd want to do was build up their aggression; they had all they needed. But B-CC was another story. Hell, these kids needed it. Badly.

The most important thing, what a coach had to do, Bob felt strongly, was "get a 17-year-old kid to believe he is a man. He wants to believe he is." A man, of course, took nothing from no one; he gave as good as he got—better, in fact; he never backed down. He was a fighter; he reigned supreme; he presented an invulnerable front to the world.

He was, in fact—at least, in this conception—almost a caricature, like a mask one pulled down over one's head, purposefully. And on one level, both the coaches and the boys knew this. After all, none of their fathers fit this definition. Alex's father had been a fighter pilot commander, true—yet he was a thoughtful intellectual who despised macho posturing and found games ridiculous. Both Toby and Geoff had fathers who were utterly and unapologetically unathletic. Geoff's father, a social worker with a somewhat clerical mien, had in fact done most of the early caretaking of his sons since he had been, he felt, temperamentally better suited to the task than his wife. Billy's father, a onetime high school player, was known for his gentle disposition—"the sweetest man I ever met," Toby called him. Sal Fiscina, Rick's father, was the soft touch in the family, the one who cried at movies.

So being a man—being *the* man, as the boys said—involved

striving for something amorphous and not quite real, certainly nothing they had ever truly encountered in their own lives; a mythological pursuit which took its color and shape from the movies they'd seen, the culture they'd been born to. In a sense it was almost a joke, and they knew it . . . few could even say the words "the man" without the hint of a self-amused smile flickering over their faces. And yet, and yet . . . the concept held enormous power. They were, after all, at the most idealistic age of all—the age at which boys go to war.

Pete was not overly fond of some of the tactics his assistants had fastened on for motivating the boys—they offended his notions of sportsmanship. Yet aside from a comment or two, he did not intervene. Maybe it would do the boys good to be exposed to an entirely new coaching approach; maybe it would help the whole team. After all, Bob and Mitch were the ones who really knew football, not him. He was still, he knew, a student.

Bob knew Pete was not completely happy; he even understood why. "When you think about it, it's not a very gentlemanly thing. I'm sure a parent doesn't want to know I'm telling their son to cuss that guy out, punch him in the face." But it was all part of the image, part of football, he insisted. "You don't have that in other sports . . . a 17-year-old male trying to be a man."

Some of the coaches' suggestions for honing toughness almost sounded silly at first to the boys. Tae Uk, for one, had a hard time not giggling at one of Bob Plante's directives. "He was like, today, why don't you go a little crazy. When you see your mother and she touches you, tell her, Mom—get off me!" And the coach shook himself, demonstrating, his face clenched in grimace, a grenade about to explode.

"I was laughing at the time," Tae Uk said. "But after a while you start thinking, all right, I will."

"He was trying to get us into a state of mind," Toby realized. And bit by bit, it was starting to work. You couldn't help going along with it. "There is no other way, if you're into the sport, if you're gonna play football. You've gotta believe it, listen to the coach, get on his wavelength." Once you had made the commitment to play, to try to become a real football player, you listened to the man who was telling you how to do it.

"You play like the coach that coaches you," said Kong simply. "Mitch coached us, and it reflected on us, how he is. He's not a bad person to reflect, he's a good person—but he can be out of control sometimes. I guess defense is more Mitch-like, offense is more like Coach White."

Bob knew his offensive line was smaller than most in the county, probably even than Wooten's. In the week of practice before the first game, he did his best to turn even that to an advantage. Oversized linemen were like big, floppy dogs, he told the boys— now, which would you rather be? A floppy dog who was going to fall all over himself or a pit bull, small and deadly, who could chew up someone's balls? So okay, they weren't huge—they'd have to be pit bulls. Right?

Tae Uk weighed a scant 140 pounds, though he generally gave himself a few more when asked—for the program he had upped his weight to 155. Of course, all the vital stats listed in the program were inflated, but that was no big deal; every school inflated vital stats, it was yet another exercise in intimidation. But since Tae Uk was the smallest lineman, Bob Plante began a ritual this week that would last throughout the season.

"Hey, Tae Uk, how much do you weigh?" he hollered almost daily.

"Uh—one fifty-five, Coach," Tae Uk yelled back.

"No way—you weigh two hundred!"

"Right," the little Korean would gulp manfully. "Right, Coach, two hundred."

On Friday, September 9, the day of the first game, the boys showed up at school looking sharp. Last year, Pete's first season as varsity coach, he had instituted a new custom—every member of the team would wear a shirt and tie to school on the Friday before a game.

"Somebody told me when I started with this that they wouldn't do it. I said, well, number one, they'll do it, they'll do it or else, but I don't think they'll disagree. I told them my reason, that I thought it made 'em stand out." There was another reason, too, though. "If someone's going to be a fool on Friday, it won't take a teacher but one second to figure out who's got a shirt and tie on."

But the main reason for the shirt and tie was "you're somebody just a little special in the school, everybody knows who's wearing the shirt and tie." And in fact, the boys—almost none of whom had ever donned a shirt and tie for a school day at B-CC before—had swiftly come to appreciate this. No one balked, and no one ever forgot.

So on Friday every team member showed up scrubbed, pressed, in shirt and tie, instantly distinguishable from the rest of the student body, still in scruffy shorts and T-shirts, legacy of the summer just past. The boys strode through the halls with dignity on this day, standing a little taller, walking a little slower. Their excitement was palpable. A glow seemed to surround every one of them. Even in the dark halls, they shone.

All yearned eagerly for the hours to pass, the contest to begin, but none with the same single-minded focus as Geoff Smith. Not that football Fridays were anything new for Geoff. They'd been a ritual for years, ever since he'd played in local Peewee teams, a skinny kid, barely seventy pounds, all arms and legs. He remembered the way he'd put his uniform on the night before the game back then, lovingly, then lie there on the bed in his pads, staring at the ceiling, dreaming, waiting, unable to sleep. Nothing new, this feeling, yet the excitement never waned, never grew stale. He awaited the start of tonight's game, the first of his senior year, with breathless impatience.

Football didn't run in Geoff's family at all. So far as anyone knew, there had only been one other athlete born on either side— his mother's uncle, another skinny blond boy, full of energy, a Yugoslavian who had been executed by Tito's forces in the early days of World War II. Geoff was, his mother fondly believed, a throwback to this boy, born with the same easy grace, the same boundless enthusiasm.

Certainly his athletic talent was unique in his immediate family. His dad jogged around the block occasionally; that was about the extent of his physical activity. His older brother, Chris, now at college, had steered away from sports for years—a brilliant guy, admittedly, but never an athlete. Geoff thought maybe he'd run away from it, in a way, because of him. Though he had recently gotten into lifting and developed some formidable muscles, which considerably annoyed Geoff, who was still skinny. "I want to say, you've got the mind, why don't you give me that body—what do you need it for?" Geoff said.

But Geoff had taken to the game from the moment he saw the sign at the little park across the street from his house in Chevy Chase calling for prospective players. He was going into sixth grade then, and Rick Fiscina, he knew, had already been playing a year at the Boys' Club—even then, there was a rivalry between the two. So he'd signed up. He'd had a great coach, used to yell at them all the time, Geoff had been really intimidated, but it was good to have a guy like that as your first football coach. Playing soccer, he'd had nothing but women coaches, pampering them with orange slices. This felt more like the real thing.

It was quickly apparent that this was his game. In fact, Geoff became such a dominant force on the Peewee team that at times the refs had insisted he be benched just to keep the competition equal. "If you scored more than eighteen points, you had to sit out." And he'd kept playing from there on in, even though his first year at B-CC had been a little hairy. "I was five-four, a hundred four pounds—petite." Some of the guys, even on Jayvee, had been enormous. "I came home, Mom, Mom, it's not like it used to be."

But he hung in. Football may not have run in Geoff's family, but tenacity did. It came down from his maternal grandfather, a Yugoslavian aristocrat who had ridden out with the cavalry to face the German Wehrmacht in the early days of World War II, been taken prisoner, and managed to escape by convincing soldiers—he was a superb linguist—that he was Italian. It came from his other grandfather, too, son of missionary parents, raised in China, who directed intelligence in China under General Clare Chennault during World War II, earning himself an honored place in cartoonist Milton Caniff's *Terry and the Pirates* strip as China Smith.

But it also came from his mother, Lana, who was small, dark-haired, and bubbly, the very picture of a demure Chevy Chase matron, but who had, at age four, escaped from Yugoslavia with her parents, walking at night, hiding in barns by day, from Italy to the border of Switzerland, finally arriving at the clearing where the Italian soldier leading them had thrown down the small suitcase carrying their belongings, waved his arm toward the horizon of flowers and tinkling cow bells, and announced dramatically: "*Siete liberi*"—You are free.

It had been another six years, hard, nomadic years, before the family had made it to America; Tito's first action had been to wipe out citizenship for those Yugoslavians who refused to accept him— they were literally without a country. Down to his last few banknotes, all the jewelry they had smuggled out long gone, traded for food and lodging, Lana's father had marched into a casino, dropped his entire cache down on the roulette table, and walked out twenty minutes later with enough money to buy their passage to America. A slight five-degree tilt of the wheel either way, and B-CC might have been deprived of their star receiver for all time.

They arrived in New York penniless, jobless. "Get a job, get a place to live, and, for God's sake, cut the kid's name in half," a friend urged them; so Svetlana became Lana from then on. Her parents spread out *The New York Times* classified in their rented room and went through the ads one by one; a day later her mother had a job as a seamstress. Lana, who at ten was fluent in Croatian, French, Italian, and Spanish as a result of their travels, had not known a word of English. She had learned by listening to radio soap operas after school with fierce attention, piecing the meanings together word by word, learned so well that long before she arrived at Bryn Mawr as a freshman there was no trace of accent in her voice. Years later coaches in the county would marvel at Geoff— not just for his catches, but for his seemingly infinite ability to take all kinds of punishment and somehow emerge unbowed. "Like Timex," said one, shaking his head. " 'Takes a licking and keeps on ticking.' " They did not, of course, know his mother.

Back then, it had seemed more important than anything to her to be American, a real American girl, with roots, a place, a home. She had been ready to turn her back on the love of her life when he wanted a foreign-service career; Lana knew she could take no more travel. Luckily he had seen the light, switched careers, and they were able to get married. It had all worked out. And last year, when she had stood in the stands at the Einstein game, with her parents, her husband, and her oldest, Chris, home from college, and watched her youngest son pull three balls out of the air for touchdowns, heard the crowd explode, it had been a pinnacle, of sorts. A golden moment, the sense of a goal having finally been reached. "The three generations, all together, like a moment caught, an eternity caught forever," she felt. Safe, together, rooted. How far they had come, all of them, to reach this field.

Football fever had not come easily to this family. Geoff's grand-parents, who lived nearby, were horrified at the game. "They'd watched Chris grow up doing his homework. He was such a per-fect little guy, and me, I'm going out to bang heads in the park. They hated it." Danger was something they had known too well in their lives—you avoided danger, you didn't deliberately court it. But Lana, his little indomitable mother, had stood up to her par-ents fiercely. "She yelled in defense of me," said Geoff proudly. She knew how important the game was to her son, who truly didn't know what he would have done if she herself had objected. "I'm sure I would have been more of a rebel."

Finally, she had been able to convince them to attend a high school game, three years ago. One game was all it took. When Geoff had made the all-County team last year, his grandmother bought a pile of newspapers and sent them to every relative still living in Yugoslavia; his grandfather now sported a sweatshirt pro-claiming "My grandson wears Number One." Their house was filled with pictures of Geoff in uniform. They had come around.

He knew he was good—yet, in a way, he didn't want to be too aware of it. "I think once you understand you're doing great, you're not going to do great anymore. It has to be natural." On his way home after the Einstein game last year, his friend Trey had stopped him suddenly at the door of the car. "Geoff, I want you to realize—you just played your best game ever," he told him. Yet it had never really hit him, not even when the *Washington Post* called to tell him he had been selected player of the week, not until this past summer, when he watched the tape of the game and had to admit he did look pretty damn good out there.

And now the season had started in earnest; it was Friday. "Fri-days in my house are like a priest would view a Sunday," Geoff said. He had a strict schedule. He'd come home right after school, take off his shirt and tie, and nap for an hour. Then he'd wake up, put the dinner his mother had prepared for him in the microwave, read the note she always left him, and eat. And all the time, even while sleeping, be conscious of anticipation. "That feeling—like I had been given a million dollars." Because tonight he would be on the field.

"I'd feel so sorry for the people who weren't going to be able to experience it. I'd feel on top of the world because the best thing ever was going to happen, Friday night. And only thirty or forty other people could experience that! And I'd feel so sorry for everybody else—for Doug and Tony and them, guys who don't play—they wouldn't ever experience it." Because to Geoff, the game was food and drink, religion and art, rolled into one—the most important, indispensable part of his life.

By five, the boys had started drifting into the locker room one by one. The atmosphere was relaxed, warm, familial—it would be at least an hour before they started gearing up in earnest for the game. Now was the time for fooling around, teasing, lounging on benches half in, half out of uniform, arguing about which tapes to listen to, go-go, rap, or heavy metal.

The excitement was there, bubbling just below the surface, yet in some ways this was the calmest time of all, this hour. Geoff loved it.

"Everybody walking around, putting on pants, getting in pads, such a relaxed feeling—that nobody else but a player would be able to identify with. Such a feeling of security. You felt like you could identify with these people . . . the aroma about it . . . that's what I love so much." In a way, it was this part, "the behind-the-scenes that is 50 percent of the season" that he loved most of all.

Black and white players divided sharply on the issue of locker-room music and yelled disparaging comments across the room to each other, mock insults. "The white guys like their music and we totally *don't* like their music," said Mike Mitchem, although there were other players, like Alex's friend Dimarlo Duvall, who though black refused to let race dictate his taste—"Damn it, I like Pink Floyd!" he insisted—and Toby, a confirmed reggae freak, whose nickname was occasionally expanded to "Rasta Farney." And everyone wanted to hear the rap song Dave Bardach brought with him, "I'm Getting Ready." "It got you really psyched," admitted one player who was generally not a rap fan.

Locker room in the early pregame stage was the place for horsing around, dancing—Geoff, who was utterly uninhibited, often did a few ballet twirls in his tights—a place for the ancient rites of grab-ass, probably first performed by cavemen congregating before games at Stonehenge. "It doesn't really mean grab your ass," my son explained patronizingly, although at times it certainly did. "You don't want to take a shower in there," one player joked. "Shane and James are always grabbing at you, not just in back either. They're major homosexuals, of course." ("Yeah, sure, you can say I said that; then you can write my obit, too," he added.) And it was a place, too, for riffs, for mimicry—even this early in the season, Toby already had Bob Plante down perfectly. "Who's a fucking pussy?" he roared in his booming voice, stalking the aisles.

A few of the boys, though, had already begun more serious preparations for the night: Kong sat on a bench, slowly and carefully circling various parts of his body with rounds and rounds of tape—fingers, ankles, wrists. It was not only protection—it was a method, his method, for getting himself into the proper state of mind.

"Everyone gets dressed their own way, everyone tapes up, everyone wants to become a road warrior before they go out on the field," said Rick. "Some of them look mummified when they walk out." Along with the tape, many players applied black streaks under their eyes, down their faces, which supposedly guarded against sun glare but was also, Rick knew, "the same idea as make-up."

"I read this book that said the football player is the matador of the future . . . the face is insignificant, covered with the helmet, big shoulders, thin waist. I was reading it like—yeah! Matador of the future! That's me. Because it is like some futuristic warrior."

Every player had his own special method of preparation; some had even launched the process before arriving back at school. Mike Mitchem and Rene Grave de Peralta often listened to an hour's worth of hard, driving music, played at peak volume. Alex, the military maven, preferred a careful viewing yet again of his favorite movie, *Patton*. It reminded him of the state of mind he was trying for, one of cool, effective authority. But generally, the process did not start in earnest until the boys had been in the locker room a time, often nearly an hour, had gotten some of the silliness out of their systems, and were ready to concentrate.

They called it "pumping up," but the phrase was not entirely descriptive; pumping up was only part of it. A great deal of the readiness process involved an attempt to focus their minds utterly on the coming struggle—one's own part in it, one's role, one's job—with a pure distillation of concentration that was beyond thought. Thinking was wrong; conscious thought was the enemy. Thinking players were hesitant players, players who froze, balked, shrank back for the tiny extra millisecond that could prove so deadly on the field. They wanted to be without thought. What they strove for was a state of mind in which they would have absolute awareness of the moment, pure heightened awareness, with no extraneous intrusions—a state in which they would be able to move freely, with absolute freedom.

"You look around the locker room, guys are sitting there, rocking back and forth, trying to get into it. You don't have to be athletically gifted; it's the mind, more than anything," said Rick. "Zen and the art of football.

"Everyone tries to situate themselves—one, with their uniform, two, with their mind. You try to come in contact with yourself before the game."

It was no more than what seers, mystics, wise men, and others had sought down through the ages, through meditation, prayer, discipline, and, of course, drugs. Some professional athletes had even started using a name for it: the zone. What was amazing was how many of these boys, undisciplined, untrained, not only understood what they were seeking but were able to find it, all on their own, on a high school football field—and know it for what it was.

For Geoff, it was the absence of sound he noticed most on the field, in this state—the way the raucous noises of the crowd, the band, the screams of the coaches all clicked off suddenly, completely, during a play—only to resume instantly, the minute it was over. Like a volume button—off, then on.

For Rick, it was visual: his arm back for a long pass, he could see, not just the outline of the waiting player, many yards downfield, nor even just his face, but the actual whites of his eyes, the pupils making contact with his.

And for Billy, too, it was sound—one specific sound, always the same, which he had heard during every game he had ever played, the sound of a girl's high-pitched, drawn-out scream. Always the same girl's scream, ringing in his ears, every game.

"When I'm running the ball, I think about something else," said Brendan Symes. "Try to keep my mind free. I think if I think really hard I'll mess up. Every time I'm running the ball, like a song is going through my head . . . or I'll talk to myself, say, 'All right, Brendan, you can do this.'

"What I try to do is block out the crowd and everything, just play, like I'm on the playground, don't think about it, just do it. My dad calls it instinct."

Distortions in time, in sensory perception, "vaguely like LSD," one player who had done some experimentation described it. Yet at the same time, wholly different. There was no escapism, no avoidance involved here—the boys were striving to grasp the actual moment itself, seize the very core of it, and hold it in their hands like a nut. Or a brown leather ball.

By an hour before game time, the locker room had grown a great deal more quiet. Not completely—this was, after all, a room filled with 16- and 17-year-old boys. But the difference was noticeable.

Alex was doing his best to keep the offensive linemen together, isolated from the rest of the team, and silent; that was his main job right now, as he saw it. Nothing was more important than proper preparation, the right kind of mind set; you controlled that, you controlled the line; control the line and you controlled the game.

Only it wasn't that simple to do, especially with some of these guys. Take Toby, for instance. Here was a guy almost allergic to isolation. Every time Alex thought he had the whole line together, off to the side, he'd turn his back and Toby would wander away. "Goddamn it, get the hell back here," he'd roar, furious, knowing he wasn't exuding calm leadership but unable to help himself. By then Tae Uk too had wandered off. Grimly, Alex continued trying to round them up.

As the players prepared, Dave was finally forced to admit it to himself—he would not be able to play tonight. Up to the last minute he had kept hoping. He'd shown up long before everyone else to test his ankle. Removing the air cast, he jogged around the field, trying it out. It was no good—he could hardly move. Deeply disappointed and at the same time filled with foreboding—if he wasn't out there to direct the defense, what would happen?—he sat down heavily on a bench in the locker room. He would dress anyway, just to feel a part of the night. You had to do that.

Billy Stone, too, knew he would not be playing—his operation, long postponed, had finally been performed two days ago. His throat felt ripped raw; he himself felt terrible and had spent the day lying flat on his bed, which was clearly where he still belonged. He could hardly stand, but he had managed to pull himself up, gritting his teeth, in order to come tonight. He had to at least be here.

His absence on the field would mean a double loss—he not only played tight end on offense but was also the linebacker slated to take over from Dave. Now a lot of the defense would be riding on the shoulders, the newly massive but still largely untested-in-actual-combat shoulders, of James McDonald.

James, though, was feeling no doubts. True, he'd had little game experience so far, but he knew he was ready. All that work this summer, honing his body, had led to this point. He felt loose, confident, and supremely lucky—like an understudy when a star breaks a leg. Too bad about Dave and Billy, but, hey, it's an ill wind . . . James was feeling no pain.

The coaches, when they strode in that night, issued directives in a manner fitting to each, which meant directives were issued in sharply variant manners. Pete White, of course, was calm as ever on the surface. This was a time, he told them all, to be quiet, to concentrate on their individual roles, the plays they had worked on. His voice was low, even, his tension betrayed only by a private mannerism. Pete tended to add the word "whatever" to sentences, almost as a sort of punctuation, and this habit escalated sharply under pressure; at times like this, the "whatevers" almost seemed to dominate his speech: "Whatever, we'll go out there and play, whatever," he said more than once, often adding yet another "whatever" or two for emphasis.

Mitch, as usual, was tuned to a higher pitch. A few days ago, watching them drill, he had exploded suddenly: "Goddamn it, you guys aren't excited enough—you've got a game Friday night, you should be coming in your pants!" Now he assembled his crew in the back of the room for an emotional last-minute charge. Bob Plante, cooler as always, took the offensive line aside to quiz them on plays. Unless you knew them, you wouldn't get out there, he warned. Then, when one kid gave a wrong answer, he said grinning, "You're wrong"—pausing for effect—"but you play anyway!"

Now came the real pumping up—slapping helmets, gritting teeth, roaring. The boys had an almost religious belief in the efficacy of this ritual, even though Coach White's warning, oft repeated, rang in their ears: "Emotion will only take you through the first ten plays." Still, that first few minutes could set a tone for the whole game.

They lined up in the hall outside the locker room, their blue-and-gold uniforms ablaze with newness, tensely waiting for the moment the door would open. "Attitude!" screamed Geoff, who considered himself the team's chief motivator, stalking the line, slapping helmets. "Fucking attitude! Get it up!" The heavy doors clanked open and the 1988 Barons roared down to the field.

The stands were packed and milling. The audience at a high school football game is an endlessly restless one, constantly in motion. Fresh-faced young girls with cascading hair—black, brown, blond—whirled around repeatedly, checking out the crowd. Various boys swaggered down the steps between the bleachers with the èlan of visiting heroes—inevitably these were the stars of other sports, basketball, soccer, and baseball, or, occasionally, returning football veterans. B-CC's band, assembled square in the middle of the stands, crashed their way through a belligerent "Joshua Fit de Battle of Jericho" dominated by drums and cymbals.

Far down in front the cheerleaders huddled together, conferring. Cheerleaders at B-CC had their work cut out for them. B-CC was a notoriously hard crowd to get going—there were too many diverse clots, small separate chunks of humanity almost impossible to orchestrate into one raucous unity. In the stands were separate and distinct groups of white, black, Hispanic, and Asian kids. They were separated by sex as well—black girls in one area, white girls in another. There were a number of exceptions, of course—a white girl sitting in a sea of black girls, one or two black boys surrounded by white. But the exceptions only underlined the more typical separation. Greetings were tossed between groups occasionally. One black girl jumping up to embrace a white boy returned to assure her group, "That's my little buddy," in slightly embarrassed tones. Enmity seemed absent, yet a visible wariness existed nonetheless, simmering slightly between them. The lines were distinct, firmly drawn. An observer would have been hard put not to reach the same conclusion any intelligent urbanite had long since arrived at—that the melting pot, America's cherished ideal, was indeed a crock.

Yet when the Barons themselves, resplendent in their new gear, tore out onto the field, the entire disparate crowd erupted together in roaring welcome. At this distance, in their uniforms and helmets, it was impossible to pick out individual characteristics among the team members. You could not tell who was black, white, or Asian; they only looked like football players.

The parents of team members huddled together in a few separate areas. Jo-Ann Fiscina sat high up, near the concession stand, poised, her hair neatly coiffed, her face set in an expression of calm amusement, one which would vary little throughout the game, no matter what emotions were stirred up. By mutual agreement, Sal was nowhere around—she could not stand to sit beside him at football games; not only was he tense and funereal, always expecting the worst, but he tended to engage in nonstop commentary she found particularly irritating.

More than one married couple reflected a similar dichotomy in viewing style: one intense viewer, one more calm, removed. Lana Smith had already seated herself several benches below and was watching the field closely, her black eyes vivid, expectant; while her husband, Jim, his back to the field, was involved in a pleasant discourse with another man about Florida retirement homes. I myself was already tense, close to bursting; my husband's casual conversation with my father—about the coming election, or some such inanity—was like a mosquito buzzing around my head, I longed to slap it away. The band now launched into a lusty rendition of the old doo-wop chant, "Come Go with Me," giving it a hard edge the Del Vikings would have been hard put to recognize, had they been able to discern it between cymbal clashes.

Moments later a taped version of the national anthem exploded out of giant speakers. Everyone stood, Judy Burgess's powerful voice soaring easily above the crowd. On the field, the boys were nervous, tense, yet optimistic. All the ploys in the world couldn't change what they knew in their hearts—this was a team they could beat. They knew it; they felt it. They grouped together for the last team roar: "Are you ready? YOU BET!"

They ran out on the field. The crowds cheered. The whistle blew for the kickoff—

And it went bad right from the start. Very bad, spectacularly bad, the way it can be when football games go bad—not just a slight downward slide into mediocrity but a huge, cosmic avalanche of rolling, unstoppable horror.

It started right after kickoff, with the Barons' first play from the line of scrimmage. Rick, rearing back, Rick the four-year pro, the county's number-one passer, the consummate athlete, threw the ball straight into the moist, waiting hands of the opposition. Eagerly Wooten seized the treasure, jumping in the air, howling, waving fists—and within moments had marched the prize proudly down the field for a touchdown.

Edgy, anxious, thrown off kilter by such an unspeakable start, the boys continued to roll downhill throughout the first quarter and into the next. Rick threw another interception for another Wooten triumph, then—Holy God, was it possible?—yet a third. Even Jo-Ann Fiscina's calm face looked a little sick. This wasn't how Rick played—what was going on? At times like these, she felt all too visible on her perch. Everyone knew she was the mother of the quarterback. Her strongest emotion, though, was gratitude for the fact that her husband was nowhere near her.

"No protection; my son's not getting any protection," Sal was muttering, from his own perch far up on the other side of the concession stand, while Mike Reese, Panther's stepdad, shook his head, commiserating, yet somewhat amused—when the chips were down, Dr. Fiscina had trouble seeing anyone on the field but his son, he felt. The offensive line looked terrible, Sal thought; compared to last year's powerful linemen, this year's was a bunch of undersized amateurs, none of whom seemed to know what they were doing. Yeah, maybe it wasn't Rick's finest hour—three interceptions in the first quarter was pretty bad. But what could he do with a line like that?

It was a good thing none of the parents of offensive players were sitting up here. Actually one of the reasons he liked to sit so far up was so he could grumble without offending anyone. A kind man, generally, but during a game his identification with Rick was too intense to allow for civility. Identification was the wrong word, really—it wasn't you down there, playing, where you might be able to do some good; it was your kid, for whom you could do nothing but watch and shudder. Especially during a game like this.

Down on the field, Rick, never the most serene of players, had lost his cool completely. "Who was supposed to block that guy? WHO?" he demanded in the huddle, as the linemen, thoroughly confused, each pointed fingers at each other. "HE was!"

"There's a point at which Rick turns into the devil," Billy had said once. The point had been reached. When John Han ran up to him after a Wooten player had tossed him to the ground—"Rick, Rick, are you all right?"—Rick stared daggers at him. "Don't touch me, Han," he spit. "Just don't—touch—me, okay?" Tae Uk, running to try to reclaim the ball from an interceptor, found himself shoved to the ground heavily—by Rick, running past him, his face fiery red.

Toby knew Rick's anger was justified; the line was green as grass and showing it badly. "Of course there was no cup blocking at all," he said. "Rick, he's like—fucking do it! We did feel pretty responsible." At the same time, the quarterback's demonic fury struck him as funny. Losing or not, Toby was feeling good tonight. At least it wasn't like last year, when he hadn't even been able to get on the field—that had been terrible. At least now he was here; good, bad, or indifferent, he was *here,* in the thick of it. The knowledge filled him with exhilaration.

Rick, though, was not enjoying himself. Too much praise when you win, too much blame when you lose, that was a quarterback's lot, Pete often said, and Rick couldn't help agreeing, especially tonight. What did the crowd, what did anyone out there know about lousy blocking, bad snaps? All they knew was what they saw, and interceptions were all too visible. At this point he could have cheerfully murdered the entire line and gone to the chair with a smile.

Theoretically, by all calculations, Wooten was not as talented a team as B-CC. But calculations had been skewered tonight—by the absence of Dave and Billy; by the awkward newness of the offensive line ("Hit somebody!" Alex barked at the rest of them furiously. "Just hit somebody!" Although Alex too, playing center for the first time, was having some trouble getting the snap back, thus denying Rick precious extra seconds he needed). Skewered too, perhaps, by the determination of the Wooten Patriots themselves, who had spent their two-a-days honing defense as a newly hired coach howled the same two-word imperative at them again and again: "Reckless abandon! Reckless abandon!"

And of course, calculations may have been thrown off by Rick's performance as well. New line or not, he was not playing at the peak of his game. Perhaps mainly because of the new cast of players, his timing was off—and Rick's precision timing was so much a part of him that the team not only counted on it to be there, without question, but literally did not know what to do when it was not.

The Barons had become accustomed to relying on passing; it had worked like a charm the year before, God knows. Pete did like to throw it, as Montgomery Marty had said; he had not really concentrated on developing a running game. So if the passing wasn't working out—if, to be brutally specific, Rick wasn't able to connect with Geoff—they were in deep trouble.

Of course, it would have been a very dull opposing team who had not by now figured out that Rick liked to throw to Geoff a great deal, and taken defensive steps to prevent that. Wooten, though hardly a champion team, had clearly put that equation together. So even while Geoff, endlessly optimistic, assured Rick again and again he could make it this time—"I can get free," he insisted, in the huddle—it wasn't proving quite that easy.

B-CC's defense, on the other hand, was actually not doing badly at all when they hit the field, considering the absent players. Certainly they were fulfilling at least one of Mitch's demands to the letter. Kong, James, and several other players were bad-mouthing Riggs—in fact, nearly every Wooten player they ran into—with riotous enthusiasm: the air around them was blue. "Ugly fucker! Think you're something? You ain't nothing, asshole," they howled happily.

The referees were doing their best to turn a deaf ear. High school refs generally gave enormous latitude to on-field name-calling, and with good reason. To deal with every incident would multiply penalties by the hundreds, slowing a game down indefinitely. It helped, too, that no one in the stands could hear the boys' comments—otherwise they would be forced to do something about them. Pete himself knew he had a much easier time getting his Georgetown Prep baseball team to clean up their language. "All I have to say is, next time you talk like that I hope it's your mother standing there." Baseball crowds not only sat closer to the field, the game itself was quieter, more refined. Football was explosive—a game of grunts, groans, helmet collisions—and, inevitably, talking trash.

But there were limits to what even a football ref would take, and in the second quarter Kong crashed through them. He tackled Riggs, who was running with the ball, bringing him down. Lying on top of him, under the protective coating of a huge pile of players, he vented himself with wild abandon—Riggs's performance, mother, family all came in for denigration. In his enthusiasm, he failed to notice that the pile had been cleared. His last bit of venom, unfortunately, was delivered right in the referee's face.

"I started talking to him while everyone was on top of us—but then the ref started pulling everyone off and I was still talking to him," Kong said sadly. He was called for unsportsmanlike conduct; a furious Mitch bawled him out and refused to talk to him the rest of the game. He had violated their understanding—he had gotten caught.

Mitch knew he was being a hypocrite, but he knew he had to rip into him too, in front of everybody. Secretly, though, he was pleased. "He did what I asked him to do." Kong, he felt, had the makings of the best kind of a player—a mean, nasty, take nothin'-from-no-one player—he even had that arrogant way of walking, like a black guy, he thought.

Another player, Toriano Seagears, a junior, was managing to get a few shots in against Riggs—in one pileup he socked him in the stomach a couple of times and Riggs yelled at him, so "the next play I took a cheap shot on him. He was standing there, he would always tell you what he was going to do. He was lazy. If it was a running play he would just stand up, have his hand on his hip, one foot back—so I hit him and grabbed him, held him up—and then I said, 'My fault.'

"I think that scared him more than anything else, when I said that. He just looked at me and walked back to the huddle, shaking his head." (After the game, Riggs, obviously still puzzled, shook Toriano's hand warily. "You're . . . confusing," he told him.)

Mitch was pleased to see Toriano, too, following directions. However, Geoff, playing free safety on defense, was pissing him off. He was charged up, all right, and playing hard—but again and again, he did something Mitch could not stomach: after he'd knocked a guy down, he'd help him up! Even pat the guy's ass!

"Goddamn it, if I ever see that again, I'll kick your ass," he spat at Geoff from the sidelines. When you knock a guy down, you don't help him up. "You stand over top of him, you *walk* over top of him—that's part of the game." Geoff was a terrific player, but unless he got that goddamn B-CC niceness flushed out of his system, he was never going to go all the way.

Despite the score, James was feeling good, playing the best he'd ever played, he thought—"I didn't know I had it in me"—throwing tackle after tackle; damn, this *was* going to be his year, Oklahoma State, here I come, I'm going to break records this season, he was thinking. If only the offense, if only Rick, would do something once they got back out on the field. "We kept stopping them, but then they'd get out there and pop another interception." Finally he went to Geoff, pleading, "Geoff, it's our senior year—you score, I'll keep them from scoring, okay?" Geoff assured him he'd do it.

But Billy and Dave, on the sidelines, were not happy with the defense at all. They sat on the bench, sick and injured, alternatively wincing and groaning. James wasn't impressing either of them; as far as they were concerned, no one out there was filling their shoes. "We had nobody who could play linebacker, since Dave and I couldn't play—they'd just run straight in the middle for fifty yards—since we couldn't play, they had nobody else who knew how to play," Billy said.

"The middle linebacker has to first tell everyone else where to go, then worry about himself. If you put yourself first, everything is screwed up," said Dave. James wasn't bad, but he was no veteran—he still had to think about himself first out there. He wasn't used to directing other guys.

To the crowd, the first half of the game seemed to drag on interminably. The single shaft of sunlight was a final drive, late in the second quarter—including a beautiful long pass to Toriano—which disintegrated when Corey Dade lost his hold on the ball. Yet another turnover! As a final blow to the heart, Wooten kicked a field goal. The score, as the players moved off the field—Wooten leaping, B-CC walking heads down, shoulders slumped—was 17–0.

Once, at a similar juncture—and there had been many such junctures in his time—the old varsity coach had spent halftime telling his players how much they sucked. Bob and Mitch had no problem screaming at players, as a rule—but both were savvy enough to know this was not the time. The boys in the locker room stared at them with wide, tragic eyes. This was a time, if ever, for guts, pride, steel. His voice ragged, Mitch told them about his brother, who had played at Springbrook—about the playoff game, where they'd been getting their tails kicked and it was one minute before the end. One minute! And his brother had said to his friend, "We're gonna win, we're gonna run the kickoff back for a touchdown." And they'd done it! Because they never knew how to lose! Even then, one minute left, they weren't thinking losing, they were thinking, how do we win this game? That was the key, the key to it all.

Bob, too, was kind, almost gentle, with the linemen. "We thought we were doing awful," said Toby. "But I guess his expectations were so low, at turf level—he thought we weren't doing all that bad." And Pete, as usual, was equable. The boys sucked on water bottles—those who were going both ways, like Geoff and Tae Uk, slumped on benches, exhausted. Rick stood a bit apart, isolating himself ("No one talks to Rick at a time like that," the boys said). Yet by the end of halftime, there was a new sense of vigor, determination. "We got to give him more protection," the offensive linemen urged each other. It was a new half, a new chance. They ran back on the field ready to go.

At once the air was charged with a new feeling—even before the whistle blew, we in the stands could sense it. The aura of defeat, which had hung so heavily over the field during the first half, had somehow dissipated. Only in sports, it seemed to me, could one pick up a change in tone, a shift in direction, from the very air itself, even before the play began—as if actual molecules of energy, of purpose, flowed up and off the players to be picked up by any viewer alert enough to catch them. We sensed—no, knew—that the boys were ready to fight.

And it was as if, after an entire half of first-game jitters, the Barons finally started to play. Finally, finally, Rick connected with Geoff for a beautiful, soaring spiral pass—a pass that rose like hope itself, high above the field, into the harbor of Geoff's hands, and safely into the end zone. Cheers at last exploded from the stadium—we were coming, we were coming, at last. Wooten, still staunch, rebounded almost at once with a touchdown, their third— they had no intention of caving in—but the spell had been broken, and now the stands were raging, freed like the boys themselves from the deadly first-half paralysis. "Get it back! Get it back! You can do it!" we howled.

Of course, at this point the chances were dubious, at best, and studied pessimists like Sal Fiscina—in reality a romantic who had trained himself in pessimism, at least on football fields; you were so much less likely to be disappointed—refused to be swept away in an orgy of expectation. The boys had dug themselves a large hole; it was unlikely they could climb out.

But for the rest of us the battle on the field was now so much sharper, crisper, harder than before, that saying no to hope seemed almost a betrayal. And truly, there seemed so much to admire out there suddenly. How much tougher it was to continue to fight against such odds—for James, for Brendan Reed, to press on so determinedly, tackle after tackle—for the line, in the face of all their inexperience, to hang in, push on, determined to get it right.

Even when Rick, in the third quarter, hurled another interception, to everyone's groaning dismay, James continued to hope. If Rick could just get set in his game, even now, they could do it. He knew it. "I felt—we can win this, we've known each other for so long, I've known Rick and Geoff since sixth grade, they're all too capable." "Just don't fade out on me, guys," he muttered under his breath. "Don't fade."

Mitch had gone up to the score box, high over the stands, for a better view; he was yelling his advice down to Bob over headphones. "He wants to talk to you," Bob said, handing the headphone to Brendan Symes. Brendan, who never played defense and had had little contact with Mitch, was mystified, but picked up the phone. The disembodied voice crackled out with deadly sincerity: "You go in there and score," Mitch said. "If you don't score, I'm gonna kill you."

"Okay, Mitch," said Brendan in his soft voice. "I'll score."

He was ready. The game had been getting to him—all that screaming in the huddle, Rick so mad—sometimes it seemed to him Rick felt he had to do everything himself—constantly trying to pass to Geoff, not giving Brendan a chance to run it. The Wooten team was getting to him, too—one of their defensive tackles had sneered at him, "You little nigger, I'm bigger than you, I'm gonna kill you." And, yeah, he was smaller, all right—but try hurting him. It wasn't that easy. Brendan liked to laugh at them when they started talking like that. "It just makes them so much madder, then they mess up more."

But he was definitely ready to get something back. And out on the field a few minutes later, now in the fourth quarter, as Rick handed off the ball to him, and Toby, astonishing himself, managed to connect with a decent block for once, Brendan tore downfield eight yards for a touchdown—even managing to flick a wave in passing at the guy who'd bad-mouthed him. See ya, sucker. Howling with happiness, he and Toby embraced each other as all the players—and the viewers in the stands—threw their arms in the air—a freeze frame of joy—joy made all the more intense for its proximity to despair; a taunt to death, a savage volley—take that!—hurled against the oncoming night.

It rolled in, though, despite everything, that night, heavily, unavoidably, not long afterward. A whistle's bleat, and all hope deflated like a tired balloon. The game was over. Wooten leapt to the sky, whooping. In the bleachers, many of us stood unmoving, not wanting to believe. We'd been doing so much better, couldn't they grant us just one more quarter? We shrugged, scowled, shuffled, attempted to return to our daily selves—just a game, after all, so silly—even as sadness squeezed the heart of every parent, however briefly: the first game. Joking, "*I* don't want to be there when he gets home, not me," we moved toward the gate, smiling, talking casually, all the while keeping an eye on the line of players now stalking up the stairs, through the crowd, faces pale, strained, and still, their eyes far away, avoiding everyone. And we ached, knowing we could do nothing at all. It had been, finally, too little, too late. Despite the second-half effort, the outcome had never truly been in doubt. "The kind of game that leaves a bad taste in your mouth," said Kong. A lousy start. Wooten, Wooten—the long vowels gave the words themselves some of the rueful sound of loss; and Wooten, Wooten, the boys would mourn, down through the season. A game they should have won. The one that got away.

CHAPTER FIVE

THE BOYS WEATHERED a bleak, desultory evening after the Wooten game—who felt like partying?—before coming home and falling into bed. If only another player could understand the comradery of the locker room, as Geoff had said, certainly only another player could understand the feelings after a loss—and all were adamant about not wishing to communicate with anyone but another player that night. Parents, siblings, grandparents, even pets gave the boys a wide berth, out of both sympathy and self-protection. For despite Bob and Mitch's belief that the Barons were gentle, mild pacifists, their families knew better. However civilized they might be on the surface, they had all had their moments, and they were all at this point in time, we assumed, large, pissed-off male adolescents. It was much the better part of valor to stay out of their way.

However, the truth was that those of us who were family members—parents, grandparents, siblings—did *not* really understand a great deal; did not understand, for instance, that nearly every game had so many moments of sweetness, despite the final outcome, that it was impossible for a player to feel only one emotion.

Toby, for instance, was deeply proud that it had been his block that had allowed Brendan Symes to run in a touchdown—and that pride had gone straight to the place inside where he held his belief about himself and his ability to improve, strengthening his confidence. James was sincerely overjoyed with his numerous tackles—it was one thing to brag, to flex your muscles, quite another to prove you could succeed to yourself. Geoff, the emotional kaleidoscope, was both hugely disappointed at the loss and hugely pleased with his own performance. And Billy and Dave, unable to participate, felt the keenest frustration of all: if they had been in there, they knew, things would have been different. All the reactions were more complicated than any parent knew, below the surface. Yet trying to explain was useless, so the boys kept their distance.

However, a loss was still a loss, and by the next day, left to their own devices, the boys would not have minded burying all memory of the game—why dwell on defeat? Pete, at least, understood this. He had been involved with baseball, with basketball, over the years, but somehow, no loss hurt as much as football. Football losses went deeper, and seemed to stay longer, he thought.

Yet a brisk twelve hours after the boys had finally cleared out of the locker room, well before any scab had begun to form on the wound, they were gathered back at school, specifically, in the Blue and Gold Room above the gym. Object: a careful viewing of the previous night's disaster, in all its humbling totality, on videotape.

Mitch particularly was a staunch advocate of videotape. What better way to show a kid what mistakes he was making? He had spent the evening after the game viewing the tape again and again, making careful notations on every boy's performance.

Despite their disappointment with last night, the boys were not totally unhappy with the prospect of viewing the game. Last year's tape sessions had been fun, win or loss, with lots of catcalls and wisecracks. Face it, everyone liked to see himself on television, at least, everyone in this group. Football rarely attracts people who shrink from the spotlight, and this year's team featured more than its share of center-stagers, especially among the seniors. There were times when almost all of them accused others of being cocky— Geoff, Rick, James, Dave, et al.—and it was hard to miss with an accusation like that, because nearly all of them were. A humble, almost self-effacing kid like Eric Knaus puzzled everyone.

But it was obvious from the minute they walked in the room that this year's tape sessions were to be different. For one thing, Bob and Mitch dominated the scene. Pete White stood off to the side for the most part, a bit subdued, letting the young coaches have their way.

Their way involved a great deal of heavy bloodletting. Nearly every member of the team came in for his share of browbeating. Even if he had acquitted himself well on a particular play, even if the entire team had acquitted itself well, there was always room for improvement, that was their stance. And of course, this first time around, the fact was that almost no one had acquitted himself all that well.

There were boys who took it in stride, even at this first session. Brendan Symes, who took plenty of flack that day for what one player called his "inverse problem—mistaking holes for piles" had a mild temperament. Even Mitch's repeated howls—"Christ, Brendan, you did it again, goddamn it! What the fuck are you doing running in that direction, the hole's over there!"—did not truly bother him.

"I guess some of the criticism I deserve," he admitted; he did not find it really upsetting. The way he saw it, the football team was like your family, Coach White was like your dad. "So when you get screamed at, it's like at home. I'm getting screamed at because I did the wrong thing. They just want me to do better, that's all."

For John Han, though, tape sessions would quickly become a tense, unbearable exercise in torture; he sat stiffly, silently willing the tape to pass by his less skillful moments so fast that neither coach would pick up on them. "Sometimes you'd be watching and you kind of know where you messed up and you know it's the next play . . . and you're watching . . . and all of a sudden, someone else makes a great play and they watch that—good job, Brendan!—whatever—and you see yourself screwing up and it goes by.

"And then some idiot in the back goes, Coach, can we see that again? Then of course they're gonna rewind it and then Mitch or Plante says—Han! What the hell's that?"

John felt a guy should be able to talk himself out of anything; he did his best. "You think of something. You gotta cover it up. When they say, what the hell was that, you can't say, well, Coach, I was stupid. I missed him. I stank. So you say, well, Coach, I thought that was a 21-Y or something. And they'd say, Han—bullshit."

Most of the boys found silent acceptance the best approach to the tape session—though as the year continued, more than once they would catch themselves on the field, after a bad play, muttering a quick prayer, I hope that didn't get on the tape! Christo Doyle, the junior linebacker Mitch called Goose, who had a hair-trigger temper, once smacked an opposing player in his helmet, and found himself less worried about the ensuing penalty than the next tape session. Please, God, he urged, let me have been off screen for that one!

Kong, who approached football very seriously, found the tape session immensely depressing. "They'd just cuss you out for what you were doing wrong. Even if you made a tackle, if you threw somebody off you wrong—you're supposed to hit them with one arm, throw them with the other—if you didn't do that, they'd just critique you on back. Even if you made a nice play. They would *never* compliment you."

"I'll tell you what," Mitch announced now, as the tape unfolded its sad story in front of them. "Goose—you tell me when you make a tackle, okay, son? Jesus Christ, just let me know, okay?"

The boys did not know it yet, but this would become a running theme with Mitch. "He'd say, 'Goose, tell me when the fuck you make a play. As far as I'm concerned, we have ten men on defense right here. You're a little puss—you know that?' " said Geoff.

This bothered Geoff more than anything else the coach had done before; he knew Christo well and ached for him. "Christo took so much pride in his football, then the defensive coach tells him that—he just must have felt like shit. But he didn't resent it. Instead of turning it into anger, he turned it into depression."

Rather soon, Christo would come to detect the affection behind Mitch's words—and other players, seeing it too, would even come to view him as "Mitch's little pet." ("Goose gets me so upset I can't stand it," Mitch commented once, watching a tape, "I guess it's because I see such potential for goodness in the kid.") But certainly at the first session there was no such comforting realization; Geoff was right, Christo did feel like shit.

Geoff himself though, whose buoyant spirits could rarely be dampened, was one of the few getting any real pleasure out of the screening today. "Look at this one coming up." He nudged someone. "I have a really good play coming up here."

Both Mitch and Bob turned to him simultaneously after the play. "It wasn't all that great," they assured him, in chorus.

"You think you have to make every play, don't you, Geoff?" Mitch added nastily. "That's the sort of person you are, I bet. You're the only man on the field. I got to do it all, I got to be king, right?" Geoff just smiled, barely abashed. They had to say something, he figured. Coaches never complimented you—hardly ever, anyway. It was always—I don't care if you do it perfect, there's a better way. And what could you say to that?

Rick, though, had a hard time letting insults roll off him; it was times like these that people forgot he was only half Italian. It was hard to believe that temper wasn't 100 percent Neapolitan. "Well, congratulations," Mitch said to him caustically, after his unprecedented series of interceptions came to an end on the screen. "You threw the ball to one of our players, for once." Another player cracked up, quite unwisely, since he was sitting next to Rick, who punched him hard in the shoulder, knocking him out of his chair. Pete called sharply for "a little maturity."

Rick was even more infuriated when both Mitch and Bob insisted he had refused to "step up into the pocket." He'd been out there on the field—they hadn't. *What* pocket? "What pocket? Geoff, you see a pocket?" he hissed to his friend. Geoff just grinned; he thought Rick was silly to react that strongly. Rick, he knew, hated criticism.

"Now here we see Buttenheimer trying to make a block," said Bob with heavy sarcasm, "and we see him getting spanked. Fucking bopper, can't you do nothing right?" Toby squirmed. Bob had begun to toy with the concept of adding "Butt" as a prefix to names—Buttenheimer worked better than most, he thought. Toby, though, knew it wasn't just the name. Bob was singling him out more than the other linemen, tossing more sneers, more nasty comments his way. He knew it was because he was big, that Bob was expecting a lot out of him and not seeing much yet. It still felt lousy.

Yet for the most part Bob held his fire for this first session; he did not unleash vast amounts of ridicule on the line. Aside from the potshots at Toby, he held himself down to few blanket taunts. "Christ, you five can't block *anything*," he commented several times. "Worthless pussies." There were even a few kudos mixed in.

"Not bad, Tae Uk, not bad." Alex was impressed with his restraint. "With the old coach, every single word you said was wrong . . . with Bob, things could get rough, but he used positive reinforcement—rip you down one play, move you back up next one.

"A high school student tends to look at a coach with a certain amount of awe. If the coach tells you you're nothing, you feel like nothing, instantly. And if he tells you you're something, you feel like something." Bob, he thought, was handling things properly; he approved. Alex, of course, considered himself more of a platoon leader than a member of the infantry, thus capable of analyzing the situation from slightly higher ground; he felt most comfortable in that role. When he himself was criticized, the barbs tended to glance off. His detachment made a good armor.

Other players, too, were struggling to see the session in a positive light. "A necessary aide," Mike Mitchem thought. "I made a lot of stupid mistakes, and you'd see them clearly and see what you did. And watching Mitch and Plante go off on people—it was sort of fun." (From the beginning the boys invariably referred to the assistant coaches as Mitch and Plante; their reasons were vague, though it seemed reasonable to conclude this reflected their different perceptions of the two men. Despite their similarities, Bob did strive to be more aloof; Mitch admitted he had difficulty drawing that line of separation. Pete, on the other hand, was always "Coach White." He alone was the father figure; no one ever made the mistake of seeing Bob or Mitch in that role.)

Others, too, felt the session helped. "Gets you thinking about what you did wrong," one said. And of course the wisecracks could be fun, especially when they weren't directed at you: "That was a nice play, but what are you doing here, playing with yourself?" Mitch taunted one boy.

A few, like Geoff, had the kind of confidence no comment could puncture, and for them, the criticism had little impact. "It goes in one ear and out the other," one player said, shrugging.

But not everyone felt that way. Rene Grave de Peralta, for instance, was having a very hard time dealing with the tape session. But then, he had been having a hard time handling Mitch in general.

"Some people don't mind if coaches are on them, but some

people do mind, pretty much," he explained carefully. "If you made a mistake, they'd rewind the tape, look at this, look at this— always yelling." A guy like Coach White was so nice, he deserved to be head coach, Rene thought. But a guy like Mitch . . .

Throughout the tape session Rene sat quietly, obviously uncomfortable with the scene. From the start of the season it had felt like Mitch was constantly yelling at him, "saying how stupid I was, saying that I wasn't very good. I don't like it when people scream at me in front of my face.

"Some people," he said wistfully, "have other problems."

Rene had had his share. He had come from a background few of the other players could even comprehend, so foreign was it to their lives. He was born in San Diego; his mother was a beautiful, talented Cuban woman, from whom he had inherited his light hair, his green eyes. The daughter of a well-to-do family, she had been a contender for the Junior Davis Cup in tennis when she was only fourteen, before the coming of Castro had forced her family into exile in Miami. She supported herself by working as a dancer in various clubs. Rene had never known his father.

His childhood had been one of constant turmoil, constant change. His mother had developed her own nightclub act, then chased success around the globe, sometimes taking him with her, sometimes parking him with family—a grandmother, an aunt and uncle. Over the years Rene had lived in Mexico, Miami, Los Angeles, Spain, Greece, Egypt; before coming to B-CC he had never once completed an entire year of school in one place. Nor had he ever stayed long enough in one school for them to become aware of any gaps in his knowledge, any problems he might be having. He had simply been passed along, grade to grade, school to school, country to country, one set of hands to another. "Every time I would have friends, I would leave."

She was a beautiful woman, his mother, but a strange one as well—frustrated, unhappy, bitter. "She used to hit me a lot when I was little," Rene said. "And when I got older too. She had problems . . . and she put them on me. If you're married you can take it out on your husband, I guess, but she took it out on me." Two more children were born after Rene, each with different fathers—a boy, then a girl.

Almost worse than the blows were her words. Rene's mother had a violent hatred of anything she considered weak, and she felt her son was too sensitive, too compliant. "She thought because I was nice that I was going to become a faggot." She pushed him into football herself, when he was only thirteen, hoping it would toughen him up. At the same time, she told him she had never wanted sons; if her daughter had been born first, she would never had had any more children, she taunted.

She railed at him constantly. "Every time I went home she would say things to me, put me down." And when he was at school, it was hard to concentrate. "I couldn't learn because I was always thinking of her." Her voice, her words, drowned out everything. "I was always afraid of her, always."

At last his aunt and uncle, terribly concerned—they had taken him in before, but his mother had always returned to demand him back—managed to convince her to let Rene live with them in Chevy Chase while he attended high school at B-CC, where their own son was now a senior. At least let him have his last four years of education at a good school, uninterrupted for once.

He had walked in utterly unprepared for what he would find; worked diligently late into the night on homework he could barely understand. There was almost nothing for him to build on; his erratic schooling had been all but worthless. The frustration and hopelessness had brought him to tears often that first year. Finally, they realized the extent of his difficulty; he was tested, adjudged learning disabled, and began to receive tutoring in special-education classes. It was late in the game, he had missed so much time, but Rene continued to work hard, very hard, trying to master skills he had never been properly taught.

"I survived," he said quietly. "I think when I was little there was a point where I was trying to become crazy like her in a way. It took me quite a while when I came here to adjust. I felt like a bird in a cage . . . and they let the bird go. Free. That's how I felt. It was scary. I had never had that."

But the past is not so easily shed; he knew this. "My grandmother says, well, that's the past, it happened in the past, you shouldn't dwell on it, you have to go to the future, but I have a lot of trouble concentrating, still. My mind wanders off."

Yet against such formidable odds—only one other player had experienced anything remotely as harsh as Rene's childhood—he continued to struggle, searching unrelentingly for footing, for the path that would allow him finally to climb up out of the desolate valley of his past.

"I'm a very hard worker. I have two jobs, one in a Japanese restaurant. Then in the summer I worked on this house, helping with construction." The owner had been so impressed with his dedication he insisted Rene work at his computer store, where he had learned many of the basics of computer technology. Afraid of losing him—no other boy worked as hard as Rene—the restaurant had then doubled his salary, so he continued to work at both places. At the Edison Center, where county high school students were trained in various trades, he was learning construction techniques, helping to put together two houses "from scratch." He hoped eventually to become a plumber.

Even more important, there was his girlfriend. He worried sometimes. "She has high classes, and I don't know that much." But it didn't seem to matter to her. "She says I'm different, I really care about people, that it's hard to find people like me. That's what she says," said Rene.

"You did everything you set out to do," she had told him recently. "On your own. Look at all the things you can do. I'm very proud of you."

"Being loved . . . I never had that, so it feels special to me. I told her my problems, she told me hers. She says I'm different, because I can open up."

He liked the other kids on the team, he was close to several, but there were times when he felt jealous, a little, he admitted. "They've had a good life. A mom and dad. Stay in one place, know everybody." Not like him. He himself would never hit a kid, he knew, or try to push him into anything. "I would see what he likes." Also, any kid of his would have a father; that would be the biggest difference right there.

His skill at football had improved a great deal since he had moved here. His uncle had encouraged him to join the team; he thought it was a good way of making friends, getting into the school, and in fact, it had worked out that way. "Before, it was her pushing me. Now, it's for me." Playing well gave him a feeling he had had too little experience of over the years: it made him happy.

Or rather, it had, up until this season. Coach White, who was never unkind to any boy, had been a perfect coach for a boy like Rene. Mitch was not. It was hard for him to shrug off the sort of poison darts Mitch liked to throw, the ones that rolled so easily off the back of James or Geoff. There had been too much cruelty already in his life, too many moments of shame and humiliation. The vessel was full; it could take no more.

Though only a few of the other players knew the actual facts of Rene's past, most of them sensed a fragility there; they could see Rene did not have the same armor they did, that casual barbs sank deeper, did more damage. Toriano, who dearly loved to talk about his own prowess, and held regular boasting contests with other players, like James ("that's the battle of the egos right there, me and James") was puzzled, even disturbed, by Rene. "He would be down on himself a lot," he said. "Say, I should have made that tackle, I messed up." It amazed Toriano. He couldn't imagine talking like that about himself.

And Geoff, with instinctive empathy, found himself seeking to bolster Rene's ego on the field. Knowing nothing of Rene's childhood, he nonetheless sensed strongly the boy needed to feel someone had faith in him. "You gotta have a fucking attitude, man!" he'd yell at him. "You gotta care about your ass!" That, to him, was primary—Rene had to care about himself. You couldn't play unless you did. And it worked, it worked, Geoff said proudly— often, after he yelled those things, Rene would go out and make the tackle. And Geoff would grab him and hug him, feeling exactly like a proud father.

Though few boys reacted to criticism as strongly as Rene, the tape session took its toll. Most filed out of the room feeling as if they had weathered a second defeat. Pete, watching them, wasn't entirely sorry he'd let Bob and Mitch have their sway; it seemed to him the guys should be down, after last night. It was only fitting.

The Wooten game had been a big disappointment to Pete and a surprise as well. "We had a great week of practice, then we go out there and stink up the joint." It felt terrible. "Losing to Wooten, a coach thinks, God, I can't believe it, how could we look so crummy?" and watching the film just made it worse. He knew, though, that by Monday, the kids would have sloughed it off and would be ready to go to work again. Boys always had an easier time getting over a loss than coaches did, Pete noticed.

"No matter what happens, by Monday the kids are pretty much ready to get on with their life, get on with the next game, oh, we're gonna kick these guys' butts." It didn't matter, either, that they might have just lost 89–0 to one team and were about to face a team three times as good. "Coaches may be, oh God, this might be even worse, but the kids are not.

"I guess that's the great savior in athletics. The kids . . . very few of them have any touch with reality. Which is good. Which is great."

The tape session had been important for a number of reasons, Pete thought—and one of the main ones was, it gave coaches a chance to redress wrongs: "You find yourself during the game yelling at the wrong people. You know what the play is, what went off, but your eyes can't catch everything—you see where something's happened and maybe you're yelling at the center, you figure he should have blocked this way, but come to look at a film and you'll see—well, that guy from Wooten slid down, so actually the center did the right thing, it was the dumb guard didn't figure out he should have done something different—but here comes the center off the field and you're already yelling at him and here it's not his fault." A tape session could result in a more equitable distribution of blame.

"That's why we tell them, whatever's said out there between the lines, there shouldn't be any hard feelings. What's said on the field is nothing personal, just business." Though a lot of the kids, he knew, were having trouble understanding that, with Bob and Mitch, who "took no prisoners."

Bob Plante knew he had carved out a hell of a job for himself. Wooten had just made that fact all the more plain. Could he really take this disparate, skinny, undersized group of guys and weld them into a force—a line capable of wreaking some genuine damage on the field? All Wooten had done was show him just how far he had to go. Tae Uk, now, was quick and gutsy; Marc Gage, too, seemed to know something about what was going on, but, Jesus, neither of them topped five-seven. If he was ever going to get anywhere, he knew he'd have to count on the bigger kids, like Oppenheimer.

Toby Oppenheimer was at this point just about worthless—pitiful! Big, strong, and practically a complete waste on the field. The kid knew nothing! A blank slate! Well, damn it, he was going to turn this guy into a lineman if it was the last thing he did. That'd be his special project.

Alex Burgess was a big guy too, even bigger, a veteran as well—yet there was something about Alex that gave Bob the feeling he'd never be able to have much impact on him. This was a kid, he sensed, who wanted to be up on his level—an associate, a co-director, not a grunt. Nice guy, bright kid, but Bob had a hunch he wasn't going to be able to do much there. No, he was going to concentrate on Toby—raw clay, fresh for molding.

Linemen were made, not born—that's what Bob believed. No one ever willed himself to be a champion running back or wide receiver; all the effort in the world couldn't help you there, you were either born with the talent or not. And of course, those were the guys who got all the glory on the field.

But what a lineman got was something even more important, Bob thought. He got a concrete lesson in the work ethic that would stand him in good stead the rest of his life. A lineman got used to working hard to achieve any kind of success; he kept going, he didn't expect things to come easy. What better training could you get for going out in the business world?

And that was the best part of all about football, to him. "It teaches you to attack life. So many elements in the game are involved in being successful in life—the working together, the physical contact, competitiveness, as well as mental competitiveness. It also teaches—and I'm a perfect example—that you don't have to be the biggest and the strongest and the best to be the most successful."

Bob was convinced he could tell right away whether or not someone had ever played football. The guys that hadn't had "an air . . . they don't have that thoroughbred mentality. When they're knocked down they don't know how to get up. There wasn't ten guys standing in the huddle, saying get up, they don't know how to work with the support of other guys; a lot of time they don't have a lot of class." Sometimes, waiting in a supermarket line, watching some bozo try to push his way in front, Bob would nudge his fiancée, she'd look at him—by now she knew him pretty well—and they'd say it together: "That guy never played football."

"She's learned a lot about the game from me, but she's at a disadvantage in the business world. I tell her, sorry—you're smart but you never played football, so I got the advantage." The game had taught him everything, he thought—how to pick himself up, get out there, and fight. It also taught him—and this was something women rarely got a chance to learn, he felt—how to deal with competition. "At the end of the game, you take the helmet off, the war is over—and say, man, you really nailed me. But next time I'm gonna nail you."

These kids had a lot to learn about football, and they had to do it fast—it wasn't going to be easy and it wasn't going to be pleasant, either; sometimes you had to humiliate them, it was the only way to challenge their manhood. But the end justified the means, Bob felt, and what better end could you ask for? He was going to turn them into football players.

Pete, walking by on the field during practice that week, stopped to watch Bob drilling the line. Again and again he would run them through a play; each time, he'd shake his head, wrong, one shake, and make them do it again. Over and over. Never shook his head yes; only no. Now and then, he'd grab someone by the shirt—"Get out." Or just say to someone else, "Get in for Toby, go ahead." And make Toby stand behind the line—"What're you doing? Taking the day off? That's all you're doing today?"

"Bob was not going to take mediocrity. Even if they weren't great football players, he was not going to accept it," he realized, impressed. "And no excuses, either—if your toe hurts, your butt hurts, whatever, get out here and do the job or get the hell off the field."

Bob wasn't the most talkative guy in the world. When Mitch got started, he could go on forever, it seemed, but Bob kept himself down to a few well-chosen words. One of those words, though, was a powerful one: courage. "That's a word that always cuts right to the quick," said Pete. "He'd say, 'You have to show a little courage—if not, we're gonna have to get somebody else in there.' Bang. They'd get the idea."

Toby knew Bob was leaning on him particularly hard, yet already he was starting to realize something else, too, about the coach. "He wasn't going to just blow up in front of us, because he was part of us in a way," he said. "He'd try to teach us . . . it was like we were doing it for him, his pride. It wasn't yeah, you did it wrong, you're all shit . . . it was come on back, do it again. Let's fucking do it right. He was never just going through the motions. He really cared, and that's what made you work harder. So we just tried to do good for him, a lot of people did, because he was the only one watching." Sure, Bob yelled, yet somehow he was able to do it so you didn't feel it was at you, exactly—he was telling you to do better, as if he knew you could. And you believed him, that was why you kept trying.

Nobody, in Pete's estimation, ever worked as hard as the linemen on a team. "They work and they work and they work. You never give them a minute off." Yet they hardly ever got credit. "If you throw a good pass, everyone's excited; they want to shake Geoff's hand if he caught it." But who ever ran out on the field to shake a lineman's hand? "They have to draw from themselves, and from their coach."

Yet in truth, "everybody that coaches, or plays, knows pretty much that's where you win or lose. I think everybody on the team understands how important their role is, and they do too." But linemen traditionally got more than their share of abuse. A quarterback, even if he was playing terribly, you couldn't really yell at, he was the leader, whereas linemen were upbraided in front of the group almost religiously. There was a point to it—you were making them bond together, and trying to get them to the point that they'd react without thought. But in reality . . . in reality . . . what you were asking linemen to do was practically impossible. "You give a guy a job to do that can't be done, almost."

Pete still had a picture in his mind from last season. Somehow it had burnt itself into his memory. A freeze-frame: the offense coming off the field, Rick, flushed, talking a mile a minute, totally hyped up, manic, the words tumbling out so fast Pete could hardly understand them; and looming behind him, silent, unblinking, un-complaining, like a solid wall—the offensive linemen. Waiting for instructions. Waiting to go back out there and do their job. The dray horses, the blue-collar workers, the anonymous ones—the core of the team.

As the week went on, both Bob and Mitch continued to rail at the boys almost constantly—"You suck! Worthless bags of pus!"— infuriating many, puzzling some. "It wasn't like I hated them," said Jimmy Loreto, who as backup quarterback had pretty much re-signed himself to sitting out most games this year—Rick never got sick a day in his life. Next year would be his season, he hoped.

"It was just like, what's your problem? Something up your butt? They were so tight about everything, you wondered, how can you possibly act like that to people? Who would ever like you?" When he filled in on defense, both coaches would "yell, cut on me, say what a wimp I was. I guess they were doing it like a fear thing, to get you mad, but if you don't know why they're doing it you just feel, oh God, they hate me."

Billy, who had valiantly suited up for practice on Monday, a scant five days after his operation—Jesus, he had to play, they were starting to slip some dumb junior into his position—was getting a lot of abuse; as usual, the sight of an ailing player spurred both Bob and Mitch to even greater heights. "Stone, you are the ugliest white man I've ever seen," Mitch spat at the kid who'd been last year's junior Homecoming King. "You look like you're on skates out there—can't you do nothing right? Crummy, worthless piece of—" And Billy would stand there, taking it, boiling inside.

Yet away from the field, even the wariest boys had begun to discover something else about Bob and Mitch—these guys were funny. Hilarious, actually. Once you got them away from the field, off maneuvers, you could sit around and shoot the shit with them for hours—no subject was taboo. Only eleven or twelve years older than most of the players, more like older brothers than the father figure Pete was, they had no qualms about filling the boys in on the X-rated details of their personal lives. Qualms, hell—they were absolutely raring to go.

These bull sessions—"Mitch and Plante's sex lectures," one

player dubbed them—were raunchy to a fault, an exercise in macho overkill. "Do you know how many women I've had? I have had eight thousand women," Bob announced oratorically. "Yeah, sexual tyrannosauruses, you better believe it, that's us," Mitch bellowed. Bob, now engaged, had of course cleaned up his act considerably in recent times; even Mitch now had a steady girlfriend. But they'd had their innings, all right, though perhaps "quarters" would be the better word in their case—both separately AND together—and with their keen football-honed recall skills were fully able to account them play by play.

"Yah, we did tell 'em some stories," Bob admitted to me (having the grace to flush slightly). "But that's all part of men being men—well, actually boys being boys. I'm a typical male."

"It's all part of the theatrics, too—even that stuff," he added, eager to point out the philosophical underpinnings. "They see, wow, that's our coaches, that's great, and in their eyes we're even better than we were before—I'm your coach, I'm the greatest thing since sliced bread and I've had eight thousand women. You guys want to wear the uniform, be like me, have all the women, right?"

They also told the boys how much money they made, as another way of impressing them, he added, even parading some of their fancier toys—like their new twin Harley motorcycles—in front of them.

Significantly, not one player responded with much interest to the money angle; these were not children of deprivation who could be awed by toys. "Yuppies," said one boy dismissively. "I've got about ninety cousins just like that." Truth to tell, the boys weren't exactly impressed by the sexual bravado either—but it was a lot of fun to listen to, anyway.

The coaches launched their reminiscences originally during two-a-days, and continued them throughout the season, an endless catalogue of superstud exploits, for the most part. Yet occasionally a glint of reality, even humanity, emerged between the layers of guff. Early on, Bob had walked into the weight room one day to find several boys gathered on the floor, earnestly trying to outdo each other with tales of sexual endurance. Thirty years before, the conversation would have been slightly different—then, each boy would have had his work cut out for him trying to convince the others that he had actually, in fact, done the deed, let alone done it skillfully. Today baseline experience was assumed automatically (and generally, validly); the competition had moved up to the higher level of technical expertise.

Bob stood for a moment, slouched against the door, listening, then said exactly the right thing. "Hell, when I was your age, I hardly even stuck it in—wham!—that'd be it," he told them, dropping the braggadocio for once. It was the sort of reassurance only an older brother could ever give, that only an older brother, probably, would even know to give; it made every boy in the room feel better instantly. "It was, you know, a real male-bonding thing, he was telling us something real about himself," one explained. But confusing, too—"because here was this guy who was being such a dick to us on the field." Yet he had another, more human side too, apparently.

CHAPTER SIX

THE SECOND GAME of the season was Blair. Blair was an away game, one; a Saturday afternoon game, two; and the follow-up to the Wooten embarrassment, three. Those were the bad things about Blair.

On the good side, Blair, a Silver Spring school with a high minority rate, always seemed to have trouble when it came to B-CC. It didn't make sense, really, certainly not to Mitch, who nearly drooled with envy when he saw those humongous black players they had, but there it was. Last year, in a home game, B-CC had been whipping them up one side and down the other, when the game had had to be called on account of a sudden, torrential rainfall. Actually, everyone would have been more than happy to sit out the rain and wait, even B-CC's principal, Nancy Powell, that's how well things were going—but one of the referees suddenly announced he couldn't wait any longer, he had promised to pick up his daughter somewhere, a seizure of parental commitment so ludicrously ill-timed that the entire crowd saw it as a transparent attempt to save Blair's ass, and voiced its opinion accordingly.

But the following Monday, faced with a whole new game to play, start to finish, B-CC had wiped up the field with them all over again! So much for referees' daughters! So actually, it was as if they had beat Blair not once but twice last year.

Pete, though, was making no predictions. "They might not be the best team, but they don't just lie down for you on the field," he warned. Certainly as far as player size went, Blair was a force to be reckoned with, a lot more than Wooten, and look what had happened there. He concentrated his energies on making sure the boys had a solid, serious week of practice. The opening game had been bad enough. Two in a row and B-CC was going to be the laughingstock of the county.

Dave was determined to play this time. He had friends at other schools and had gotten wind of what they were saying. "Everybody was downing our defense because of what happened against Wooten—they thought they could do whatever they wanted to us." He went out for practice, hoping by some miracle his ankle would feel better. It didn't—it still hurt like hell. Bending over to examine it, he saw something unnerving: a group of ominous little black spots on the skin. A friend of his mother's, a doctor, looked at it that night, and told him the spots meant internal bleeding, and to stay off it, for God's sake.

Miserably, he hobbled into Pete's office the next day to tell him he would be unable to play again this week. Pete sighed. "It's too bad, it's your last season," he said sympathetically. God! As if he didn't know that! He marched unevenly into the locker room, taped his ankle up and tried, once again, to hop out on the field— he hated to admit he'd have to sit out another game. If Billy were out again too, which looked likely, that meant James would be back at linebacker again, and they needed James on the line—not to mention the fact that James's ego was expanding at an alarming rate and sorely wanted cutting down. They needed him! That's who they needed. Jesus, he wanted to play. Horribly frustrated, Dave swore to himself that this would be the last game he'd miss, no matter how many black dots popped out, no matter if the damn thing fell off.

"You have to, just have to be a part of it," he said. "It's one of those feelings, it makes you want to go ahead and give it all you got and do whatever you can. It's upbringing. My parents—they never told me to quit. I never learned how to quit."

They were both determined people, his parents. His mother, Joan, was a small-town Kentucky girl, a pert, freckle-faced blonde who'd been football queen her senior year at high school; she and

Dave's father Rick had come to Washington in the sixties, after college; he worked for the Human Resources Department of the D.C. government. Both had gotten involved in volunteer programs with kids in the city, and this had led directly to their adopting Dave.

"It was our first real contact with blacks on a personal level; Kentucky was very segregated," Joan said. "And when we were ready to start a family there were a lot of minority children not getting adopted. We didn't have real strong feelings about having to have a biological child."

They decided to adopt a black child—but first, they made a number of other decisions about their lives. "Our life had to be a life that a child from a minority group would feel comfortable with; that was important. We wanted to stay in a diverse community.

"And we decided to adopt first, because we felt the firstborn has some advantages in being first—and thinking that there were going to be some disadvantages, in terms of society, we wanted to give him an extra little edge—and so we got Dave." Their second son, Teddy, was born two years later. If the marriage had lasted, they had intended to adopt another black child, a girl.

The original plans had worked out—the family had always lived in mixed neighborhoods, and Dave was an almost prototypical firstborn; certainly he was the son his father identified with, pushed the most scholastically—like all firstborns, he was convinced his younger brother tended to get away with murder. Growing up in an all-white family had advantages and disadvantages, Dave felt. "One of the advantages is, I can cope with any situation, white or black." One distinct disadvantage was that his mother had had no idea how to take care of his hair for years. "A lot of things people take for granted, you have to learn on your own pretty much," he said. "Because there's no one there to say, here's how you comb your hair. My mom used to try as hard as she could, but . . ." Being adopted, Dave admitted, felt "a little strange. But I'm not obsessed." Later on, perhaps he would pursue it, find out more about his roots—mainly his medical background. A person should at least know if there is heart disease in his family or not.

In many ways, his unique situation offered him a real opportunity, Dave thought, particularly when it came to one of his favorite activities—breaking stereotypes. "I love breaking stereotypes. I love proving people wrong." Visiting his grandparents in Florida, in an all-white community, he loved to "say a whole lot of complicated shit . . . and everybody's like, wow.

"I don't change my identity. If anything, I inform people who I am and what a black man is like. It pisses me off, but that's all they've been taught . . . they don't know anything about me. So I get to break stereotypes."

A good student—"school's always been a getaway for me, where I'm always happiest"—Dave had taken his share of honors courses. But he was always aware that "teachers from the time you're young will let you know that you're black, and will treat you different than they will white kids. Will expect less from you." It was a struggle, at times, to keep from falling into that trap—expecting less from himself, just because they did. At one English class, in junior high, the teacher had spent the last day congratulating the three black students fulsomely—"because black kids are hardly ever in honors classes, but you three made it." Toby had also been in that class; he came home from school that day looking sick but not knowing why. It had sounded, he told me, as if she were complimenting them. Why did he feel bad? And I tried to explain, proud of him for knowing enough to be repelled by patronization—even if he did not yet know its name.

To Dave, though, this was an old story. This year at school, Dave was a peer-tutor coordinator, helping to lead a program of students aiding other students. The principal had assured him that she, too, wanted to break stereotypes. "She said, I want black guys tutoring white girls." Dave was stunned. "I thought the point was to pair up people who needed help. I wanted to say that so bad." He didn't; he just mentally shook his head. There were, unfortunately, so many incidents like that, tiny ominous black dots speckling the world. Some kid's father had even told a friend of his mother's not long ago how wonderful they'd been, his parents, to adopt Dave. "Like I'd be nothing without them, like they dragged me out of the gutter," he said bitterly.

There was no question in Dave's mind that black and white were polarized, at B-CC and throughout the country, and that, if anything, things were getting worse. Somehow, though, it was different with the team. All that stuff was beside the point; football transcended it. "We always do racial jokes, because nobody cares," he explained. "Everybody jokes around. So much fun."

Recently, he, Toby, and Billy had gone to the country club Billy's parents belonged to for lunch. It was hysterical—he was black, Toby was Jewish, probably neither of them could've joined on a bet. But there they were, big as life, and twice as loud, too. Funny thing, the food was awful, actually . . . except for the onion soup.

Guys on the team like Rick or Billy, Brendan Reed, Jimmy Loreto, Toby . . . once you were their friend, you could count on them forever. That was important to Dave: loyalty. It was what had impressed him about the old coach, and was what he thought he saw in Mitch, too. There were even kids on the fringe of his own school crowd—the "black elite"—that he didn't trust that much to stand up for him. "Not as much as I do my boys." You played football with someone, you depended on him out on the field, and somehow it flowed over into real life.

The biggest problem he'd ever had to face in his life had had nothing to do with racial prejudice—it had been the divorce of his parents, when he was eight. His father had only moved down the block, to stay close to his sons, but somehow that had almost made the rift worse. Dave began to have stomach upsets regularly at school; nearly every day he was in the nurse's office. Naturally he didn't make the connection. He was only a little kid.

Then, when he was thirteen, he stopped talking at home—just stopped completely. And Dave had always been a talker, just like his father—his father loved to talk more than anything. He didn't know why he did it; it was nothing he had planned, it just happened. But he could hardly have hit on a device that would get more immediate attention, in his family. What happened finally was the entire family ended up in therapy, because of Dave's silence. And at long last began the slow, painful process of real healing.

He'd traveled a lot in his life—another one of those things that his mother thought was important. Spain, France, Mexico, camping trips all over the country. But the trip he remembered most had been a few years ago. His mother had taken him and his brother to visit friends in the Peace Corps in Ghana.

"We'd gone to this village, they were having some kind of parade . . . and suddenly all the villagers came sprinting down, to the car." His mother and his brother had been the only white people there—"I'm African-American, our friends were African-American."

Nearly a hundred villagers surrounded them, fascinated by the pale faces of Dave's mother and brother. They reached out gently, to touch his mother's freckles, marveling. While Dave sat, watching them, this crowd of people, all black, like him.

"That was right after I'd started talking again." It wasn't anything you could analyze, but somehow the moment marked a change, a shift in his own internal atmosphere—like when the clouds break after a long storm and the sunlight streams down. Funny how a scene like that could stay in your mind so clearly, something you could keep with you forever.

He was enjoying his last year of school, but he wanted to be ready when it came time to go to college the following year. Though he could see his mother was already having trouble; lately she had taken to following him *outside* when he left, up to the door of the car, even, asking him when he was coming back; Jesus, she hadn't done that for years. They had always been pretty close, but still, this was getting ridiculous. "She's not gonna have an easy time letting me go," Dave said.

But as for him, "I keep thinking that the best is still to come, I want to be ready." He didn't know quite what he'd do yet, but that wasn't the most important thing. "I know who I am."

There was a story Dave had heard once that he liked a lot. A man walking on the beach had seen a small boy standing near an enormous pile of starfish, throwing them back in the sea. "That's a big pile," the man had said. "I don't think you're going to be able to really help much."

"I know," said the boy. "But I can save a few." That was how Dave felt, whenever he busted a stereotype, whenever he was able to argue with someone and change their mind. Like he was saving a few starfish, anyway. Not the world, maybe. But a few. It seemed like a worthy thing and something he was capable of doing.

Everyone had to recognize their limits, though, Dave knew—that was the other point of the story. And he knew his. Even if he was the most necessary man on the defense field, he was still a guy, at least right now, with only one working ankle. They'd have to do without him again this week. At least until those creepy black dots disappeared.

That determined it for Billy. The fact that neither he nor Dave had played last week hadn't in all likelihood been the entire reason they'd lost—it was never just one person, or even two, in football. But it sure hadn't helped, either. And he was damned if it was going to happen again.

His father, who was in real estate and could make his own hours—"Actually, I'm not really gainfully employed," Matt Stone described it pleasantly—took him in for his postoperative appointment on Friday. The doctor was ringingly unequivocable.

"These were the worst tonsils I've taken out in seventeen years," he said. "There are stitches all over the back of his throat. If he plays football tomorrow, he could bleed to death on the field—got that?—very easily." If he did play, and did start to bleed, do him one favor, the doctor said. "Don't come to me, okay?"

"Sorry, Bill," Matt Stone said to him on the ride home.

Billy sighed. "Sorry, Dad," he said. That was how Matt Stone, at least, came to realize that Billy was going to play no matter what. A reasonable man, he saw his course clearly. He would go to the game, sit in the stands, pay close attention, and be prepared at all times to run down to the field, scoop up his son, and rush him to the hospital, should the need arise.

He was not a laissez-faire father; actually, he had always been deeply involved with his three children. It was more a matter of principle. Matt Stone truly believed in the importance of free will. Even for teenagers. This was why he had allowed Billy himself to decide where he wanted to go to high school, after eight years in small, protected private schools. He'd shown him the options, discussed the benefits of private education, but in the end had let him make the decision on his own. He still wasn't completely sure Billy had made the best choice, but he had believed it was his to make. Just like this one.

The question was not unlike the one my husband and I had faced when Toby had wanted to play football. When do you decide to let a child make decisions about matters affecting his own body? At six? At sixteen? Or do you simply make every decision until he goes away to college, at which point you will be mercifully spared the question and can only pray that your kid, reins finally off, does not go into a dangerous tailspin. For me, it had always seemed important, as time went on, to turn over more and more decision making, more and more control. For control was the point—control, and the absolute necessity for parents, over the years, to relinquish it, bit by bit, for the sake of the health of the child.

A close friend of mine was born to parents who had already, tragically, lost a child to illness. With fearful dedication, the mother set out to protect this new baby from every germ in the world. Her environment was completely sterile; she was kept away from strangers and crowds. Sometime during her second year she caught a cold. It came close to killing her. I heard this story long before I ever had children myself, but its moral had stayed with me. Overprotection, too, had its dangers—and some of them could be fatal.

Matt Stone was sure of his decision, which sprang directly out of his own deep-seated belief. However, he did think on the whole it would probably be better not to mention it to his wife. As a nurse she tended to be touchy about possible hemorrhage.

Billy, of course, knew full well he had been suiting up for practice all week, playing with full pads—something his father, his mother, and his doctor were completely unaware of. He hadn't bled to death yet, had he? And anyway, it was his throat, just like it had been Toby's spleen. He could handle it.

Since Blair was a Saturday game, the players had a ten-thirty curfew Friday night, a rare thrill for parents, most of whom had not seen our sons this early on a Friday night for several years. Friday night was such a big party night in the area that few parents had not at least once witnessed their teenager, sick all week, make a miraculous recovery Friday morning so as not to miss the evening festivities.

Pete had a simple system—each of the captains (Rick, Geoff, Billy, Dave, Alex) was responsible for phoning and checking up on a group of boys. Rick was always relieved to find them home. "I don't know if I could actually rat on someone," he admitted. As it was, he was positive at least one of them had been "bonking some girl" when he answered the phone that night. "You could hear her in the background."

Saturday rolled in gray and misty, with a promise of imminent rain. The boys were thrilled. Not only was rain a good omen, considering what had happened with Blair last season, but everyone loved to play when it rained. "Goddamn it, I love rain," Mitch announced happily. "I always get a hard-on when it rains!"

The bus ride over to Blair was quiet—Pete was adamant about that. You didn't talk, you spent the time concentrating on the job you had to do, holding on to your focus. It was easier for some of the boys than for others, as Alex had already noticed last week; once again, Alex found himself getting infuriated with some of the players—you'd think they'd act a little more mature. Before a game was not the time for messing around. Today two of the juniors had shown up barely ten minutes before the bus left—one kid said something about having forgotten his socks, that was why he'd been late, he'd had to go back. That sort of thing made Alex see red. Arriving at Blair, he once again tried to assemble the offensive linemen off to the side, striving to get them into a frozen, preferably immobile, state of readiness, again with mixed results. Screw it, might as well let Toby wander around, that guy was never going to respond to any notion of military precision.

Alex was pissed, but he figured that was okay. He'd just turn it against Blair. He hated Blair anyway—"a bunch of thugs; into the spitting, kicking, foul play." If he couldn't take it out on his linemen, he'd take it out on Blair. Alex was psyched.

The Blair players, congregated on one side of the scruffy Blair field, were every bit as enormous as promised. One of them loomed at what looked like at least six-seven, a hulking tower of an adolescent, every inch of height solidly packed, his uniform filled to the bursting point. Tae Uk, spotting him, had the ominous gut feeling he'd soon be getting the chance to study the guy close up. Very close up.

Bob must have sensed it too. "Tae Uk, how much do you weigh?" he roared.

"Uhhh, two-ten, Coach?" he answered hopefully.

"No way—NO WAY," yelled Bob, pointing at him. "Today—you weigh two-seventy!"

On the field just before the game, facing the flag, while the anthem blared out, several of the boys said prayers under their breath, as they did before every game. They were personal prayers—yet, oddly, almost invariably the same. Eric Knaus said the same brief one each time. "Let us do well, and don't let anybody get injured."

Billy prayed "that I won't get hurt, that none of my friends will get hurt and that I'll just play the best I can." The prayer he said today was no different from that before any game—actually he had almost forgotten completely about his throat and the stitches.

"It isn't that I'm afraid we'd get hurt . . . it was so I didn't have to think about it . . . I just felt safe." Billy knew religion wasn't particularly cool or popular these days—no one in his family was religious, though they were all nominally Catholic—"and I don't even respect the Catholic Church for all their views." Yet he did consider himself in some way religious. "It's because no matter how bad things get, there's always something else. People who don't worship at all don't know that. And life . . . life's such a miracle."

"I just say, it's your will, God. I pray that no one gets injured and that I play the best I can," said James matter-of-factly. None of the boys prayed for a win, and not solely out of humility, either. They might consign their bodies to God's care, but the win, they knew, was up to them. And that's how they preferred it, too.

The second the B-CC offense got out on the field, Tae Uk saw his fears had been right on the mark. The monster he had seen on the sidelines was now directly in front of him, face to face, his own personal responsibility for the whole afternoon. "I can't believe it," he hissed to John Han. "Every game I get someone over three hundred pounds—look at this guy!" John shook his head feelingly; he wanted to encourage his friend, but already he could see him lying out on the field, flat as a pancake, cleat marks firmly etched into his skin.

"How the hell am I supposed to stop this guy?" The minute Tae Uk could work his way over to the sidelines he begged the coaches for some kind of answer. How do you stop anything that big? Bob was firm. "Just slow him down," he said. "Get in his way. Delay him for a few seconds so Rick can do something." Get in his way. Christ, might as well try to get in the way of a bulldozer.

Back on the field, confronting the behemoth once again, Tae Uk became aware of something else—and it shocked him so much that for a few seconds he was unable to do anything. The guy had—by God, it had to be—a wooden leg! His skin was dark brown, and here was this light tan leg. Wooden! "Alex," he screeched in the huddle. "That guy has a wooden leg, did you see it?" Back on the line everyone made a point of checking it out. Tae Uk was right, it was wooden, all right, a dark black kid with a light tan leg, what else could it be? But what did he care? Even with one leg gone, he was still the most gargantuan figure on the field—he made even Alex look like a lightweight. It wasn't as if he had to run anywhere, either; all he had to do was fall forward like an oak tree.

"Alex, can you please help me with him?" Tae Uk begged in the huddle; the big center said he would give him a hand. Back on the line, the two boys squared off to block the kid: Tae Uk took the guy's lower half, Alex his top. "I squatted down and had my hands on his stomach, pushing in, and Alex was on top of me going into his shoulders." Two people versus one—and the guy managed to push them both back. Alex turned to Tae Uk in amazement. "Now that is an elephant," he said sincerely.

Yet somehow, despite the elephant, B-CC was marching straight down the field. Whether it was the slight drizzle, or the past history of Blair-pounding, or the bottled-up tensions from the previous week—who knew? Whatever, there was a real sense of gaiety in the air; quite different from the grim purpose that had radiated from the players during last week's second half. Within minutes after kickoff, you could almost feel the sighs of ecstatic relief. This wasn't going to be another Wooten after all, no way. This was going to be fun.

And within short moments, it seemed to us in the stands, the offense had driven all the way down. Rick dived into the end zone for the first touchdown and the B-CC crowd—smaller than last week, yet still fairly sizable—roared approval. All right, all RIGHT!

On the field, it took a few moments to disentangle the pile. In the final crunch, Alex had hit the big guy low so he fell on top of him; Rick had squirmed under both of them to reach pay dirt. But the three players were sandwiched on top of each other so tightly it was difficult to pull free. "We had this three-hundred-and-forty-pound elephant on top of us, our face masks were being scrunched together," said Alex. He, however, retained his usual cool. "Nice play, Rick," he said conversationally.

"Nice block, Alex," said Rick with aplomb. With a mighty wrench, they freed themselves from the gridlock. Eric Bachman's kick was good. In the stands, people were beginning to pull shirts and programs over their heads—the drizzle was getting a bit harder—but the mood on the B-CC side was gloriously sunny; people turned toward each other, slapping palms. Matt Stone, however, kept his eyes firmly on the field, on number 44, his son. Billy had assured him airily he probably wouldn't even be starting, after all, but he was, of course. Carole Stone had begged off going to the game; it was Matt's opinion that she suspected but didn't want to know for sure that Billy would be on the field. He, though, was here for the duration, watching. Not nervously, steadily. Prepared, as calmly as he could be, for disaster.

The defense, charged and ready, pumped to a high degree—"You don't know how to lose, do you?" Geoff bawled at them—ran out on the field, ready for action. Later they would belittle their performance. "Basically, Blair was just out there like tackling dummies for us," said one. But nothing marred their pleasure today. Rene, James, Geoff, Kong, Panther, all of them played with euphoric vigor, slamming into Blair players for hit after hit.

There were players on the team who did not like to hit—who were, as Toriano admitted, "scared as hell and fast as shit" (and in fact, what could possibly make you move faster than a genuine distaste for getting smashed?)—players who agreed with John Han's lucid observation that "hitting hurts." But they were a definite minority. For the bulk of the team, hitting was not at all a necessary evil, a byproduct, or a stern test of mettle. Hitting was the very essence of the game. Hitting was not beside the point—hitting was the point. And hitting was what they loved most of all.

"When you get the perfect hit, nothing compares to it," said Christo. "You don't feel any pain or anything."

"I'd rather have a huge hit than an interception," said Kong, an opinion that was shared by many. "I'd rather have a hit that sent somebody to the hospital. Sort of killing somebody—I think that's the whole thing about tackle football. I think that feels better than anything else."

"I love it," said Corey Dade simply. "The satisfaction of dominating somebody, asserting your macho-ness, getting an impact—getting a rush that's unbelievable. Unbelievable. Unbelievable."

"Nothing," my son would later write in an essay, "has ever felt so real."

The defensive players got their chance today. The Blair game was a hitting bonanza.

Lined up, at the ready, James, playing middle linebacker for Dave, had a sudden flash of intuition—he was going to catch the ball on the next play. He knew it. Time seemed to freeze; every millisecond expanded, like a drawn-out breath. He saw the Blair tight end looking around, obviously ready to receive the ball; he saw his eyes. As Blair hiked the ball, he stepped up toward him, aware of everything around him, the moves of every player—even, under the spell of this odd sense of timelessness that had descended over him like a glass bell, taking a moment to search out Mitch's face on the sidelines, to connect with him, to let him know—completely focused so that every line, every edge registered with preternatural intensity, yet "oblivious to everything, to anything except what I was focusing on. I just said, you're gonna catch the ball, I'm going to go get it."

The Blair quarterback tossed the ball. James intercepted it—and with a mighty whoop, the spell broken, held up the prize for the world to see as the defense players descended on him with howls of joy and the B-CC fans erupted again.

The moment was probably "my most memorable experience," James said later reflectively. The defense poured off the field, clustered together on the bench, still hugging and patting each other. "It was like we were holding hands, practically. We were all leaning on each other on the bench in the cold rain. It was great. Sometimes in practice it was like we were ready to kill each other, but we were family out there that day. That's what it's all about, you know."

The momentum continued without pause. Again the offense careened down the field. Tae Uk and Alex by now were beginning to feel more at ease with the mountain in front of them. You couldn't level him, but you could fake him out. Alex, in fact, was starting to sense certain macabre possibilities to the situation. "I was trying my damnedest to knock that leg off, freak somebody out, seeing that leg sitting there, just a sock and a cleat." Although he was beginning to suspect it might not be that simple: "I guess he had that sucker bolted on pretty tight."

Another lineman, little Marc Gage, had a chance, too, to go up against the monster. He decided to take the tack Alex and Tae Uk had been carefully avoiding—hit the guy directly in his leg. The effect was exactly what Alex and Tae Uk had thought it would be—the huge player fell directly on top of Marc, like a giant boulder, all but burying him from view. "Yow!" he yelled, muffled under the mound of flesh. "Get me out of here!"

And now Rick connected to Geoff with a flawless pass for the second touchdown, and we in the stands were on our feet, cheering wildly. The rain sloshed down hard, seeping into shirts and pants. Soon most of the crowd had retired to the back of the stands, squeezing themselves under a narrow overhang for shelter, Blair and B-CC fans together. The Blair fans were easily identifiable—they were the sullen-looking ones. B-CC fans were radiant. No one cared about the rain. As long as there was no lightning, as long as no referee had to pick up a daughter, the game would keep on.

Matt Stone had worked his way over to Sal Fiscina; after all, Sal was a doctor, even if a nonpracticing one. Sal was comforting; Billy wasn't going to bleed to death out there, their doctor was probably just a conservative type, he assured Matt. Billy himself had thought that since the doctor was a little guy, a nonathlete type, he probably didn't understand sports, Matt told him. Sure, sure, Sal agreed, that was probably it. He'd be fine. Matt was reassured. Brief as it was, this conversation would be what would infuriate Carole Stone the most when she finally learned the events of the day; the picture of the two dads chatting pleasantly, all the while Billy was out there on the field.

In the locker room at halftime, Mitch was stern. No reason for kid gloves today, the guys were winning. He pulled the defense over to one side and began to ream them out methodically. James, though, wasn't fooled. He was feeling much too happy to listen to Mitch's words, and anyway, words weren't everything. "He put his hand on my shoulder while he was talking—this is wrong, this is wrong, this is wrong—but I knew through his touch we were doing just fine."

Back on the field, the sweet demolition continued. There was nothing even about it. B-CC was soaring over Blair like a Concorde. In truth, there was a good deal of sloppiness in B-CC's play, particularly on offense; in truth, to be picky, Rick was still playing somewhat under par—not like last week, certainly, but not at his peak. Communication between him and the line was obviously still tenuous, shaky. In truth, finally, Blair was just not a very good team. But this was not a day to ponder that sort of truth. Only a giant blowout could have repaired the ego damage done by Wooten, and a giant blowout was what they were getting.

Toby was experiencing another small, delicious taste of success on a football field and loving it. "I was understanding a little bit more, even though I was still shaky." At one point, when the Blair defense was moving up the middle, he smashed into one player, knocking him down, and felt a breeze as running back Dirkey Finley dashed by him, free. "It was an incredible feeling."

For James, it just got better and better. Not only was he having a perfect day, his friends were, too; that was the icing on the cake. At one point, the Blair quarterback went out for a wide angle and James saw Rene give chase. James and Rene had known each other all through high school; they often walked together to school, talking about football. James knew Rene well, knew his doubts about himself. "I see him running to the play and I say, my boy's gonna make the tackle, and for some reason he turned around and looked to see if I was behind him. It was great. 'Cause he was looking for me, no one else—smiling."

The quarterback attempted to dodge, but James and Rene were on him. They pummeled him to the ground, then pushed themselves off him, hand in hand. "It sounds corny, like *Tom Sawyer* or something—but it was great," said James. "Especially since it was Rene. We'd spent the whole summer anticipating this, we sat together on the bus before the game . . ."

In the third quarter, Rick made a run into the end zone for the third touchdown. At 21–0, the coaches began giving some of the second-string players a chance on the field: Geoff Heintz, John Everett, Eric Knaus. "You want these guys to play," said James, who was feeling gloriously magnanimous by this point. In fact, he was even glad when Blair finally mustered the strength for a brief attack. "They had a run on us for ten yards, and I was happy, I said good, they're actually trying. I wanted them to try.

"But we kept putting it to them." From the first moment on the field, he'd had that feeling—we're gonna have a field day with these guys. And that's exactly what was happening.

Sitting on the bench with Brendan Reed, both of them covered with mud, happy as pigs, watching the second string—"We wanted to see them, they're our guys"—James witnessed what seemed to him the perfect note of the day: Geoff Heintz, a light-skinned black kid who, like Dave, had been adopted into a white family—a boy everybody liked, who rarely got in for long (he had dropped out of football after ninth grade and only returned to the team this year), made the first sack of his life.

He could hardly believe it himself. "I looked around. I thought, man, there's something wrong here—nobody's here!" said Geoff later. "I saw this guy just standing there—next thing I knew I was on the ground looking down at him . . . asking him if he still had the ball!" If the guy had managed to toss it off, Geoff knew he could get called for a late hit, "because when you go like that, it's like a rolling car, you keep on getting faster and faster, you can't stop." But he was lucky.

The Blair quarterback was not, though. He lay on the field without moving; his ankle had been broken. Later, at home, Geoff's mother was concerned. "You hurt him, you hurt his ankle," she said, upset. "I saw them take him off."

Geoff grinned, enjoying the memory. "And I was like—yeah." Injuries on opposing teams were never mourned—and never quite real, either.

Late in the fourth quarter, there was yet another glorious moment—a moment everyone on the team could relish, the true crowning peak of the day. Kong the mercenary, Kong the intense, Kong the biggest heart on the team—but also Kong the brickhand, who'd never been able to hold on to a ball in his life—pulled off an interception.

And in the shock of the moment—he, as much as anyone, could hardly believe the ball was in his hands—he began to run. Swift, fleet, faster than he'd ever run in his life. Toriano, one of the speediest guys on the team, tried to run along with him as

backup, but Kong even passed him—the guy had sprouted wings
suddenly. Straight down the field he flew, seventy full yards, for
the touchdown. And the boys went nuts. Wildly they ran up to
him, lifting him, all of them cheering, delirious, even though John
Han, in the midst of the pandemonium, had a quick, prescient
glimpse. "I knew we'd be hearing about this for a long, long
time," he said.

It was then that Pete decided to do something that made Mitch
furious. Rather than go for a simple kick, he told the boys to fake
it, then run it into the end zone for a two-point conversion.

To Mitch, this was plain unsportsmanlike behavior; it was time
to call off the dogs. Rubbing their faces in it was wrong. "You can't
demoralize kids—if you're winning twenty-seven to nothing, you
kick a field goal and get out of there." He tried to argue with him,
but Pete insisted—he was caught up in the moment, the heat of the
win, Mitch guessed. The play was successful. But for Mitch, seeing
the Blair players standing there, crushed, almost took the pleasure
of the game away completely. You shouldn't hurt kids like that, he
felt—enough was enough.

Yet he was probably the only person rooting for B-CC on or off
the field to have that reaction. Pete White was not the only one
caught up in the win—players and fans together heartily applauded
the conversion ploy. And when, moments later, the whistle sig-
naled the end of the game—29–0—we in the stands howled our
approval long and loud. The big Blair kids stood frozen on their
own field, shoulders slumped, looking no less sick than our boys
had looked one short week before. Did it matter? Did we notice?
Hardly. We screamed ourselves hoarse.

Matt Stone, at least, did not. He only smiled—a very warm,
happy smile, true—watching the B-CC players bound off the field,
his son in their midst, whole, unharmed, his stitches intact. He
adjusted his trench coat and headed for the exit.

The ride back to school was a wild one. The boys rocked the bus
from side to side, screamed, laughed, sang, and hugged each other.
Were we bad? Are we headed for the championship or what?
Everyone threw insults at everyone else. "Kong, I never saw anyone
so scared in my life," they teased him, "you didn't know what to do
with that ball!" And, "How about Tae Uk up against that wooden

leg? Man, if you can't knock over a guy with a wooden leg, you've got real problems."

It was a rare football game that made everyone feel good, but Blair came close. So many guys had done so well, it seemed. Rene had been awarded the designated-hitter shirt, given to the best defensive player of the game—he'd had a great game, two sacks, lots of assists. You were all over the place out there, Mitch told him—one of his rare compliments. Just to see Rene feeling proud of himself, glowing, was a pleasure for the boys.

"That's the other thing about football," Bob Plante said once, thoughtfully. "You want the other guy to do well—almost, you want him to do better than you."

"Everyone had an outstanding game," said James. "Everyone was loving each other on the way back in the bus." Even the coaches seemed happy, though Mitch couldn't resist getting in a few swipes. "It wasn't that you guys were that good, it was that they sucked," he'd said; leave it to Mitch. Bob, too, had leveled a few harsh comments at his line, particularly Toby. They'd squeeze plenty more rounds off at the tape session on Monday, the kids knew. But neither of them were on the bus, and anyway, no one could take away the joy of the day. The pure, unblemished satisfaction of a mighty win.

Tae Uk, wildly excited, was caught up in the celebration—it was only later thinking back over the day that he noticed something: he had started to feel differently about the offensive line. People were always saying defense was the best, the place for real men, but Tae Uk had begun to realize he really liked offense the most. Like today, with Alex, working out how to handle that guy. You shared, on the line; you asked someone to help you or he asked you; there was a togetherness. On defense everyone was out for himself. Offense, though, took friendship and trust.

He had filled in on defense before and would again, throughout the season, but Tae Uk realized he had found his true home—he was an offensive lineman.

CHAPTER SEVEN

EARLY THE NEXT WEEK, Eric Knaus managed to get Mitch alone back in Pete's office for a few minutes. He'd played a good game at Blair, he knew it; he worked hard, and what he wanted to know now was, could he look forward to more time on the field? Did he have a chance?

Mitch's heart sank. This was the sort of thing he hated the most, having to look a kid in the eye and tell him he wasn't going to be first string, not now and probably not ever. "It was a very difficult conversation. How do you say to a kid, I don't see you playing much? During summer, two-a-days, everyone has a chance—but once you start, you have to go with the first team." Inevitably there were guys who didn't make it, even seniors—guys like John Everett, Dimarlo . . . and Eric Knaus. Yet how do you tell a boy that without completely discouraging him? You just can't do that to a kid, tell him flat out there's no light at the end of the tunnel.

The fact that it was Eric asking made it worse. Some kids you could yell at easily—you're a bum, get out of here—but not Eric. Eric was—and Mitch was not the only one who realized it—an unusual kid.

He looked regular enough, with his clean blond good looks, the sort of looks that conjured up images of Iowa farms, but there was a kind of radiance, even a purity, about Eric that set him apart from

151

the other boys in a way. "Too nice," as many of them put it. "He shakes your hand after every game," one boy complained. "It can get irritating." Yet all of them knew there was nothing false about it; it was just the way he was.

He himself did not mind being called too nice—actually it was a compliment, he thought. "Tae Uk gets offended," he said fondly. "Whenever anyone says I'm too nice, he'll call me a jerk." It was his friend's way of protecting him, he knew.

"They say nice people finish last, but I don't believe that. You're born with your looks, but your personality is something you work on. Your looks are nothing that you've earned, but your personality is."

He knew some of the kids on the team acted a little arrogant sometimes, but it didn't bother him. It was actually pretty funny, usually. He guessed guys like Rick or Geoff had a right to act cocky, they were awfully talented. But it was funny, sometimes he found himself even feeling sorry for Rick. "It might sound weird, but I think in a way he's lonely. He's kind of got a job, because he's so popular—if you're that popular it kind of turns into a job, to keep up that image all the time. That must be so hard."

Eric's dream was to get rich so he could open up a big home and take the street people off the street. "Not just to give them stuff, to help teach them about business, so they can be on their own." But even without being rich, you could still help out in some ways, he felt. When he was thirteen, he'd sent half of the first paycheck he ever earned, fifty dollars, to Ethiopia. He would have felt guilty keeping all that money when people were starving.

His parents had been divorced for several years; his father's new wife had mellowed him out a good deal, he felt. His mother had felt bad about the divorce at the time—"She wanted me to have a father"—but Eric, barely thirteen, had reassured her. She should do what was best for her, he said. Since she knew her son, she knew he meant it. They were both happier now, he thought.

One of the many unexpected things I picked up from hanging around the team was a virulent case of pinkeye; I met Eric when the disease, at its peak, had all but swollen my eyelids shut. When I apologized, embarrassed—it was not a pretty sight—he told me he hadn't noticed. "I was just looking at the blue," he said. "It's

just pink on the side, the blue is still there. Nice eyes." His own
blue eyes were kind, serene, full of light.

Eric knew he was unusual, that no one else on the team felt the
same way he did about helping other people; maybe Toby a little;
he was a caring person who had helped him sometimes in history
class. He knew his sensitivity could be a problem; girls tended to
take advantage of it. "It seems like I always end up getting hurt,
like they don't like nice guys." Girls went for the image, the star
athletes, the Ricks, the Geoffs; it was a prestige thing. Once a
pretty girl from another school had noticed him on the field and
asked to meet him—that had been nice. Football . . . football could
do that for you, it was a macho image thing. And there were times,
Eric had to admit, that he liked people to think he was macho.
"But I also want them to think I'm sensitive, and I always want
them to think I'm nice."

They always did. Facing him now in the office, Mitch found
himself using a gentleness he rarely showed. He was honest—
Eric was not going to be first string, true—yet at the same time
encouraging. He'd get a chance to go in and do some good, he
promised him. The point was to make something happen when
he got in. It was important to keep working hard. The coach,
Eric realized with some shock, was actually a nice person himself,
off the field. On the field, he had been doing his best to avoid
him. "He could embarrass you really bad." Once, he had yelled
at Eric during practice and after that, Eric could hardly think at
all, he was shaking so badly. "I just didn't know what I was doing after that—all I was thinking was, don't yell at me again. It
affects you, it really does." Coach White was so much better, the
way he never yelled, but always managed to get his point across
without hurting anyone.

Yet Mitch had taken the time to talk to him, had actually seemed
to really care how Eric felt. He would not get a starting position—
but the conversation had made him feel better.

At Blair, the Barons had bonded, shown some strength, bounced
back in full from the Wooten disaster. By all rights the following
week should have been a rhapsody of cooperation, steady work,

and good, harmonious fellowship. It didn't work out quite like that.

For one thing, the Blair win had charged everyone up; the boys were feeling their oats. When a sizable group of young men start feeling their oats, the wise adult moves out of the way. Bursts of energy tend to erupt, small conflagrations spark, mini-skirmishes break out. And so it was the week after Blair.

First James got into a wrestling match with Brendan Reed one-on-one, in the locker room after practice. The Panther was an experienced wrestler, one of the best in the county; James had never wrestled competitively in his life. "I'm the big guy with no skills and he's the little guy with all the skills in the world," he summed up, quite accurately—but after Blair, James was feeling ready to take on the world. It was a mistake: James went down badly, spraining his toe. He would have to be out for the next game, which was Rockville, no pushover. Mitch was so pissed off he refused to talk to him for the rest of the week. This was a guy he had been starting to count on in the field—fooling around and getting himself hurt like some dumb kid.

Next, an actual fight broke out. Not much of one, true—it involved, in fact, only one punch—but it contributed to the growing sense of chaos burgeoning in the locker room that week. Ben Brucker, a large sophomore who'd been brought up from the ranks of Jayvee for a trial run, had just been informed by Pete that he was being sent back—he'd be better off waiting till next year for varsity. Feeling somewhat disconsolate about being bumped back to the minors, he wandered into the locker room, where he ran into Dirkey Finley, the junior running back.

At this point, testimony conflicts. A number of players are convinced that Ben, in a sour mood, just started messing with Dirkey for no particular reason. "Grabbed him around his neck," said one. "Ben is a playful person and the way he plays can be detrimental." Another player was sure Ben had just come up to Dirkey and "started winding up a button in the back of his neck, like a machine."

Dirkey, however, is clear on what happened. "Ben had just left Coach White's office, and I was wondering why he was in there. I thought to myself, maybe he was moved down to Jayvee. So I said,

Ben, why were you there? Why, why—ah, you got demoted. I shouldn't have done that."

"He laughed, too, a kind of sarcastic laugh," another boy added.

Incensed, Ben grabbed Dirkey, who was several inches shorter, by the neck. "Dirkey goes, can you let go? When you let go, I'm going to punch you. And Ben goes, sure you are," said Toriano. "So he let go and Dirkey punched him." Just one punch, but a powerful one—enough to knock several of Ben's teeth back into his mouth. Blood spurted out. Tae Uk grabbed Dirkey to calm him down, while Ben ran to a mirror to inspect the damage.

Instantly the entire locker room was galvanized, as the boys ran to inspect the carnage. On the way, two other boys collided—one running to see, the other running to spread the news—with the latter falling heavily on the former's ankle, which began to swell instantly. The ambulance arrived a few minutes later, summoned by the disgusted coaches ("Jesus, it was like the world was falling apart," said Pete), and carted the two injured boys away. The ankle, luckily, had just been badly bruised. But Ben needed to have several teeth wired back into his jaw, and eventually, a series of root canals.

Ben and Dirkey were given in-school suspension for the next day; it was decided that blame should fall equally on both. They apologized to each other publicly, a little stiffly. Dirkey was sorry he had teased Ben about his demotion. That, he felt, had been wrong, and that was what he apologized for. Not the punch.

"It was some punch," said one player appreciatively. "That showed Dirkey's strength." It had been a good, solid one, all right. It was hard not to be impressed, and almost all of them were.

After all, with few exceptions they had all been there. Fighting came with the territory; few male teenagers attracted to physical competition confine that competition to the playing fields alone. Though in recent years, actually, the frequency of combat had toned down considerably for even the feistiest on the team. Ninth grade had been a high-water mark for many. The first year of high school was the proving ground, a time when the volatile mix of fourteen-year-old energy, hormones, and sheer idiocy led to many an explosion.

They were calmer now, more secure; making your bones—by

battering someone else's—was no longer such a paramount issue. Not to say that they didn't get a great deal of delight out of recalling those times. Reflecting on previous battles, their faces became suffused with a soft, rosy hue, the glow of reminiscence.

Billy warmly remembered his first fight at B-CC. "When I first came, I'd heard horror stories—like, better not go, man, the bad guys are gonna fuck with you, you come from a private school." Slightly wary, he did hold back—for an entire day. The second day, in gym class, when "some guy started playing with me" in the bleachers, he decided it was time to take a stand. "I was small but still fairly tough. I was used to these little schoolyard tricks." He let the guy go on, as if he were scared, backing down, and then sucker-punched him a good one right in the gut.

"It felt so good!" The two boys fell to it, right at the top of the bleachers, to the delight of the crowd, until the gym teacher broke it up. "Right after, somebody goes, you're going to get shot at— and I say, sorry, my brother goes here." Billy's brother Matt, then a senior, was no wimp. "It was convenient," Billy admitted. Furthermore, that first fight, in which he'd given better than he got, had gone a long way toward making his own reputation in the school: someone you didn't mess with.

Two of the senior players—Rick and Geoff Heintz—had gone through a lengthy precombat confrontation in ninth grade, which both remembered with affection. Actually, as so often happens, the real quarrel had not been between them at all, but between two friends of theirs. "Brendan Symes was going out with Tanya, and Trey and Brendan got into this thing, so Brendan and Rick were supposed to fight," Geoff said. The "thing," Rick recalled, was that Trey had threatened to level Brendan "so Brendan knocked him into a trash can, in the hall."

Both Rick and Geoff went to bat for their friends; Rick, in fact, even *used* a bat, Geoff recalled. "He had this bat in gym class and he was, man, you ain't all that, and I was, fuck you, man, put down the bat and come show me what *you* all and he was, come on, let's go, I was jumping over people."

Nothing happened—the fight was broken up, with both boys carted down to the principal's office, where they continued to throw chairs at each other until further deterrence was brought to bear. "We still joke about it," said Geoff; he and Rick had been good friends for a long time.

"You're trying to be a man, you're in ninth grade, you're try-ing to establish yourself," Geoff explained. "Then later you really don't care anymore." In point of fact, you could say the fight had a racial element—Rick and Trey were white, Brendan and Geoff black. Since school fights like others were generally at their core simply us-versus-them struggles, skin color could serve—and of-ten did—as a convenient dividing line. But since that time, all four boys had played football together and come to know each other well (Trey's academic ineligibility this year was something everyone mourned); for them, with each other, at least, that line had dissolved for good.

The eternal competitiveness between Rick and Geoff Smith had more than once erupted over the years, most spectacularly last year right in the middle of the Wheaton game. Rick had called an audible that Geoff failed to hear—"The band was playing so loud"—and, walking off the field, he'd screamed at him: "Why the fuck don't you run your pattern?"

" 'Cause I didn't hear it!" Geoff yelled back. Suddenly the two boys were yelling, screaming, grabbing at each other—"This is in the middle of a game!" said Geoff—only seconds away from a full-scale brawl. A senior player pulled them apart, and Pete told them in no uncertain terms to sit down and shut up. "But we would've rolled in the middle of the field, we were so ready to fight," Geoff reminisced. "We're the best of friends, but we'll go at each other's throats." At least that time it had been "about foot-ball; everybody knew it was in the best interests of the game," he said.

In general, fights were fewer now, for most of the boys on the team, and almost never among themselves, which was why the Ben-Dirkey blowup had drawn so much attention. It was rare in fact for any of the older B-CC boys to fight each other. When two nonplayers did come to blows at the end of the year, the entire class was disturbed and did not relax until a rematch was scheduled, carried off smoothly, and both boys walked off arm in arm. Most now felt you needed a real reason to get involved.

Yet the potential for combat still existed. "If you're a football player, you have pride," Geoff Smith explained. "It comes along with being a football player. You almost have to be a fighter."

And when fights did break out now, they tended to be larger and wilder, holding much more potential for real damage. Often they occurred at parties, between a group of B-CC boys and a group from another school—not so much personal vendettas as friend-versus-stranger free-for-alls. Invariably they were fueled by alcohol.

"Alcohol contributes so much to fighting," said Billy. "It's such a big factor—that's really the main reason for it." In the last couple of years, there had been a few brawls that a number of the boys had participated in: a B-CC fight with Gonzaga that had broken out at a party the year before ("Here these guys show up at one of our OWN parties") and a fight against a group of older boys, former B-CC students, known as the Sweeney-and-them crowd, that had taken place last summer.

Rationally many of the boys, especially the seniors, knew by now how silly fighting was: "The reason you get in a fight is just so you don't look like a wimp," said Billy. "That's really the reason. If somebody calls you a faggot—I know I'm not a faggot, so why would I get mad? It's weird."

"I've walked away from fights," said Alex. "Why risk getting my head bashed in just because this idiot called some stupid insult? It's a judgment call most of the time.

"Most people I have to put on some sort of an act. I'm huge, I scare everybody, everybody thinks, uh-oh, here comes Alex, he'll kill us, run away. The freshmen, they part the Red Sea. But most of my friends, they know. I don't go around looking for fights."

Yet there were other reasons for fighting, too—reasons less amenable to simple logic. The first was one of the strongest underlying tenets of all male society down through the ages: you stand by your friend. If your friend is being attacked, you gotta do something. Most of the boys by now were mature enough to turn away from a casual challenge—they were big enough now to let it go, even take it as a joke. ("I go to Rick, you know, one of these days we're gonna fight," said Jimmy. "And he goes, yeah—you'd die, of course.") But protecting a friend was still an inviolable ethic. "I can't really have respect for the sort of person who does nothing at all in that situation," Billy admitted. And B-CC had a full contingent of stand-up guys, guys who were known to go to the mat for a friend.

"It's because you love someone, you just jump in," Brendan Symes explained simply. "Everyone on the team, all of us are like brothers. I think all of us would fight for each other." At the Sweeney fight, watching Rick, he had realized it. "I felt, I really love these guys. I don't want them getting hurt."

The other reason behind most fights was even simpler. The truth was that fighting was fun. Not for everyone, perhaps—some of the boys did not like hitting during a football game, either. But certainly for the majority. "My fist just whammed into him," Toby described once, enthusiastically, while I listened, slightly sick. "Pow! It felt so great!"

"I remember Rick telling me about the Sweeney fight," said Sal Fiscina. "He had such an air of . . . happiness. So excited." ("They'd been out of school, they were all out of shape," Rick said; it had been a clear victory.)

Fights were exciting, dramatic, the way a good football game could be. Listening to the various tales ("So we all jumped in the car to go get 'em, there's gonna be a hanging today, we were yelling"; "They'd jumped him, four to one, a bunch of private-school wimps, so we went out to get them, twenty-five of us, we figured that was a fair proportion, we were gonna do some damage"), you caught the sharp flavor of frontier justice; the thrill of the posse, the gang war, the lynch mob. After all, the historical roots were undeniable; down through the years, long before television, violence had always been, as H. Rap Brown said, as American as cherry pie.

And yet just as often the boys seemed to be describing—with great enjoyment and perfect awareness—scenes more reminiscent of sitcoms than battlefronts. Monty Python stuff, not Stallone. They were happy to tell of their victories, but almost got a bigger kick relating ignominious defeats. "Suddenly, I'm up against the car and this ENORMOUS guy is about to—" "I'm flat out on the rug and this guy is looming over me practically blocking out the room—I hadn't even SEEN him—"

Also, again and again, it came through clearly—violence, yes; animosity, no. After a good fight, especially one-on-one, you felt almost affectionate respect for your opponent; hell, you probably even felt it *during* the fight. Shortly after the Churchill win the year before, Alex had found himself at a party surrounded by mightily disgruntled Churchill players. ("They were a proud team with a proud tradition, and they were pissed.") Alex generally steered away from this sort of theater, but in this case, he was forced to take on a few. Afterward, sitting on a couch with his chief opponent, both of them cleaning themselves up, they had turned toward each other and politely, almost formally, introduced themselves and shaken hands. Without rancor.

"I envy them that," said one mother, Terry Schaefer, a television news producer. "I very much envy them that. At work, women play these mind games. It goes on forever, wastes so much time. If I could just hit somebody in the face, it would be over."

The fighting "seems to be something kids just do. It's silly, but maybe kind of innocent," Sal Fiscina suggested. "Like king of the hill, a lot of kids play that when they're younger—just a way to kind of rumble. Of course," he admitted, "it can be a dangerous game. Especially in this day and age."

The boys, most of them, knew this. "I think people at B-CC understand about the shootings that have been going on at other schools," said Shane Dempsey, who had participated in his share of fights. "It scares me. Fighting I have no problem with, knives I can kind of deal with, guns I don't like. I'm surprised it hasn't happened more." Later in the year, it would, at a school just over the line in Washington, less than three miles away from B-CC, Woodrow Wilson High. The reasons—somebody hanging around with someone else's girl—would be as typical, as childish, as those behind any high school fight. Only this one would leave four kids seriously wounded. One gun had made the difference.

The Ben-Dirkey match, close on the heels of the James-Brendan skirmish, had been exciting for everyone. Yet both events contributed to the atmosphere hanging over the boys that week, a sense of things skidding out of control. A few of the boys had started skipping practice, especially early in the week. Mike Mitchem was often late or absent; he had excuses, fairly legitimate ones, but Mitch was infuriated. Dentist appointment! You get your teeth fixed off-season or not at all was his attitude.

Alex, too, was out this week—sick with stomach flu. "You all heard about that big flood they're having over in Pakistan, right?" Pete cracked. As far as he was concerned, the connection between that and the big center's stomach problems was a mite suspicious. Sick or not, though, the boys knew Alex would be back Thursday, so he could play Friday night—Alex hated Rockville, their next opponent, heartily.

Dave, at least, was back in the picture this week, out on the field every day, his ankle taped up within an inch of his life—one full roll of tape, wound inside and outside his cleat. Bucket-foot, Bob and Mitch were calling him, ol' bucket-foot—Jesus, he could hardly move on that thing. But he was going to play, no matter what. "It still hurt," he said. "It never stopped hurting," But, hey, he was a man; if they thought he was going to sit on the sidelines the rest of the season listening to James talk himself blue in the face about how great he was, forget it.

Scrimmaging the Jayvee late in the week, Toriano, the junior speed king, went down badly on a catch and hurt his leg. He decided to try and ignore it, and not mention it at home—Toriano had a vigilant mother. He was going to play. There was no denying, though, that it did feel a bit wobbly.

And in a funny way, so did the whole team. It wasn't solely because of the boys, either. There was something a bit desperate and out of control about Bob's and Mitch's harangues this week. Both of them seemed to be dumping hard on everyone, especially favorite targets like Toby, Billy, Mike Mitchem.

Then late Thursday afternoon Mitch blew up at Billy in an explosion so violent it left the entire team shaken. Billy was still feeling relatively weak; it was not all that easy, he had learned, to ignore the aftereffects of surgery, and playing in the Blair game—in pouring rain—had done him no good whatsoever. Now, on defense, he jumped up for a pass intended for Toriano, managing only to tip it. The ball ended up in the receiver's hands.

"Goddamn it, Stone, why don't you fucking listen to me! Where the hell were you?" Mitch howled.

Running back to the line, annoyed at himself, Billy muttered something. "It was some very minor comeback . . . all right, all right, Mitch, something like that," he said.

"Mitch had said, 'Where were you?' and Billy said, 'Right beside him,' " said Toriano. All the boys were clear on the fact that Billy did not swear, or even really confront the coach.

They were also clear on what happened next: Mitch went berserk. "He goes, WHAT THE FUCK DID YOU SAY? DID YOU TALK BACK TO ME?" said Billy. "Seriously, fire was coming out of his eyes, and tears, he goes, GET THE FUCK OUT OF HERE!"

A dead silence had fallen over the field; every player stood rigid, holding his breath, as Billy walked off. "Some of my friends go, don't go; I go, I'm not, I'm just gonna hang out over here." A little later, Mitch ordered him back on the field. "He needed me on defense. Then, he started kissing my ass, putting his arm around me. But I'm like, fuck you, you can't do that to me, I've seen too many of your type of people—domineering, two-faced. It was like he had no self-control at all."

The incident was memorable for Mitch, too. "The emotional things are more important to me than winning or losing," he said. "Like yelling at Billy Stone—making him cry. I made Billy Stone cry during practice! That one incident was so . . . there was no meanness intended. When he came up to apologize, I put my arm around him, he put his arm around me, we knew it was over and there was no need to say anything more. There was an acceptance." It was a moment of highly charged emotion neither he nor the boys would forget; yet their separate perceptions of that moment in their wild divergence finally only illustrated the cold lesson of *Rashomon*—the ultimate elusiveness of truth.

Pete did not appear terribly happy about his assistant's strident manner with any of the boys. Billy had always been one of his favorites; was that why Mitch seemed so intent on scapegoating him? Emotional explosions were distasteful to Pete, yet he continued to be loath to rein in Bob and Mitch—that was not his way, and, face it, the coaches did know their football. But the boys sensed he was not pleased with the timbre of the season, not pleased at all.

And this too added to their apprehension. The boys were uncomfortably aware of a certain shakiness at the top, the shadowy shakiness of a disintegrating yet still nominally intact marriage;

there was a gathering fear that the center might not hold. Something was definitely in the air this week, a friction, an unease, affecting everyone. Even at home, we parents picked it up from the boys. It made no sense to us—they had beaten Blair, they should be feeling ready for anything. Yet a feeling of tension, even foreboding, hung in the atmosphere.

And so they came down to Rockville.

Rockville was tough, Rockville was blue-collar, Rockville was a neighborhood school, all of one piece, the kind of school that produced down-and-dirty football. Rockville had had the same coaches for years; they had a snappy offense and a trigger-happy, blitz-in-your-face defense. In short, Rockville was Mitch's kind of team. Alex despised them.

"No sportsmanship whatsoever, no gentlemanly qualities at all that I've ever seen. They're very dirty, stick it to you, talk a lot on the field. I hate Rockville." He sighed. "And I've never won a game against them."

His teammates had read him right; despite his lingering flu— Alex tended to catch viruses that held on—there was no way he was about to miss this one.

The game was held on B-CC's own turf that Friday night. It was September 23—at least on the calendar, two full days after the start of fall. In truth, of course, the date meant little. There was no sharp, leafy tang in the air, with its nostalgic resonances of past football triumphs to spur players on; the humidity hung as heavy and sodden as it had the week before. Only the night rolled in faster—much faster, the sudden darkness falling like a sheet across the field, the electric lights bathing the players in odd hues. It was like an insidious reminder, that night; already the year was waning, chances were running out.

From the start the game did not go well, not well at all. The band, sweetly strident, blared its way hopefully through "Get Ready, Here We Come," yet almost from the first, one could feel a weight, like the weight of B-CC's dismal history itself, pressing against the team. There was a hesitancy, a thickness in the air—a sense of parts not coming together, a white-sweat feel of desperation rising from the field. Passes were dropped, there was a looseness in the line, the static heat seemed to lie on the players' shoulders, pressing down. We sensed the weight of it even in the stands and shifted uncomfortably.

The boys were out of kilter, all of them; the team itself was out of kilter. Rick, careening wildly into the Rockville sidelines, smashed into a girl, the team's assistant manager, knocking her down hard. The ambulance—there was always one standing nearby at all county games—roared off, carrying her into the night, red light flashing. It was only a precaution, she was not seriously hurt, the siren had remained silent. Still, even unheard, the sound seemed to throb through the stadium like a warning. It was not just the team, or the boys—something about the entire evening was subtly off, crooked, wrong.

On the field they knew it instinctively, they just did not know why. The first half of the game was a washout. Rick threw badly—"interception Rick," a few of the boys had started calling him, out of earshot, of course. But he knew the line was denying him time; they were, incredibly, playing worse than ever, even managing to foul up the snaps. Then one long drive dissolved when the ball spun out of a junior player's unaccustomed hands—he'd had to throw it to him, Rockville was ganging up, double-teaming Geoff Smith with a vengeance. Billy, going both ways—offense and defense—was quickly exhausted. "Jesus, man, get OUT of here, go sit down," Geoff said, pushing him out of the huddle. Billy stumbled to the sidelines, only to bump into what looked like a solid wall of screaming coaches. "GET BACK! WHAT THE FUCK YA DOIN'! GET BACK, STONE!" Wearily he stumbled back.

Tae Uk found himself up against another disability on the line—only this time, instead of a wooden leg, the guy was deaf; he was communicating by sign language. Tae Uk didn't know what to do about that one. However, the little Korean did manage to wrest one bright moment from the night—possibly the only pleasure any Baron got from the entire Rockville game. After one play, turning toward a Rockville player who was mouthing off, he discovered to his utter delight that the guy was Asian. "Hey!" he screamed, putting his whole soul into it. "Shut the hell up, you Chink!" The guy was so shocked he actually did shut up.

B-CC's defense, even with Dave and Billy back—admittedly, a

rather impaired set of players—matched the offense for bad play. Mike Mitchem, who held dear to his heart the notion that he could take anyone, was having that notion severely tested tonight by one Rockville player. "I had tears in my eyes, I was trying so hard, and basically, that guy was beating me. Beating me! You think you're so good in your mind, but when you see someone better . . . I tried so hard, every ounce."

Mitch, on the sidelines, was apoplectic, his eyes like blue stones behind his glasses. "We gotta go with James," he begged Pete, "we gotta get James back in." Pete shook his head. With James's toe, you couldn't let him back in, not unless they checked with his parents, and since he'd been sidelined, his parents hadn't come to the game. Toby and Billy might have been able to conceal their medical problems, but James's injury had occurred right in the locker room. No way to ignore that one.

At halftime Rockville was ahead 14–0. Second half, the boys did seem to be trying harder, repeating the pattern of Wooten. Rick finally found his old buddy Geoff for a touchdown pass; when Rockville came back quickly, he found him again, in the fourth quarter. The score was not that uneven, despite everything; a glimmer of hope ricocheted through the stands. And yet that sense of something wrong remained—vague, diffuse, palpably there.

Then all at once it focused, as if a giant arrow had appeared over the field, riveting our attention. With a shock, several of us in the stands suddenly realized that Alex was sitting heavily on the bench, unmoving. Alex, the largest player, the captain of the line, the one who directed others, Alex the cool commander who never relaxed during a game. "Football is his life, his LIFE," Toby had said. "He takes it very very seriously." Sitting. "I knew it when I saw him sitting," his mother said later.

Bob Plante was leaning over Alex, his face only inches away, barking at him tensely—short, tight stabs. "You giving up? You out of the game? That's what's happening, you quitting on us, you pussy?"

Alex said nothing. His eyes stared straight ahead; he blinked, motionless. His hand lifted slowly to his helmet, as if to remove it. Bob's face went red. "You really quit, right? You really did it! You're taking your helmet off, you're really quitting, is that it?"

Jimmy Loreto sat next to Alex on the bench, frozen in horror. "Alex, what are you doing?" he whispered feverishly. "You're intimidating him, don't do it Alex, what are you doing?"

"YOU QUIT!" Bob Plante roared, totally enraged. "YOU QUIT ON ME, YOU FUCKING PUSSY!"

Alex's voice came slowly, slowly, as if from the bottom of a deep well. " . . . No."

"YES, YOU DID, YOU—oh, my God." With the crack of a thunderbolt, the truth hit. "Ambulance!" Bob yelled. "We need an ambulance! Right away!"

In the stands, we saw a man clear the other boys off the bench, sit down next to Alex, remove his helmet: the paramedic. Slowly, like a great tree falling, the big center was lowered onto the bench, his neck held steady, tenderly, to immobilize the precious spine. Alex stared up into the night, his face utterly solemn, motionless. His large body filled the length of the bench.

The boys, one by one, coming off the field, stopped by the bench, trying for a response. "Hey, Alex, you okay?" "What happened, man, you all right?" Their fear rose up out of the stillness, gusts of it reaching us in the bleachers.

"Would Judy Burgess please come to the field?" the announcement rang out clearly over the loudspeaker.

The game continued unchecked—yet for many of us parents in the stands, it seemed to fade. The players blurred into shadow; Alex, stretched out on the sidelines, seemed to draw all the available light, as first his father, then his mother, joined him on the bench. He had been sick during the week, he should not have played. I knew it. I also knew by now that Toby had gone out on the field long before it was safe, just as Carole Stone, next to me, knew by now that Billy had played last week. We sat knowing, watching.

The game itself had lost any interest for me, though I sensed in some removed place that it had become rougher, harsher, that the boys were playing suddenly very hard, wrestling with some cold awareness that had suddenly made itself felt on the field. Now Carole Stone and I climbed down to the sidelines, picking our way through the crowd. "I'm a nurse," Carole told the Burgesses. Then, "Can you hear me, Alex? Are you okay?" A long moment passed before Alex answered yes, slowly; his eyes, far away, stared up at the night, black, unseeing.

We touched Judy Burgess, who was smiling, clear-eyed. The Burgesses, a military family, were trained in cool competence, at ease with crisis. They were divorced, too, but civil, very civil, to each other. The rescue squad finally arrived; slowly, slowly, Alex was transferred to the stretcher—backboarded, so his spine would stay immobile for the trip. I climbed back up to my seat.

The long game wound up. There was a moment when the team, miraculously, had a chance, even after everything. It could turn around, still. My husband and my father were still totally involved, tense, cheering, I noticed with an odd shock. But Rick, under fire, tossed the ball almost aimlessly. It was grabbed gratefully by a Rockville player. They had lost their chance and the game ended.

The boys marched up the steps looking straight ahead, their faces very pale, very young, expressionless as Alex. No one knew what had happened. Alex never went down; no one even remembered him getting hit. "It was scary, real scary," said Toby, when he came home. "We even said on the line, let's do it for Burgess. We thought maybe something good would happen, that God would do something good for us."

But "he was congested, he had a virus, that was it," he added quickly, with his newfound careful attention to medical detail, a football player's attention. And I thought of Tom Wolfe's description in *The Right Stuff* of how test pilots dealt with the common tragedy of a buddy's fatal crash. It was necessary to erect a safety fence at once—he did this, he neglected that, that's why it happened. With the attending corollary, of course—I do not do that, therefore I am safe.

I had already seen this process in action. Last year a high school boy in another suburb died after a football game. Within a week, each of the players at B-CC "knew" what had happened: he had been playing with an ill-fitting helmet. His equipment was faulty. B-CC prided itself on its equipment. On other teams, there were undoubtedly other explanations. It didn't matter whether they were true, not really. What mattered was that they were simple, that they could be lived with. Now the boys needed one for Alex right away, to shore up against the fear. All right, Alex . . . Alex had been sick.

Late into the night I kept seeing Alex's face—not as it was now but the way it had been when he was four, at nursery school with Toby, the green eyes, the soft blond hair, a gentle, sleepy, teddy-bear child. "Zander," his family called him then, a doomed last-ditch effort to avoid the inevitable "Alex." "Zander loves to cuddle up in a blanket and be cozy," his mother told me once, back then. A baby, a little boy—what was this child doing risking his young body? Late at night I called the Bethesda Military Hospital, where I knew they had gone. "We can tell you he's here, that's all. His parents are with him," said the doctor coolly.

In the morning, I held off—perhaps they had all gone home to sleep?—before finally calling, at eleven. His older brother, Tim—Toby's soccer coach in another lifetime—answered the phone smartly: "Alex central." So I knew it was okay. It had been midnight before he came back from wherever he was. Concussion, they said; concussion, even though no one saw him hit. "We won't know till we see the film of the game." He remembered almost nothing of the night.

"I had to tell him we lost, and he cried," said Judy Burgess later that day. She had been crisp, cheerful, brisk, matter-of-fact throughout the ordeal, but when she told me this, her own eyes filled with tears.

The film showed nothing in particular—but Alex himself was back that afternoon, suited up for the next practice. And now, the fear thrown off like an old skin, the boys jostled and laughed harshly, to regain their equilibrium. "Jesus, Alex, I HOPE you were unconscious there," said Bob Plante cheerily, as they reviewed the tape. "I sure HOPE you'd had that concussion already." And the boys howled.

And at home? At home we shuddered, another protective skein of illusion pulled away, one millimeter less safe. Shuddered and tried to forget fast, to bury quickly that sharp glimpse of horror, that nightmare moment when it had all been so starkly clear—yes, it could happen here, yes, we were all at risk. None of us could pretend anymore we didn't know the kind of chance they were taking.

And yet, and yet, "If you took all the risk out, if nobody got hurt at all, I wonder if the feel for the sport would be there?" Carole Stone said, painfully honest. "Part of it *is* the risk."

"The whole aspect of football is being *this close* to everything," one boy, Corey Dade, had told me. He paused. "This close to dying."

"The absolute," Jo-Ann Fiscina called it, musingly. "The basic, the absolute, the bottom line. Whatever the bottom line is, if you can get to it somehow—in your profession, or onstage, or in the field, or in bed, or unfortunately in drugs—something that's going to take you to that, you're going to pursue it. To have that feeling of nearing the center of things."

Like Carole, she had found it in nursing, in emergency wards, she felt; Judy Burgess at times on a stage. Myself? I wondered. Twice, I knew, in labor rooms, giving birth; perhaps all mothers found it giving birth. And maybe, on a few rare occasions, in bed. Our boys, Jo-Ann believed, had found it in football. Maybe sports, like combat, was where men found it. Maybe I had always sensed that; maybe I found it there a little myself. Maybe that was part of the explanation for my feelings about it.

Yet after Rockville—after that one unwavering glimpse of what could be—I felt a subtle shift within me. I still stood in the stands, screamed, cried, threw my arms to the sky in victory, roared with anguish in defeat. I continued to embarrass my more reserved husband. I was still on the surface as noisy, emotional, overenthusiastic, out of control as ever.

But inside, deep inside, I was always aware, from this time on, of a ticking clock. Six more games, it said; then five, then four . . . only this many more to get through. Only this many more, and my son's safe. Just these few, then I can relax.

Rockville to me had been a nightmare—a real one, like the kind that woke you in your bed in the early hours, heart pounding, teeth chattering, even after you flipped on the light for reassurance, telling yourself firmly it was just a dream, just a dream. Rockville was just a game, just a game; Alex had recovered within hours; nothing terrible had truly happened. But like a nightmare, it continued to hold me in its grip long afterward, its ugly vision like an unpleasant truth suddenly bared, a truth I had managed to dodge, one I'd hoped to avoid forever. But I had been there, I had felt the icy hand close over my heart, and I could not forget.

For me, it would never be quite the same. Yet even so, I watched, impressed, as the team—coaches, boys, other parents—moved

speedily to sew up the crack which had gaped so wide and naked
that night for all to see. And I saw it work: within short days, even
hours, every boy had managed to leave his own fear so far behind
it was scarcely a memory. "Ah, I wasn't scared for a minute, it was
pretty funny actually, Burgess, you blimp," said Toby a few days
later. They outdid each other remembering Alex's behavior on the
field that night—the concussion, it was finally determined, had
probably come during the first quarter, in a mighty helmet-to-
helmet smash with a defense guard. Alex had spent the next three
quarters stumbling around the field semiconscious, before finally
sitting down. "We kept saying, 'Hey, Alex, the huddle's over
here,' " said Tae Uk. "He's supposed to tell *us*."

"Ah, concussions, I've had them," said Rick. "I think I even had
one during Wooten. You get all woozy, you just want to go to
sleep." They were casual, calm, amused, utterly believable to anyone who hadn't seen their faces that night.

"It's nothing, concussion's nothing," said Christo Doyle. He
remembered having had one a year earlier, during a Jayvee scrimmage; he'd walked home, barely conscious, and had only come to
sitting on his porch, looking out at the yard. As he thought back,
his face changed for a moment. "It was terrifying," he said, almost
involuntarily.

Alex himself was utterly cool. "The doctor said it must have
been a buildup. We didn't see any momentously huge hit on the
film. Personally I don't think they knew what happened. A mystery
of science.

"It didn't really freak me out. I'm always pretty calm about those
things. I guess I'm like my dad. He's trained for it, I'm sure, after
seeing enough of his friends burning in flames. My mom, now—we
had a rat downstairs once and she totally freaked out, tried to climb
on top of me, going into full operetta. She's more emotional.

"On the film it was . . . this blob staring, not moving at all. I
don't remember anything. Just had a real bad headache for a day."
He took Bob Plante's taunts at the tape session with a grin, joining
in the general laughter. The bad part was that they had lost, once
again, to Rockville; that he, in his semistupor, had been unable to
lead the offensive line to victory. Other than that, he shrugged, no
big deal. No big deal at all.

For the boys, for the coaches, the important thing was to move on, to distance yourself—it had happened, it was over, you kept on going. "Hey, if that phone's ringing, don't answer it," Pete cracked to Geoff after a bad hit a few days later. But in my own mind I heard again the voice of Bob Plante, early in the season—"You guys pussies? You want to be pussies?"—spurring them on. And saw that scene—was it from a book? a movie?—which always had the feel of pure truth to me: a squadron leader rallying his men to charge down a field into almost certain death. "Come on, you guys, come on . . . YOU WANNA LIVE FOREVER?" And knew that I was praying inside that this was as close to combat as any of them ever got.

CHAPTER EIGHT

DESPITE ALL the concentrated denial by boys and coaches, though, Rockville did take its toll: the tension level on the team escalated sharply.

The fact that it had been Alex who had gone down made a difference to all of them. Not just because Alex was bigger than everyone else, but because he had always radiated such an image of cool leadership and control—the military commando par excellence. "Everyone looked up to Alex," said one boy.

"He wasn't performing—Alex Burgess, he's supposed to perform," explained John Han. "He was the leader emotionally. He had that leadership role." It was also not easy to avoid the obvious connection, the one you never wanted to make: if it happened to Alex, it could happen to anyone.

He had been the one man on the line who could be counted on. During the game, no one had understood why the offense was performing so poorly, but now, looking back, it was easy to see— Alex's concussion had hung heavy over the field the entire time. Missed snaps, inept blocks, chaotic plays—all of them directly traceable to the fact that the big center had been walking around literally in a coma. If the line was the core of the team, Alex had been the heart of that core—the effects of his injury had rippled out in all directions, rendering the offense all but powerless.

Alex's concussion had been nobody's fault. But all those fears and frustrations needed some kind of outlet, and Bob and Mitch, at least, found their relief by systematically, brutally reaming out the players at a level of intensity even they had rarely approached before, which was saying a great deal. They yelled at them in the locker room after the game, scant minutes after the ambulance had pulled away with Alex; they cursed them out nonstop at the tape session; they denigrated them viciously on the practice field.

The atmosphere on the team after Rockville was no longer subtly charged—the tension now was raging, pulsating, almost overwhelming.

"They tore the shit out of us after that game," said Billy, whose own exhaustion had been so profound he was close to unconsciousness himself. "I tried so hard—I really feel, don't tell me I didn't try."

The game had been Toby's personal nadir. Enraged by his performance, Bob had finally pulled him off the field completely— "You won't do it? You're not going to do it? Then I'll find someone who will, you worthless bag of pus"—and sent in Erik Karlson, the big junior, to replace him. "That was my low," Toby said. He'd stood on the sidelines, silent, a dark cloud of doubt rising within him, impossible to escape. Would he be able to do this, after all? Was it possible, was it, that he would never be a football player?

John Han, too, found himself the object of ridicule. In on defense, he struggled with poor success to handle an opposing player. "What the hell's going on out there, Han?" Mitch demanded.

"I don't know, he's overpowering me," said John honestly. It was the worst thing he could have said; Mitch was practically beside himself.

"Did you hear that?" he roared at Bob. "Can you believe that? This gash here says he's being overpowered!" At the tape session, he taunted John mercilessly.

"At that point," said Dave, "everyone thought the season was going to hell." He had been willing to go along with Mitch, had believed that many of the boys could benefit from harsher treatment than they were used to getting from Coach White. But even he could see it was going too far; the entire atmosphere was being poisoned. Even if he himself was not being pinpointed as a target, too many boys were, and the results were not good, there was an ugly feeling in the air. This was not how it was supposed to be. He kept his countenance, watching warily.

But Billy Stone had had enough. To him, it was clear: Bob and Mitch were raging out of control, growing stronger every day, all but taking over the team. Everyone was demoralized. The season, his last season, his senior season—the one he had looked forward to from the time he was a little kid—was going down the drain fast. It was almost a third gone already! He couldn't stand it. It was time to take action.

"After the Rockville game we went over the tape for like two hours. I've never seen such verbal abuse in my entire life. It wasn't constructive, it was like—what the fuck, you stupid piece of shit!— that kind of thing. I went home in a daze.

"I have a problem with any kind of authority that really wants to put themselves on a pedestal. I have a problem with that. I can't just say, that guy's an asshole, leave him alone—I see an asshole and I have to do something. I'm like that." In a bar, on the street, you could just punch the guy out, and certainly he had, on occasion . . . but this case, Billy knew, was going to require something more than a one-punch remedy.

That night Billy discussed the problem with his parents at dinner, sitting at the table in their large kitchen—the tyranny of the young assistant coaches, the browbeating humiliations, the terrible pit of despondency the whole team had fallen into. "The team was going through a really bad period. The players were so upset—I was so upset. Mitch was being such a cock to me I couldn't handle it. I couldn't believe the way they shit all over some of the players. I've never experienced anything like this in my life. The way they talked to Toby, the way they attacked Burgess—I mean, he was passing out! And they call him a goddamn pussy.

"They were treating us so bad after the Rockville game, and Mr. White wasn't saying anything, in the film sessions. They'd scream at you in a really impressive, scary way, almost like you'd worry about them . . . and Mr. White would sit there and he wouldn't say anything. He looked really unhappy about it, too, about the way it was going." Yet the head coach, Billy felt, was not going to move to change things; it was as if he, too, did not know quite how to handle the problem—he had let these two unruly genies out of their bottles unknowingly and had no idea how to stuff them back in.

Sitting at the kitchen table, Billy laid the whole thing out. Talking it out was the way his parents always approached problems. Actually, talking was what had brought them together in the first place, the bridge that had spanned the distance between two very different worlds. Matt Stone was the scion of an old, at one time supremely well fixed southern Maryland family, going back to the 1600s—eleven generations—and although most of the money had been lost a few generations back, Matt's father, a sharp businessman, had managed to make his own fortune in building and land development. As a bachelor-about-Georgetown in the sixties, tall, blond, and eminently presentable, Matt's dress and demeanor, not to mention the umbrella he carried, bespoke a world of country clubs, golf courses, and private schools.

Carole's did not. French-Irish, tiny, dark, and vibrant, she had grown up in the projects of South Boston, daughter of a day laborer, who had never truly recovered from the death at age three of his beloved firstborn son, Billy.

She was a born student, though, an anomaly in her family; she had attended nursing school on scholarship and was working her way through Georgetown University when she met Matt. He was dating a gorgeous German model who stayed at the house where Carole was renting a room, and came by often to pick her up. While he waited—the model took lots of time to get ready—he and Carole sat at the kitchen table and talked. And talked. As the weeks went by, he showed up earlier and earlier; finally it became clear to Carole that something was going on, and that furthermore the attraction was not just verbal.

She panicked. She had already decided to devote her life to work; a serious relationship was out of the question. How could a man like this understand her past? They stopped seeing each other for months; then Carole, missing him terribly, sent him an Easter card, and Matt got the real message. Soon after that, she came home and he was there again, and that was it. The jig was up; there was no longer any matter of choice involved—if there ever had been.

Now, a quarter-century and three children later, they were still sitting around a kitchen table talking. After spilling out his own tale, and hearing their comments, Billy knew what the answer was. It was time for the players to take matters into their own hands. And they would do it by talking. All of them together.

"I called up the other captains—Rick and Alex and Geoff and Dave—and said, you guys, let's have a meeting. This is really bad. I go, I'm a senior and I'm not going to watch the season just run down like this." Each of the other boys agreed, and assured Billy they would pass on the word to the rest of the team. The next day's practice was delayed till five, so immediately after school they would get together, all of them, to discuss the problem.

At 2:25 P.M. sharp the next day, the boys—almost the entire team had been alerted—gathered in the school library for their meeting. Immediately they ran into an obstacle. Library personnel were frankly horrified to be confronted with this large, unauthorized assemblage of male adolescents, jocks at that. Heads shook strenuously; hands pointed coldly to the exit. Not in here, they told the boys; don't even think about it. Out. Now. Then where? asked a few. They shrugged, disinterested, closing the doors firmly.

Several of the senior boys had the same idea at once—Mrs. Lockard's room. Karen Lockard, an energetic young English teacher, was everyone's favorite; she was a dynamite teacher who liked kids, and even more unusual, treated them as human beings. "I'm going to Georgetown University," Rick announced during her class at one point, pausing with his exquisite sense of timing before adding, "and I'm taking Mrs. Lockard with me." The laughter from the other kids was completely sympathetic.

She was in her room now, working at her desk, when they came to the door. "They asked if they could use the room," she said. "They said they had been trying to have a meeting in the library and they had kicked them out—they saw a bunch of jocks and thought they'd be rowdy. They just wanted to have an informal football meeting, they said.

"I said, guys, you can have it, but I'm right in the middle of something, can I stay? And they said, that's fine . . . just ignore us."

And so, settled finally, the boys began their meeting in earnest. The captains stood at the front of the room; briefly, they stated the problem as they saw it. "Guys, look. We know Mitch is going on a rampage, he's being hard . . . and we want you to know, as captains, we're gonna try and do something about this," said Geoff Smith. Then they asked for comments.

And the boys began to talk—hesitantly at first, then one after another, the words toppling out like rivers long dammed up. They talked about their humiliation, their fears, their anger and unhappiness with the young coaches. "It turned out everyone was pissed off, not just me," said Billy. "I hadn't known. I just needed to talk about it, but it turned out it was everyone. Shane was telling how Plante wouldn't let anyone play, people were saying how Mitch wasn't giving anyone a chance—everybody had a problem."

Karen Lockard realized she was witnessing a rare scene and stopped trying to do her work. This was more important. She was being given a chance to see a group of boys actually utilize the democratic process for their own ends. "I was seeing them governing themselves," she said. It was, in its way, thrilling.

She had no way of knowing, of course, that one of Billy's ancestors, another William Stone, had been the governor of Maryland who had passed the state's first Religious Toleration Act; or that another, Thomas Stone, some 150 years later, had signed the Declaration of Independence. Yet she knew what she was sensing in the room—an echo of that same historical process.

"They said, okay, here's the problem—these guys are beating us down. It's demoralizing. They're cussing us out, making us feel like shit. Now what are we going to do?

"And what was interesting was the comments. Occasionally someone would say, well, fuck 'em—off the wall comments—but they kept pulling it back. Okay, that's not productive, that's not getting us anywhere. Now, what do we really do?"

Shane remembered a lot of "Well, they're just total assholes, they're not out for us, they're out for themselves. Some of the players were thinking, let's get our parents to sign some type of petition to get them off the team—if they're not going to be for the kids, they have no right being out there."

But the bottom line, Geoff pointed out, was that "right now what we can't allow is our morale as a team to go down." That was the most important issue, the one that demanded immediate action.

Eventually, after everyone had had his say, accord was reached.

"They agreed on several things," said Karen Lockard. "They were stuck with these coaches, that was a given. Pete White was a great guy. He was doing his job but was somewhat out of touch. That was a given. And third, they had to handle it themselves.

"How would they handle it? They decided that they would have to encourage each other, since they weren't getting encouragement from the coaches. If someone makes a great play, we have to count on ourselves, guys, to pat each other on the back, to say, great play, great pass, great block. We can't assume they know it. That's what they were saying.

"We have to do that for each other. They're not giving it to us, we have to give it to each other," Karen quoted.

"We said, if Mitch or Plante is getting down on somebody, everybody's got to step in and give them support, everybody," said Geoff Heintz.

"We talked about how even if the coaches are pissing you off, just ignore them. Don't worry about it," said Tae Uk.

"We realized that instead of looking to our coaches for support, we had to pick each other up," said Billy. "Be like our own coaches."

Karen Lockard was amazed at their fairness, their insight. Some, of course, were only castigating the coaches, especially Mitch, but others would interrupt each time—wait a minute, this guy's a great football player. He really knows his stuff. Then another would add—but he doesn't understand kids. He thinks he can treat us like pro-football players, demean us and it will work. He doesn't realize we're kids.

"To hear a kid say that!" Karen marveled. "They were actually saying, we're not getting the kind of guidance we need—we need guidance. To actually hear a kid able to understand that and say it." She was so impressed by them—Billy, Rick, Geoff, Corey Dade, whom she had not known before, "who would periodically come up with these beautiful statements, so sensible, like the voice of reason." All of them, talking, listening, trying to reach a solution. Working it out.

The meeting was a milestone for the boys; perhaps the most important milestone of the entire season, and maybe even more important than that. Many months later, long past football season, well into the summer, a number of the same boys would face a very different sort of problem—a theft at a party. Yet somehow, almost automatically this time, they would know what to do, how to approach it. Gather together, all of them, the next day, and calmly, carefully discuss the situation. Lay it out on the table and let everyone have his say. No parents, teachers, or adults—just themselves. After all, there would always be problems, serious, difficult, even insoluble problems—but together, discussing, reasoning, listening among themselves, maybe, just maybe, they could find solutions, too.

There is an old story writer Leo Rosten retells in one of his books. Three men are asked what they would do if they knew, beyond doubt, that within twenty-four hours the earth would be covered by the sea. One, of a sensual bent, says he would instantly round up the best-looking women and all his favorite foods and spend the last hours indulging himself; another, more ascetic, vows he would spend the time in prayer, cleansing his spirit.

But the third is a different sort—a man of reason. And to him, the answer is clear. Why, what he would do, of course, he says, is assemble all the wisest minds in the world in one room. Together, they would begin studying the problem at once. Together, they would learn how to live under water.

For an English teacher like Karen Lockard, who had taught William Golding's *Lord of the Flies* often enough, the meeting was particularly memorable. In Golding's book the dark, savage side of human nature overcomes and eventually obliterates the impulse toward reason in a group of young boys. Perhaps in the overall scheme of things that is how the bets lie. But that day in her room, at least, Karen Lockard witnessed a clear triumph for the other side.

Most of the boys found a deep relief in venting their anger that day, but not all. Toby, for one, found himself feeling somewhat bothered by the entire scene—it seemed a little too much like a giant gripe session to him. "Mostly they were mad about Mitch, the defense guys. He was a little crazier than Plante. But it seemed like the defense linemen were feeling sorry for themselves. It sort of annoyed me. They were getting shit on—but I'd been getting shit on, and I wasn't complaining. I felt like maybe I should have been, but everybody would've been like, why are you whining? But now they'd got together to share common complaints so they wouldn't feel like pussies. It sort of bothered me in a way."

Yet the final consensus reached—that they needed to concentrate on supporting each other, all of them, and find their strength among themselves—pleased everyone. And this was no abstract resolve, by any means. The meeting had been important to all of them, because the season was important, because football was important. The decision they had come to was unanimous, heartfelt, and concrete. The boys who left Mrs. Lockard's room were charged with purpose. They knew what they had to do.

And the change was instant. Instant. Not one boy at that meeting had been faking it. Their determination to turn the season around—to forge themselves into a true team, no matter what kind of coaches they had to deal with—was so powerful that the effects were apparent on the practice field at once.

Immediately they began to do what they'd agreed to do—pick each other up. Shout encouragement. Yell appreciation. Smack helmets, slap backs. Be there for each other, not occasionally, but all the time.

They had always done it during games to a certain extent, of course, but this was different. This was a crusade. Now it was all of them, acting together; now there was a real reason behind it. They were fighting for their survival as a team. If support was the key, by God, they'd give support. Each of them, all of them together.

"It worked," said Billy simply. "Right from the next practice, we started picking each other up. We were all psyched, we all had a great attitude."

None of the coaches were aware of the meeting and what it had meant, although Pete White, who always found out everything, had gotten a few complaints from the library people by the next day. He called some of the boys over to read them the riot act. "I hear you guys were down there having some kind of bitch session, acting like assholes," he told them sharply. The boys didn't argue, though they did try to tell him it hadn't exactly been like that. But they didn't attempt to explain about the meeting. There was no real way to explain, and the meeting had been theirs, just for them.

But the effects of the meeting were apparent to everyone, coaches included. Not only were the boys working much harder out on the field, all of a sudden, but the jangled tension that had been hanging over the team suddenly dissipated, as if a clean breeze had swept through. Mitch still screamed as loud as ever; Bob Plante still growled and sneered. Yet it was apparent even to them that their slings and arrows were not drawing quite as much blood; they rolled off, deflected, as if by some mysterious shield. The coaches had no idea what was causing the change in the boys; they sensed, a bit uneasily, that a shift in power had occurred. And indeed it had. The boys had finally reclaimed some of it for themselves.

Ironically, events had actually followed Mitch's own professed game plan to the letter. "You have to break them down to the point they hate you, so they bond together as a team," he had said. But of course, Mitch had been speaking theoretically—no coach considered high school boys capable of agreeing to or implementing a comprehensive plan of action all on their own. Then too, Mitch saw himself as sole producer and director of this particular scenario. It never occurred to him the boys might decide, or have the wit, to take control of the script.

Maybe the new atmosphere contributed; maybe it was bound to happen that week anyway. But on Thursday afternoon, in the middle of a hitting drill, Toby finally made his breakthrough—he came to roaring life all of a sudden, passed through the gateway, cut the Gordian knot that had been restraining him with one swift, accurate slice. He became at long last a football player.

"We were going one-on-one. And I realized—I can't hold back anymore. Because there was always something holding me back, some fear, I guess, because really, I'd just started, it was really my first year. I was always feeling inadequate. And then suddenly, I wasn't afraid anymore."

And with that realization—which surged through him all at once, in the space of a split second—he let go completely for the first time, with all his strength. "I went as hard as I could. I realized, right then, that I *could* go as hard as everyone else. I made myself go, not thinking about it.

"And it didn't hurt anymore, it didn't feel any worse, it was just like an inner fear that was holding me from doing it." In that moment, letting himself go, letting it all out at last, he overcame what had been standing in his way, and knew it for what it had always been—only himself.

"It was an incredible feeling. I felt like a new man. I had done what I needed to do, what I finally felt was adequate—that intensity. Which I didn't think I could do, but obviously I could. If I just let it go. And wasn't afraid anymore."

The difference was so startling that the coaches noticed it at once. "Right away, they saw—right after that first hit. They could see, with me, the new improvement. And they were all suddenly saying, great, that's the hardest we've ever seen you hit. If you play like this in the game . . .

"It was weird. One hit, and they knew." He had come on his own to the same realization the boys had come to together at the meeting: we can do this ourselves. They're not the power, the controllers, the masters: *we* are. Lewis Carroll dramatized just such a moment when at the tail end of his dream story Alice suddenly rises to her full height and exclaims, "Why, you're nothing but a pack of cards!" The realization, as always, is as sudden, as shocking, as freedom itself.

CHAPTER NINE

LIKE ROCKVILLE—EVEN more than Rockville—Einstein, the next school they would play, was no pushover. In fact, Pete White's heart sank when he thought about the five games left to play in the season. To be brutally honest, there was really only one team left, Walter Johnson, who might be considered an easy win, and even that he had no great hopes for. After all, Wooten had been an easy win, supposedly, and look what had happened there.

Sitting that week with a group of us parents who were planning the end-of-season football banquet, Pete was dryly acerbic. The most popular feature of last year's banquet had been a videotape of the season's highlights. "I guess this time we'll just have to keep running the Blair tape again and again," he joked, to groans. We, of course, knew nothing about the boys' meeting. All we knew was that the season seemed to be disintegrating around us with frightening speed.

The banquet business over, we discussed injuries. Alex's concussion had sensitized everyone. Christo Doyle had torn a ligament in his thumb at practice that week, a fact he'd managed to conceal until the following morning, by which time it was so swollen he was unable to put his pants on by himself. His mother, Terry Schaefer, had taken him to a regular doctor, who'd wrapped it up and ordered him not to play the next two games. Christo had nodded, smiling so pleasantly that his mother was impressed. "I've never seen you act that nice when someone told you not to do something you wanted to do," she complimented him in the car going home. Christo continued to smile and nod. Terry caught on. "Oh. You're going to play anyway, aren't you?" she said. Resigned, she asked Pete for the address of the sports clinic.

Initially she'd had a million doubts about football. "I felt it was a bunch of guys running around, being macho, knocking each other down—who needs it?

"I was afraid football would be one of those things that makes men who they are—in a negative sense. I was afraid it would foster all the wrong things. He's a very sensitive person and I didn't want that to be crushed." She knew, too, that Christo had still not completely come to terms with his parents' divorce. "He was angry about this, angry about that, and I thought it was just going to fuel a fire that didn't need to be fueled."

But a family therapist they had gone to after the divorce some years back had said something that stuck with her. "He said adolescent boys need to get into a contest, either with their father or some outside force, if the father's not around—they need to get into a contest and lose. And then they can develop who they are. They have to get tested and lose. One time. One big time."

At first, she had reacted defensively. "I said, excuse me, wrong, boys all over this country are living with their mothers, and they develop into valuable people. I thought basically he was saying that if they're not with their dad, you're preventing them from this and they're going to be messed up."

But later, she came to see it differently—and to think maybe he did have a point at that. And she came to feel that perhaps football itself had served as Christo's outside force, the immovable wall he could throw himself against, and that maybe such an experience was necessary after all. "You learn the world is out of your control. You can't shape how everything works. Which takes some of the heat off. When you're first growing up, you think you have power over everything. But you learn on the football field you don't, and it doesn't make you a bad person—all you have to do is give it your best shot. And the world doesn't end. You can pick yourself up and go on from there."

She had come to see that there were many men in the world who had had troubled relationships with their fathers and were still struggling to understand this basic truth. Even in her own family ... Terry was one of six children who had grown up in an atmosphere of wealth and privilege; her father owned both a marine hardware company and a railroad company, inherited from his father. Yet there were strings to that privilege: "Where we lived, what you did, when you were in ninth grade you got sent off to boarding school. So by the time you were fourteen you were out of the house." Her own brothers had missed that experience; her father had not been there for them during those years.

And finally, she realized that the therapist had not been saying she needed a man in the house, just that she should be aware her son needed to confront such a force somewhere.

In time Terry had come not just to accept football, but to have a deep respect for its effect on her son, on all boys. "It has changed him profoundly. It's taught him things—that he is capable of doing hard things—it's tested him in very positive ways. It's taught him how to be on a team and not put his own interests first. And that if you get hurt, you pick yourself up and keep going."

Of course, that last could admittedly be an uncomfortable concept for a parent to deal with, but Terry had faced one of the paradoxes of football straight on: "It's the things I've learned to respect and appreciate about football that scare me to death.

"But that's true about life, too."

The relationship between Mitch and Mike Mitchem, simmering for several weeks, came to a head just before the Einstein game. Mike had been late for practice several times that week, and Mitch, infuriated, decided to come down hard—Mike could go in on special teams, but he would not play defense at the Einstein game.

Mike knew he'd been a little lax, and was fully prepared to take his punishment—he'd just expected that punishment would be in the form of running hills, some sort of detested drill like that. Alex had just as much tendency to be late, he knew, and no one was keeping Alex out of the game. It didn't seem fair. Besides, they needed him on defense.

But to Mitch, it was a matter of principle. It wasn't fair to other players, particularly second-string players like John Everett, Dimarlo, Eric Knaus, guys who showed up every day, who never missed practice, to let Mike Mitchem get away with this. He was going to make an example of him. It didn't hurt, of course, that Billy, James, and Dave were all off the injured list for once; Mitchem was a good player, but the defense was strong enough to survive without him this time.

With Alex, of course, the question was trickier. After all, he had had a concussion only a few short days ago, and while neither coach was the type to coddle an injured player, there was nonetheless the feeling—unstated but strong—that if such a player wanted to play, you owed him the chance. In fact, Alex had been coming late to practice this week too, but Bob felt this was not the time to land on him. Later, perhaps.

The game was on Saturday afternoon and on the other team's turf, just like Blair had been—good signs, if you were superstitious, as few football players were not. As the team stood outside the Einstein locker room, Billy and Geoff marched up and down the length of the line, like officers parading in front of cadets, smacking everyone in the helmet, calling out charges. "This is it, guys—let's see attitude, fucking attitude! Get it up! You know you can take this one! Let's hear it!" All the boys knew how important this game was—this was the game that would show whether or not they could change the season's drift; whether they could really put the meeting plan into action. Billy found himself feeling better than he had all season, full of enthusiasm. It wasn't just the fact that he had finally recovered from his surgery, either. He was beginning to feel he might have helped bring about an important change on the team. Geoff too was totally charged. For once, everyone seemed ready, committed, seriously involved, the way he liked to see them.

A day before, James had gotten into an argument with one of Einstein's top players, running back Ivan Charles. "Oh, man, we're gonna beat you so bad, we're gonna run you over," the guy had bragged. James immediately told Coach White about the conversation—he knew the coach was always looking for a goad to spur the team on. Pete seized the comment eagerly and gave it top billing. "That's what they're saying out there, that's what they think, they're gonna run you over," he told the boys. Everyone was beginning to count B-CC out, especially after last week.

In the stands we waited nervously. Knowing nothing about the meeting, and given last week's fiasco, we saw little reason to hope. But the team that slammed out onto the field at Einstein was a different team from the one that had been so demoralized the week before. We saw it at once. The first-half tentativeness that had plagued them up to now was nowhere to be seen. The boys were roaring, rough, and ready to play. A new rhythm throbbed in the air; we sensed it immediately. Somehow, in some strange, unfathomable way, something had changed.

Not that the game was going to be easy. There was already one handicap, Mike Mitchem's forced absence from the field. Then, within minutes, there was a second one: Toriano, whose leg had been feeling strange since he had gone down hard over a week ago, before the Rockville game, suddenly found himself unable to run at all, a terminal disadvantage for a wide receiver. Although the paramedic who looked him over a few moments later assured him it was probably just a bruise, Toriano decided it might be a good idea to tell his mother about it after all. (It was: X rays taken the next day revealed a long stress fracture, and Toriano's leg disappeared under a cast. It would be at least four weeks before he could even consider playing again, and that, of course, would still be against his doctor's recommendation.)

But in spite of these handicaps, the boys were playing hard and well. The shock was visible on the faces of the Einstein Titans—they'd had no reason to expect a real fight out of B-CC. Toby's sudden emergence as a real player had strengthened the entire offensive line—other linemen no longer had to play nursemaid, giving him extra help; the defense, with Billy, Dave, and James playing closer to peak performance than ever before—although Dave still had trouble running—was offering tough resistance. Geoff, playing offense and defense, as usual, was taking a beating—every team in the county by now knew it was worth taking a crack at number one, since so much of the Barons' scoring potential seemed to rest in his hands. But wide receiver or not, Geoff had the heart of a defensive player; he not only didn't avoid contact, he loved it, the harder the better. No matter how hard they landed on him, somehow when the pile was cleared, that skinny form would bounce back to his feet, a wide grin splitting his face in half. There was a challenge in that bounce: Gimme your best shot, go on. Think I can't take it? You guys ain't nothing! Nothing!

Of course, Einstein had no intention of rolling over. For most of the first half, the two teams squared off against each other fiercely and evenly; a live chess match between stubborn, well-matched opponents. Neither would back down; neither would give an inch. Back and forth went the ball as each team jockeyed for an edge. The stands were rife with tension—good football tension, for once. How long could this seesaw continue?

Then, late in the second quarter, the breakthrough came. A number of separate elements suddenly coalesced into a moment of perfect grace—Toby's newfound power, Geoff's seasoned skill, Corey Dade's speed. A hole opened miraculously. Corey sped through it and ran seventy-five yards for the touchdown. We all screamed ecstatically, as the players ran to hug the running back.

We had no way of knowing—certainly I did not—but of course, the hole had not opened up miraculously at all. Toby had just thrown the block of his life, something Bob Plante would later swear was "the best block thrown on a Montgomery County field all season"—a block that Geoff, who had just thrown a superb one of his own, later assured me they would all remember at their thirtieth reunion. "I'll just walk up to him and say, Toby, Einstein game, senior year, you and me, greatest kick-out block ever—he's gonna know exactly what I'm talking about."

He would have successful moments again, throughout the rest of the season, but no moment, no one play, would ever be quite as perfect, quite as satisfying, as this block thrown on a Saturday afternoon on Einstein's field. I never saw it, nor did his father or grandparents, all of us sitting in the stands; no one announced it over the loudspeaker; no one rushed up to shake his hand. And it didn't make any difference. He knew—*he* knew—what he had done.

"They didn't really say anything," he said. "But it felt so good. It wasn't that incredible, it was just a good angle for me—it worked out, the play was right. I pulled out, Geoff took care of the cornerback, the safety came out . . . I just slammed him, hit him, and

Corey's so speedy, he just went by. It was so amazing. I was jumping up and down, yes, go, go, running after him."

The lack of recognition "didn't matter at all. Obviously the only
important thing to the offensive line when you come down to it is
Bob Plante, his recognition, his acknowledgment, that was all we
were really playing for in a way. But starting with that game . . . it
was for me."

Far up in his usual perch, though, Sal Fiscina, who had the
advantage of having actually played himself, and tended to take in
more of the game, knew exactly what had happened: it was clear to
him that Toby "had got to another level. It had all kicked in, all the
effort . . . coming back after mono, the delayed gratification . . . he
had gotten to the point where he could go.

"He had made choices, accepted responsibility, stayed with it,
not turned around and said to Plante, I don't need this shit. And
he'd gotten there. Where else at this age can you get that? Who else
could have provided that experience? You? When all is said and
done, it's one of the real positive things football can provide—
because in many ways, it's a real silly sport." Toby, Sal realized, was
finally becoming a lineman. And with that realization, his own
hopes began to stir—with a line, a real line, protecting him, Rick
might be able to do something at last.

Even without knowing the technical details, though, the rest of
us knew something important had happened out there—that this
touchdown, late in the first half of the Barons' fourth game, had
been an earned touchdown, brought about by skill and hard-fought
effort, not luck, not opponent error. Something had come together
at last; we roared our approval.

On the field, the boys gathered for the kick. By now Eric Bachman's kicks were accepted almost as a matter of course—he rarely
missed an extra point (in fact, over the season he would rack up an
incredible 18 for 20 successes, almost unheard of for a high school
player). But this time, there was a minor screwup—one of the
players, Eric Knaus, was long seconds late coming onto the field.
He squeezed himself in finally, but the delay had done its damage;
Eric Bachman missed the kick. My father, on my left, shook his
head funereally—he reacted with Ancient Mariner gloom to all
missed kicks, no matter what the score. "It'll come back to haunt

them," he predicted dolefully. I shifted away, still reveling in the glow of the touchdown, stifling the urge to use one of his grandsons' favorite retorts: "Hey, man, don't rain on my parade."

Gored but far from dead, Einstein reeled out on the field after halftime, snorting and seething, ready to wreak some damage by fair means or foul. Moments later Geoff was knocked down very hard—a collision manifestly worse than any of the others he had been in so far. The sight of Geoff, the invincible, smashed to the ground, cracked through my euphoria like a whip, instantly reviving the terror of the week before. I gasped and clutched my husband's shoulder; Carole Stone crossed herself quickly. For one long moment we held our breath, the image of Alex lying motionless on the bench throbbing in our minds. Only after he stood, finally, to be helped off the field, hands out in his usual I'm-okay manner, did we begin again, raggedly, to breathe.

We were not overreacting. Geoff himself later admitted it was the hardest hit he had taken all year. "I didn't know where I was—I went up in the air, my whole body went numb, that tingling feeling—it was scary as shit. I fell down. My eyes were open, but I was seeing black. I didn't know where I was until the coach woke me up.

"The hit was on the side of the head, but it was so hard, like two eggs cracking. My nose bled. I was out ten or fifteen seconds. I was walking off the field, my whole jersey was bloody." Minutes later, though, he was right back in the game. There was something almost magical about Geoff's resilience, though to Einstein at that point it might well have seemed demonic. Whatever, there was almost no way to get rid of him during a game—he just kept coming back at you. Bloody, unbowed, grinning like the devil.

But not every player had been granted Geoff's near-supernatural ability to bounce back from extremity. And now the forced absence of Mike Mitchem on the defense line was beginning to tell. With Mike gone, James found himself dependent on lineman Csaba Hadas for protection. A big guy, a good athlete—he was regional shot-put champion for the state—but Csaba was making his football debut this year, and it showed. "His playing is like his English, full of broken connections," Rick put it once—but it was hardly Csaba's fault. He simply had never played the game before in his life.

"Hungary doesn't have football—and doesn't really know what aggressiveness in sports is," said Csaba, whose father worked with the Hungarian embassy, and who off the field seemed to have no trouble whatsoever expressing himself. "And that was what I couldn't get. I don't have that killer instinct. My parents always told me, don't start a fight, don't take advantage of your size. So I always grew up with that in my mind and I got to be I think a too nice person. The coaches were expecting me to get more aggressive, and I couldn't." He had wanted to play. Football was such an American experience, he felt he should go through it. It would be something to tell about when he went home the next year. But he had felt like an outsider on the team from the beginning. "I know nobody can expect that the world will get used to him, he has to get used to the world." Still, it was hard, feeling like you didn't really belong.

Now James, who had a much calmer temperament than some of the other players, like Dave, who tended to explode—"I'm a more analytical type"—kept his temper and tried to direct Csaba's play. "It's critical to stop them. They're gonna run right at you. One's gonna drop you, one's gonna try and run you over, okay?" he explained. Csaba would agree—"I will stop them"—but then manage to handle only one man while the other ran by.

James took a bad hit, then another—two in a row. There was one Einstein player, a huge guy with a black mask, "He looked like something out of the Dark Ages," who kept coming at him again and again like a bad dream. James begged Rene to have a try at him. Kong, too, was doing his best to help out. "Kong's such a tough little character, so big in heart, if he could've willed the guy down he would have, but you can't will somebody down." The guy kept coming.

On the sidelines, watching this, seeing James's problem clearly, Mike Mitchem was all but weeping with frustration. "Please, please," he begged Mitch, "let me go in. They need me, can't you see? The line needs me—James needs me." Mitch was icy. "It'll be a cold day in hell before you get in this game," he told the boy.

"James kept coming out to me, oh, God, Mike, I'm getting killed. I wish you were in. Csaba's getting me obliterated. Please ask Mitch again if you can come in." Csaba was a great guy, he had incredible physical strength, Mike knew, "but I really played to hurt people. When I tackled someone I wanted to hurt them. And I'd been playing since freshman year. He had nowhere near the skill I had."

Again, he begged Mitch to let him go in; stonily, the coach stared away, shaking his head. He refused to back down, no matter what.

"A lot of people told him to put Mike in," said Rene. "But he didn't. It hurt us—they started running to that side a lot."

The strain was obviously telling on Mitch too, though, and moments later, he erupted into rage. Not against his players—against the referees. When the opposing offense was grouped in their huddle, Mitch used the time to send signals in to Dave, who would tell the rest of the defense what to do. This time, though, the ref was talking to Dave; Mitch wasn't able to get his signals across. "Then, when the offense breaks the huddle, the official says let's go. And I went crazy."

It was a serious mistake. Referees do not back down for anyone. B-CC was given an immediate 15-yard penalty, but Mitch's tantrum was to prove more costly for him than that. One of the county's athletic directors was at the game, and instantly wanted to know who Mitch was. According to county rules, only full-time coaches could be on the field during game time. Mitch and Bob were extra coaches, at least theoretically, unpaid volunteers, not officially on the books. Pete White calmed the man down for the moment, but from there on in, Mitch and Bob would not be able to stand on the sidelines during a game. They would be relegated, both of them, to the tiny box far above the field, and forced to scream their exhortations through the speaker phones.

Out on the field James continued to fight for his life. It was the fourth quarter; Einstein was driving hard, inching down the field bit by bit, determined to make it to the scoreboard. "Hold them back, hold them," we pleaded. His head throbbing from the earlier hits, James smashed into a huge pile of players, felt several others fall on him, and heard a tiny, distinct, blood-chilling pop in his knee.

"It didn't really hurt," he said later, almost dreamily. "I screamed because it seemed the right thing to do. It was a strange kind of pain." He sensed, though, that it signified nothing good. He waddled over to the defense huddle, bending down, testing his knee cautiously, probing for the nerve. Spotting him, the referee ordered him out.

The minute he was out, on the very next play, Einstein drove far down the field. Tears streamed down James's face. Oh God, why is this happening? he thought. Several Jayvee players clustered around him, clucking annoyingly, "Oh God, James, your knee, man, look at it, man, it's really bent, oohh, that's bad."

He gritted his teeth, pushed them away. No, he would not accept it; he refused to. "This is not the way I'm going out," he vowed. "Not like this." He told Mitch he was still in the game—and as soon as his leg was taped up, James was back out on the field.

And in the stands, we knew. That was the awful part, that we knew. We had all seen James hobble off to the sidelines, obviously injured; we knew he should not be back on the field. And we knew, too, that without him the defensive line was collapsing like tissue paper— Einstein would be scoring within seconds. So we cheered when he came back out, cheered even while we exchanged furtive looks of horror—horror at ourselves. There was no easy balm for any of us; we knew exactly what could happen, we had just seen a short week ago what could happen, we had just been reminded moments ago, and still we wanted him out there. Caught up in the sweep of the moment, the blaze of the team's new intensity, we wanted only one thing—to win this game. Chills swept through me; I knew I was no better than the most rabid coach, the harshest sergeant, the father down the street who pushed his son so avidly to practice tennis late into the night. They were me: I was them. I had surrendered my high moral ground forever.

Out on the field once again James still kept his confidence, even now, even with his knee, even with Einstein far down the field. He was still convinced they could stop them. He and Brendan Reed, the best tackler on the team, together they could do it. "It was killing me, I had tears in my eyes, but my brain just overrode the pain. I said, Csaba, it's too late, just don't get me hit."

He willed himself to push, to tackle, even while he was realizing in one cool detached part of his brain that there was nothing left to push from—his knee, he knew now beyond doubt, was completely gone. He and Brendan closed in on Ivan Charles together, trying to hold him back—but it was no good. "Brendan, I'm losing him," he howled. Einstein made it to first and goal. Then, though they were trying, trying, still holding on against the odds, against reality itself, Einstein finally slipped through to the score.

And back on the bench, all James could feel, watching Einstein's kick soar straight over the uprights, clean and true, was—this isn't the way it's supposed to be. I'm supposed to have an all-American season, this was supposed to be *my* season. I wanted it to be perfect! He looked at the clock, saw there was one minute, thirty seconds left, and knew there was nothing he could do. He was out for good—for him, it was all over.

At 7–6, with the clock running down fast—my father had been irritatingly right on the nose, the extra point had come back to haunt them—options were limited, but not impossible, not at all. They had gone so far, tried so hard; surely they could bring it home. We held our breath as with cold determination now, the B-CC offense moved down the field, taking no chances, playing it safe, moving carefully, with precision, as if they had all the time in the world, making their way into field-goal position.

And then they were there. Thank God, they were there. Thirty-seven yards—that was all that was needed for the win—a thirty-seven-yard field goal. It was no piece of cake, of course, but a probable shoo-in, certainly, for Eric Bachman. He had done much more, often enough; a year before, at a Jayvee game, he had kicked the exact same distance to win the game. Pressure, sure, there was always pressure on a kicker. But Eric didn't mind; he actually liked that sort of responsibility. "I like to have it on me," he had said. Well, he had it now. It was up to him. He knew he'd done it before—same exact situation, same yardage, same amount of time.

Tae Uk was to snap, Jimmy Loreto to hold. Both boys stood tensely on the field, waiting, their thoughts nearly identical. "I was thinking, if I mess up the snap, everybody's going to kill me, 'cause everyone knows Eric can kick that far," said Tae Uk. "I was like shaking, the ball was shaking in my hands, breathing so hard."

"You're not supposed to mess up ever as holder, if you mess up once you're the worst holder ever. I was so scared—I knew if I screwed up it was totally my fault, they would have blamed it on me. There was no question Eric could make the field goal. He'd been kicking all season, why would he miss?" said Jimmy. Just before going out on the field—they had called time out—he thought he had seen concern on his friend's face. "Eric, why are you even worrying? You're gonna make this, of course," he told him.

Then when Tae Uk snapped the ball, for all his fears, it was soft as cotton, a perfect snap, Jimmy had to catch it. And he did—caught and held it perfectly, as Eric's foot connected, spinning the ball up, up, as every eye in the stadium followed it, the long seconds ticked by, it seemed to take forever, "like slow motion, I felt it took five minutes," said one boy. It had the distance, the angle, it was going to make it—

But it fell short, brutal inches short. And James, on the bench, nursing his battered knee, stared up at the bar, shaking his head, face still wet with tears, and smiled in spite of himself—at the irony of it all. "Because . . . this is life, you know?" As the whistle blew.

"Eric surefoot," said Erik Karlson. "But surefoot backfired. I died. I just lay there."

It was over; the game was lost. They had tried so hard, they had missed by so little, one point, but it was over. Exhausted, the boys stood on the field, many of them crying; they moved toward each other protectively as if to ward off the rest of the world, comforting Eric—as we stared, still motionless, still disbelieving, from the stands. Arms around each other, they began the long procession to the bus. Csaba picked James up from the bench, cradling him in his arms like a little kid; his face ringed with sorrow, the big Hungarian carried the injured boy off the field to the bus.

And slowly we moved out of the stands, all of us, standing helplessly outside the fence, watching them walk to the bus, eyes straight ahead, seeing none of us, taking in nothing. Had it really been only a few short years before that we parents could make them happy with one casual suggestion? How about a pizza, a movie, a bowling alley?—why, there was nothing to it, no matter what they were feeling bad about, one tiny wave of the wand and their eyes would light up. Imagine all that power we'd had, all of us! And accepted so easily, as if it were a right. Was it all really gone without a trace? Was there really nothing, nothing at all we could do to make it better?

Standing outside the fence, fighting my own tears, I knew it for the first time: it was not just the boys who were up against an immovable wall. We were all powerless, every one of us; that magic had slipped away forever. There was nothing we could do anymore to take away the pain.

They had played their hardest game; the defeat was more crushing than any they had known. And in their defeat, in their pain, they discovered something very strange. That it was not Bob Plante or even Pete White that they could turn to—unemotional men, they were uncomfortable with the boys' pain, wished to avoid it. No—it was Mitch. Mitch the wild man, the lunatic, who had humiliated nearly every one of them in the past weeks—Mitch, who, in his stubbornness had undermined the defense line, perhaps even crucially. Yet it was Mitch now who understood and did not turn away.

He stood with them in their locker room when they got back after the long, silent bus ride home, his own eyes a little red behind the glasses. It's all right, guys, he told them, this tough no nonsense all-Met athlete. You can cry, you've earned the right. That was a hard game, you were tough all the way. Go ahead, let it out. It's okay to care.

He let them know that their grief was well earned, their tears not unmanly, that they should not be ashamed, it was natural, even important, to cry. He had given them problems, he had inflicted hurt, he had made mistakes, he would do so again. He had also managed to teach them some things about football. But he would never give a better lesson than now, when standing in the locker room after the Einstein game, he let them know it was an honorable thing, to feel.

"Einstein was the hardest game I ever played in," said Geoff. "After we lost, I was completely devastated. And yet Coach White was—right after we lost, on the field—okay, put your pants and girdles in this hamper, take home your jerseys, leave your shoulder pads. I was like—don't you care? He never showed emotion, he was never upset.

"Mitch—people knew that he cared. He was upset too. He talked to me, Geoff, man, you played well, everybody played hard. White didn't . . . know how."

Only Dave was bothered—Dave, who had gotten along well with Mitch almost from the beginning. "I don't cry—I was just raised that I shouldn't cry. It's bad, I admit that . . . but I hate people crying. It seemed like it wasn't right for them to cry and me not to, especially people like Eric Knaus, who didn't even play. I'm the one who was on the field, I'm the one who was working hard, I'm the one who gave it all my all . . . and I'm not crying.

"Mitch was saying it's good to show a few tears. I don't have to cry to show you that I care! They know I worked as hard as I could, even with a messed-up ankle—they don't need to see me cry to know I tried my hardest." It was the one thing that annoyed him most about Mitch—he was so emotional. Dave just wanted to be left alone when he felt bad, like after a loss; his whole family was the same way, he felt. "As long as I understand myself, I don't need anybody else to tell me how I feel." He couldn't help resenting the young coach's approach. Let it all out! It was his business what he did with his pain, no one else's. Stonily he removed his uniform, giving Mitch a wide berth.

Eric Bachman was racked with guilt. The field goal had been the worst moment of his football career. But one by one, players and coaches came up to him. We should've done better. We shouldn't have left it all to you. It's not your fault, Eric, we had the chances, we missed them, it's not your fault. The pain didn't disappear, but the warmth of the boys comforted him. "It's what I remember most about it all," he said later. "How the players reacted. They didn't put an ounce of guilt on me." Later on that day, a few even teased him. "Christo kept saying, thirty-seven yards, Eric, thirty-seven yards, but that didn't bother me, I knew he was just joking."

John Han, though, had a slightly jaundiced reaction. "They were saying, you guys went out and played a hell of a game, we shouldn't have put that much pressure on Bachman. I was thinking, tough shit, man, that's his job. A kicker doesn't have to go through all the pain." He himself had gotten a bad blow to the ankle just before the half and had nursed it with an ice pack before going back out. Then after the game Bob Plante had told the team he never wanted to see anyone put ice on an injury again, then go back out on the field. If you're hurt you're hurt.

"That's what they were drilling into our heads—unless you break something where I can see it, forget it. They believe so much in killing yourself."

James, who had pushed himself to play while injured and now could hardly walk, refused to allow them to take him to the hospital. His parents had not been able to attend, and he wanted to go home first, to tell his mom in person, so she wouldn't have to be called to the hospital—he could at least spare her that. Initially surgery would be recommended to repair the ligament damage to his knee, and scheduled, but a second doctor would assure his parents that a month in a cast was treatment enough. Toriano, too, would have a cast in his future—yet even he would not consider for a moment that his loss was equal to James's. Toriano, after all, was still a junior: he had his life, specifically his senior season, still ahead of him.

"James should've gotten a medal," said Brendan Symes. "He was awesome. To have your knee hurting and play—that takes a lot of courage.

"You know you're gonna get hurt, you know something's gonna get banged up. Something always happens. That's how football's like life; that's why my Dad always made us do sports. It teaches you about life."

Despite the loss, despite the injury, James had still managed to wring a sense of satisfaction out of the game. He had done his best against tremendous odds; he had refused to quit; he had gone out like a man. Even with the pain, he was feeling better than Mike Mitchem, who'd had to endure such gut-wrenching frustration, standing impotently on the sidelines. For Mike, the Einstein game had been an almost unbearable experience; it had genuinely embittered him. He would not allow himself to care that deeply again.

But for most of the other boys, Einstein was a true oxymoron—the hurt that felt good. They knew they had played hard. When Bob and Mitch complimented them, not just after the game but at the Monday film session, they were pleased but took it in stride. For they knew something else—they had pulled this off themselves. They had done what they said they would do—shifted direction, realigned their attitudes. They had stopped the season's slow slide over the cliff, wrenched it back from oblivion at the last moment. It would have been nice to win; it would have been the perfect storybook finish. But it was not necessary.

"We played so good, so hard," said Billy. "We felt so sorry for Eric, too. We had the game in our grasp and lost it.

"But it wasn't a real heartbreaker. Not to me. Even though we didn't win, we had it back together. We all played together, all of us, and that's the most important thing. So it was kind of like a personal victory."

They had done what they said they would do, drawn together, helped each other, pulled the entire team up. Not their coaches, not their parents—them.

"We did it," said Billy proudly. "We seriously turned the season around."

CHAPTER TEN

MOST OF THE PLAYERS had walked off the Einstein field anguished yet unbowed. They knew the truth—that despite the final score they had held on, they had not given up, they had, as Pete said, played "four quarters of pretty tough football against a pretty tough team," and there was a pride to that knowledge which could not be denied.

But for the school as a whole, unfortunately, another truth loomed paramount. The Barons had lost three of their first four games. The wild hopes that had danced through the halls early on were now almost thoroughly squelched, any chance at the state playoffs so slim as to be virtually indistinguishable to the naked eye. (For perennial optimists like Geoff there was always the long shot, of course—a team who won seven games still had an off-chance of making it to the state, and there were still six games to go.) Disparaging comments were rare, probably less because of any special sensitivity on the part of the B-CC student body than the fact that many of these boys had achieved a certain stature over the years; they were commonly viewed with respect, if not awe. They were, after all, the men; it was considered impolitic to piss them off.

Nevertheless, in the school at large, it was obvious that the aura surrounding the team had dimmed several watts from last year's high-voltage shine. "You guys are going to find that if you keep on winning, some of this school stuff is going to start getting pretty easy," Pete White had promised the team at one point during the last season's sudden flurry of success. Quite uncharacteristically, but then, Pete, too, had been carried away, as were they all, by that first tantalizing taste of honey on the tongue.

Well, the honey had been snatched away, most likely for good. They would not take it all this season, that much was clear, and while they might console themselves like James with the realization that "this is life, you know?" there was a poignancy to that understanding, even so, the poignancy of all lost dreams.

Then there were the girls; specifically, the girls on B-CC's varsity field-hockey team, the Lady Barons. In recent years, keeping pace with the rest of the country, women's sports had expanded at B-CC by leaps and bounds. They were not considered the audience pleasers that men's sports were, not yet; they did not attract the alumni or receive the attention, they were not generally performed to the accompaniment of bright lights, packed stands, cheerleaders, acclaim, busy concession stands, pregame rallies, or post-game dances, the whole glittering panoply of stardom that surrounded boys' sports, which the boys themselves accepted without question as the natural backdrop to their efforts.

Yet they did exist. And were getting stronger every day. Terry Schaefer, who was no stranger to the professional, i.e., mostly male, world, was upset when she attended her first B-CC field-hockey game—so few fans in the bleachers, so little attention being paid. Then she caught herself, coolly. Maybe it was better this way. The girls out there on the field were learning something it had taken her several years to figure out—that you had to give 150 percent if you were a woman, work that much harder for that much less. Unfair, maybe, but true; indisputably true. There was no point fighting it, this was the way things were. Maybe it was just as good they learned it now.

For the girls on the field hockey team were learning a great deal this year. And much of it was exactly the sort of thing so many men, particularly athletically inclined men, truly believed women were, if not incapable of learning, certainly unlikely ever to encounter. "I've got the edge over you in business, since you never played football," Bob Plante had told his fiancée with cheerful disdain.

Perhaps he had a point. But would the edge still hold if she had played field hockey? On a tough, aggressive, undefeated team?

Because that was the plain reality this year at B-CC: the Lady Barons, whose season paralleled the boys' football season almost to the day (minus the two-a-day preparation period), had yet to lose a game, even to be scored on; their goalie was beginning to feel superfluous. They had immersed themselves in the basics of team-work and physical skills, just like the boys, but now they were discovering something even the boys did not know—what it felt like to be on an undefeated team.

There had been a time, some thirty years back, when girl athletes at public schools were branded damningly as odd, unfeminine figures of fun. Certainly this had been true in my school, I remembered.

No more. The field-hockey players came from the ranks of the most popular girls at B-CC; inevitably, it followed that the connections between the Barons and the Lady Barons were complex, tangled, and close. Geoff Smith dated one of the forwards; Brendon McReady, a junior, was deeply involved with a defensive player; Rick Fiscina had an ongoing (and, at times, offgoing) relationship with star forward Jenna Siegel that went back an unbelievably lengthy five years. And all the boys knew all the girls extremely well; they hung out together at parties, they were friends if not romantic partners, they had spent four years, often more, in each other's company.

Indeed, perhaps the biggest sign of changing times was that there were far more interconnecting links between the Barons and the Lady Barons than between the football players and the cheerleader squad. Only one player, Shane Dempsey, had a long-term relationship with a cheerleader, although Jimmy Loreto did have another sort of connection with one—his sister, Susan, was on the squad.

The two teams had continued to socialize, despite the growing disparity in their win-loss records. For the homecoming dance the following Saturday, Rick, Geoff, and Brendon were all going with field-hockey players. But the girls' winning streak had definitely begun to grate. Rick fantasized grabbing a gun and "picking off plaid skirts" (the Lady Barons' uniform); another player, seeing a busload of victorious girls after the Rockville game ("Ha-ha, we beat Rockville, you didn't!") contented himself with giving them all the finger. Geoff strove for contempt: "It's disgusting. They talk about field hockey every day," while remaining quite aware of his real objection.

"I go around saying it's disgusting, but I'm jealous as shit. I want people talking that way about football. It's hard. The girls are so good and they aren't hesitant about letting you know."

To Jenna Siegel, blond, bubbly, and self-possessed, the problem was clear. "It's this guy-girl crap. The guys gave us a real attitude. They couldn't handle it, they went crazy. It got to the point we had to mess back with them, 'cause they were so obnoxious about our winning.

"They weren't at all happy," she mused. "We'd have been so happy for them. They would've been cocky if they'd won, but we would've been happy for them."

"They'd say, hey, champs, what's your record?" said Geoff. To which the boys would respond with quiet maturity. "We'd hit 'em. We'd fucking hit 'em, you know?" He shook his head. "I hate them."

It was the ancient story, but with a twist. Unquestionably the boys were as put out as their fathers and grandfathers would have been in a similar situation, and the girls knew it. The difference was that this time they refused to knuckle under. It was too bad the boys couldn't accept their success in good spirit, it would be nicer for everyone if they could, but the girls weren't about to change for them, or pretend for one moment they weren't enjoying their victories. It might be a millennium before boys could accept such one-upmanship with real cheer. But the girls weren't going to wait. If the guys didn't like it they could lump it.

The one encouraging change this time around was that no one's social life suffered from any of this. Only a few short years ago, a boy, especially a Rick or a Geoff, could turn his back on a competitive girl, secure in the knowledge that there were plenty of other cute girls around. But what did you do when the competitive girls *were* the cute ones?

Rick certainly knew that there was not all that much difference between field hockey and football; both were tough physical sports.

"There is physical contact and they do go after each other. They're out there slapping each other, just as competitive. No difference, absolutely no difference." Not long before, on his way to practice with a few other boys, he had seen the girls in the bus, coming home from another win. "I heard a girl say, let's show them what a winning team is all about! Wooo, screaming, hooting, hollering, yeah, we're winners." He shook his head. "And we're so aware and they're so aware. It's strange, the parallels, that kind of girl . . . But it can be"—he paused and grinned—"attractive."

Most of the boys, whether irritated by the Lady Barons' success or not, had at least moved to a point beyond that which their fathers had reached: they were much more comfortable with the whole idea of physically aggressive women. Shane, who often accompanied a friend when he went to visit his girlfriend at a nearby Catholic school, Immaculata, found himself becoming something of a guru to the all-girl baseball team there.

"You've got to be really aggressive," he urged one girl. "Think about being in D.C. You're getting robbed. Or mugged. Or raped. And you have a bat. You're gonna hit the shit out of that guy. Picture that ball, just hitting it."

Satisfied, he watched her connect for a solid hit. "She's like, I never thought about it that way," he said.

Of course, there were differences between the two B-CC teams; plenty of them. "Girls are a lot different," said Jenna. "Bitchier, in general. You know how girls are so testy to each other . . . and on the field, it's the same thing, shoving, pushing. They don't really hit like the guys, they nudge. It's snottier."

Another big difference was "attitude checks. We'd stand at the bottom of the hill and Mr. Carroll (Mike Carroll, the coach) would walk up and down, lecturing us on how to be more intense, more dedicated, how we had to stop fighting, getting in bad moods, getting an attitude.

"Girls' teams have head problems. Someone is always mad about a boy, and it does affect everybody. There's always someone who—what's the matter? Nothing. Come on, what's the matter? Nothing, leave me alone. Fine, I'll leave you alone. Then they're mad at you . . . that kind of thing.

"And so Mr. Carroll, he was, okay, time for attitude checks.

Does anyone have a problem tonight? Reminding us that everyone had to be a team."

Maybe the strongest difference of all between the two teams lay in their totally opposite takes on that one simple concept, attitude. The boys strove for it fiercely. "Fucking attitude! Get it up! You gotta have an attitude!" they roared; the girls worked just as hard to eradicate it. Yet if they were asked, their definitions of the word would not be dissimilar. But to the girls, an attitude—putting yourself above everyone else—was considered detrimental to the team as a whole, while the boys took it as a given that aiming high, thinking of yourself as better than anyone, was a boost to the entire effort.

As the season progressed, more and more the girls on the field-hockey team found themselves forging a true unity, as they kept their eyes fixed unwaveringly on the state championship ahead. "Just having a goal that big—it was like an obsession, a disease. And it made everyone the same person on the field," Jenna described. "And after a while, those people weren't drinking at parties, so everyone was the same person off the field too. It was a real bond; it went beyond winning. The boys saw the bonds growing . . . they saw how hyped up we were getting . . . and they couldn't handle it."

Mainly they reacted with "these comments from hell. Like, if I played hockey, you know how good I'd be." Rick and Geoff were the worst offenders; others, like Toby and Billy, were "more relaxed. They weren't thrilled, but none of that if-I-played-field-hockey crap. I'd be in shock if that came out of Toby's mouth." Late in the season, Christo Doyle actually wore a field-hockey sticker for a day—or at any rate, allowed it to remain on his shirt (by then the girls were sticking them liberally on everyone). When Jenna thanked him, he tensed immediately. "Just don't push it," he warned.

Jenna, of course, had a special problem muddying the waters— her longtime relationship with Rick. "Girls all over the county know about me and Rick and get mad at me for it. I'd get shit for it during the games. I was at a hockey game and these guys were, that's Rick Fiscina's girlfriend. Look, I have a name, and it's not 'Rick Fiscina's girlfriend.' My claim to fame, Rick Fiscina."

Their relationship waxed and waned. "We grew up together," said Jenna. She added wisely, "It's not gonna really be over until we can stop fighting." They were too much alike, many kids thought, both athletic, feisty, competitive, energetic. "Jenna *is* Rick," said Toby. Like Rick, she knew her own worth; Billy never quite forgave her for telling him once, "I knew you when you were nothing, Billy—*I* was always the *woman.*" No one was ever surprised when she and Rick broke up; no one was ever surprised when they got back together.

This week, the week before homecoming, was fraught with decision for many of the boys. Who did you go with, the familiar or the strange? Did you opt, as one boy put it, for the prettiest girl, or the one who had demonstrated the most tolerance for alcohol consumption? For large dances, like homecoming, Sadie Hawkins, and the prom, were often conducted in a veritable haze of strong fumes. Alcohol had made a striking comeback at B-CC in the late eighties; drug consumption was down, and alcohol, the time-honored opiate of adolescence, had gushed back in to fill the vacuum.

Not that the boys on the team had avoided drugs completely. Although hard drugs—cocaine, crack, heroin, speed, angel dust—were eschewed by all, well over half had smoked pot at one time or another; for some, it was a steady indulgence. A handful had gone further, trying LSD, even Ecstasy, the new designer drug, though rarely more than once. One boy had given in to an odd, chilling impulse this year—he had slipped a tab of LSD into his mother's coffee, then watched uneasily as she cleaned the house frenetically for hours. The other boys found this story hilarious and disturbing, in about equal measure.

Light as their drug use was, in general, there was not one boy on the team who would not have been able, had he wanted, to lay his hands on almost anything, right away. Everyone knew who dealt at B-CC—one boy they all knew well had set himself up as chief pot supplier a few years back. ("He was a wimp, and didn't want to be. He decided he'd rather be a dealer," Toby explained it.) And the city itself was only minutes away. The drugs were out there, available. The boys stayed away by choice, and for reasons based on healthy fear. "I know me," more than one told me. "I'd be an addict, I'd be the biggest addict in the world. I can't take the chance." Several were sure that without sports, they would have, as one said, "delved more deeply" into that darker world.

The very pervasiveness of that world, the fact that it loomed so omnipresent, forced every boy to confront the question of drug use many times over. They did their best to face it with the bravado that befits a football player. If they *did* get into drugs, they would not just be addicts, understand—they would be the biggest addicts of *all time*.

Alcohol, though, was the most common drug of choice. Most parents had an easier time facing alcohol than drugs; it was, after all, what many of us had done too. But there was a new slant to the problem—the drinking age had now been boosted to twenty-one in every local municipality, with Washington itself being the last to climb on the bandwagon. Of course since most high school students were under eighteen anyway, there had never been anything legal about their drinking in the first place. But the rise in the age of consent had the unfortunate effect of giving underage drinking a more dangerous, hence more glamorous and seductive allure.

The laws were based on a legitimate concern: they were meant to cut down on teenage drunk driving. Actually, in recent times, the massive media attention given this problem had resulted in an impressive new awareness on the part of most kids. To a large degree, they no longer drove when drunk; designated drivers were a common fact of life. (Common enough so that some of us now automatically winced when our sons announced they did not need the car on a particular weekend night. We knew what that meant.)

But the laws themselves were not good, because they did not work. Sometime earlier I had shocked a group of my older son's friends by telling them that if I had my way, the drinking age would be lowered right back to eighteen. The tack I would take to combat drunk driving would be much simpler and far more effective: I would raise the minimum driving age to twenty-one across the board. When I left the room they still had their mouths open in horror.

As it was, the new higher drinking age had merely ushered in a new age of Prohibition, not only in high school communities, but on college campuses as well, and it was currently working about as well as the country's first stab at it, back in the twenties. Perhaps even worse. College students were now keenly aware they could be penalized for doing something their parents and grandparents had done at their age with utter impunity.

At the same time, beer commercials clogged the airwaves; it was not possible to watch a sporting event of any kind on television without getting the message loud and clear: You're no man unless you've got your hand around a cold one. Hell, you're probably not even having a good time, fella. This—slurp—is as good as it gets. Toby, at least, knew enough to poke fun at these spots. "Guys," he would say, his fist cupping air, moving his hand up and down in the universal gesture, "this is as good as it gets." Nevertheless, the boys received the message beer companies wanted them to get: sports, fun, and beer were inseparable.

Impressively, though, there was a large group of boys on the team who did not drink at all. Some readily admitted they had gone through a drinking stage and moved beyond; others had simply never been interested. "It's just not for me," said James. "I don't feel a need for it. They say, hey, drinking, what a time— well, I'll just have to miss those times. I'm kind of into being in good health." His grandmother had a saying—wholesome in everything—which had always appealed to him. "I can have a good time at parties without it."

"I don't want to harm myself," said Rene. At one time it had looked to him like maybe he needed to do it, to make friends. "But I realized that's not what I really wanted."

"I don't drink, personally," Toriano said. "I play sports and I talk about myself. A lot of people on the team don't do anything— drink, smoke, or do drugs."

"I'm on the side that doesn't touch anything," said Mike Mitchem. "Don't drink, don't smoke." During football season, of course, you were not supposed to do it anyway, but Mike was not the only player aware that a large handful of his teammates were among "the premier drinking crowd" of B-CC.

"I'd say 80 percent of the players at some time or another after a losing game go out and kill their brain," said John Han. "I guess the friends I hang out with don't see the point to that. People who say, damn, I can get wasted, I can handle all this beer—that's just another macho effect. Trying to prove something. People think alcohol is safe. I just feel, it doesn't taste good, what's the point? I figure there's more to life. It'll screw you up, and once you're screwed up, it's hard to get back."

All three Asian players, John, Kong, and Tae Uk, said they actually disliked the taste of alcohol. John, however, admitted he would probably drink in college—after all, you were supposed to drink in college, weren't you?

So there were unquestionably players who avoided alcohol. But there were also unquestionably many who did not.

"Ah, your typical clean-living jocks . . . you really don't find them anymore," said Jon Adelman, a senior nonplayer who was a close friend of many of the team. "They started out clean-living, but nearly everyone drinks beer now.

"I don't think it's hurt anyone at our school. We've had no real problem, no big accidents caused by drinking or drugs. We've done our fair share of being teenagers, yes, but no one really did it to excess, certainly none of the sports kids.

"Everyone was too afraid of burning out at an early age."

Drinking, however, had been responsible for one of the largest arrests ever made in the B-CC community, two years ago—an arrest that had earned a number of the senior boys on the team a juvenile citation. It had been a mild spring evening, and twenty-two of B-CC's sophomores had gone to a secluded branch of Rock Creek Park in the county known as the Mountain, for a picnic, with beer. Unfortunately, the area was less than secluded at the time; park policemen lurked behind every tree, waiting for an inter-school gang rumble and/or a large drug interchange—they had been told to expect both. When they jumped out from their trees, guns at the ready, to face a bunch of picnicking fifteen-year-olds, they were frankly furious; not surprisingly, they handed out cita-tions to all. The boys—and girls, too, of course ("It wasn't the alcohol that was important," Toby told the juvenile officer, "it was the male-female interaction.") were each given fines of forty dol-lars. They emerged with a firm respect for one of the area's basic unwritten laws: whatever you do, don't do it in the park. Park police were a vigilant crew.

And drinking had also contributed to another now entrenched B-CC ritual: the use of limousines at major dances. At one time, limousines appeared only on prom night, but in the past few years, they had been cropping up at social events around the calendar; most of the boys intended to arrive at the homecoming dance this year via this route. Choosing a date for the evening was only one, relatively minor, consideration. It was infinitely more important, not to mention more time-consuming, to arrange for the proper limousine. Limos were expensive, they needed to be lined up far ahead, there were only a finite number of them operating in the area. You certainly couldn't say that about the girls.

Parents were not thrilled at the idea of handling the extra expense of a limousine, even though that expense was divvied up several ways, since most limos carried four couples. But the bottom line was that teenagers in limousines—drinking, nondrinking, whatever they were doing—were not at the wheel of a car. Given that, most of us forked over the money fairly readily. Pay up and you'd be able to spend homecoming night calmly, without jumping out of your skin at every stray siren. Peace-of-mind insurance—in the end, well worth the price.

There was another reason for the popularity of limos. Although almost every boy on the team had a driver's license, and most had access to a car, this did not mean that all were driving. Maryland insurance companies cleaned house regularly—three moving violations were enough to get you booted, and the area was a hotbed of moving-violation opportunities. B-CC High School sat on top of a hill on a busy street. It was rarely possible to descend that hill without picking up speed; it was completely impossible to descend it daily and not eventually run into the cop who waited at the bottom, varying his position often enough to throw everyone off track. Few boys had avoided that trap; scarcely a nun at the nearby Our Lady of Lourdes School had gotten off free.

In addition, the county was full of wealthy enclaves whose residents had been able to convince officials to ring their boundaries with signs forbidding rush-hour entry. This lent a maze-like challenge to the experience of driving through Bethesda, and was the direct reason why Billy, who lived inside ritzy Kenwood, had lost his insurance. On several occasions, around dinnertime, Billy had lost his head. He had tried to drive straight home; they caught him every time. Several other players were also currently serving out a term of enforced carlessness—once you were cut you had to wait a year to get back on an insurance company's good side, unless your parents were willing to put out an astronomical sum, and few were. Limos made sense, in more ways than one.

CHAPTER ELEVEN

THE WEEK OF PRACTICE following the Einstein game was relatively easygoing, even pleasant. The film session on Monday had been the calmest one yet. The coaches understood how hard the boys had tried at the game, and in reaction not only held their punches for once but even doled out a few grains of praise. Bob Plante's approving comments made Toby's confidence swell, though he knew the coach had a special reason to be pleased with him. "After all, I was his creation."

"The kids had fought hard, played well as a unit, you couldn't fault them," said Bob. He and Mitch had felt terrible about the loss. "We didn't coach the game right. We should've been four and oh at this point. We had the talent to be." After the game, after all the kids had gone home, the two coaches had spent hours sitting in a car in front of a 7-Eleven convenience store, cursing and throwing paper cups. "We should be four and oh! And it's not the kids' fault!" The following week both were notably chastened; a kinder, gentler duo for once.

There was, however, a certain amount of nervousness about the coming Friday-night game against Walter Johnson. Not that they would be going up against a particularly good team, not at all. Located a mere four miles away, out Old Georgetown Road, in Bethesda, Walter Johnson had a reputation for consistently turning out teams of small white boys. My dentist's grandson played on the team, which somehow seemed to sum up the situation in a nutshell, logically or not.

In addition, WJ was having an even worse than usual time of it this year; they had lost their first four games roundly, barely managing even to score. By all rights, the game should be a rout. Therein lay the worry.

"We play good at Einstein, but we lose, we lose," said Pete. "So of course you're scared to death of playing WJ, because you know they're poor. They're not a very good team. But you know over at WJ they're probably sitting there thinking, well, if there's one team we got a chance to beat this season, it's B-CC. Maybe not so and so—after all, coaches are pretty realistic—but B-CC, yeah. And we know what they're thinking."

There was another ominous note as well: B-CC's long-established tradition of losing homecoming games. Everyone remembered last season's disaster only too well; that had been the game that wrecked their playoff hopes. Cocky, flushed with success from the amazing Churchill win, they had taken up arms against Wheaton almost cavalierly—and lost. Not by much, but enough, they were out of the running, and no loss had ever felt so bad. So spiritually depleted were they all, in fact, that Pete had given them a stern talking to in the locker room. "Look," he'd said. "I know how you feel. But tonight's the dance, and the girls have been looking forward to it, and I don't want any of you being assholes. Leave your mood at home."

"I came home and sat in my den and cried for an hour straight," said Geoff. Finally his friend had called to say they had to get ready to go to the dance. "I didn't want to. It's supposed to be a great time for every kid, homecoming, and I didn't want to go." He dragged himself up at last, got dressed, and went to another friend's house to wait for the limo. "His dad poured me a Bud and we talked. He understood. It was the end of the season, and that had been such a good season."

So Walter Johnson or not, no one was taking bets this year; they'd do their best, that was all. Perhaps expectations in general had wound down a bit around the locker room.

By pregame Friday night, though, Alex was thoroughly pissed.

He knew it was homecoming weekend, party weekend, everyone was ready for fun, sure, but this was ridiculous. These guys were just goofing off! This time it wasn't just Toby. *None* of the linemen would agree to stay together in the small weight room and con- centrate on their preparations the way Alex thought they should; the minute he went out to get water or something, all of them immediately left.

"I was punching people right and left, trying to get them to go back inside." Finally he gave up—"Screw you people!"—and con- tented himself with hitting the wrestling mats hung up on the wall again and again, so he at least would be in a state of readiness. And to think just a week ago he had thought he was the unemotional one. Didn't any of them care at all?

Last week's game had hardly pleased Alex, but he hadn't gotten hysterical about it. That wasn't his way. "I know how to deal with loss better than a lot of the other guys. I meet things more head-on. I don't think, oh God, we lost the game, my whole world's gonna crumble, I might as well slit my wrists. Geoff's a lot of show—he'd make millions if he could just get someone to pay him—he gets into games very emotionally. I guess he's just more emotional than I am, but . . . look, sometimes you eat the bear, sometimes the bear eats you."

As far as Alex was concerned, the line had been improving steadily—they were moving toward being a consistent, organized force, thanks to Bob—and him, too, of course. After the team meeting, he had given his own directive to the linemen. "Look," he'd said, "just ignore Mitch. Ignore whatever he says to you. Look at him, shake your head, say yes, Coach, and ignore him. Listen to Bob or me."

At Einstein, he had felt "we did everything we could, fate was just against us." It was history now. But the WJ game hadn't even begun. At this point, thoroughly disgusted, Alex was sure B-CC was in for another loss—perhaps the most humiliating one of all. And that, of course, would be it for the season.

In the stands, too, every one of us was aware, even as we noted the packed house, the festive atmosphere, the blue-and-gold streamers, the yellow pom-poms like exploding chrysanthemums, the gathering array of oddly festooned floats lined up already for the halftime parade. The spirit of homecoming was alive and thriving; the whole school, teachers included, had turned out for the spectacle. There was even, in honor of this special October 7 game, a new crispness in the air that actually had the taste and feel of fall, at long last, and was blowing up in small, sharp gusts here and there over the field.

But facts were facts. The team had been down, the team had been up, there was a world of difference between their playing at Wooten and their playing last week. But the statistics were unavoidable. One more loss, we knew grimly, and the season was dead in the water.

Waiting for the game to start, we exchanged quick details about tomorrow night's homecoming dance. Not that we knew much beyond the minimum—who our boys were taking, who was going in whose limo. Only a few short years ago, all of us would have been closely involved, carpooling, waiting outside restaurants. No more. But we liked to keep a hand in as much as possible, even if right now the only relevant information had to do with money. Crassly, shamelessly, we exchanged numbers, searching for a golden mean. How much are you giving Toby for the restaurant? How about Billy? Tony? Rick?

But as kickoff came closer, we grew silent, tense, we clutched hands, we muttered prayers—please make it work this time! Please, please . . .

And then, for all our fears, the boys stormed out on the field like seasoned troupers and systematically proceeded to kick ass all over the lot. Wildly, for four riotous, rollicking quarters. They threw the Wildcats up in the air like straw men; they tromped them into sawdust under their feet. There was never a doubt, never an inheld breath, not for a minute; the game was never in question, never evenly matched, never even a concern. There was a gala air of celebration, even a mania about it, much, much more than at the Blair game. This was the reward for their hard work the week before, the reward for all the season's work. This was party time, yes it was.

And did we regret the lack of hardy opposition? Yearn for a more worthy adversary? Feel at all for WJ's victimization? Not a bit of it! We loved it, reveled in the slaughter, screamed and laughed and cried for more; we pounded backs and threw up our arms to embrace the entire glorious night. And how loud the band! How fresh-faced the cheerleaders! How crazily colored the floats! How brilliantly the lights shone down over us all!

Did it matter at all that, as Mitch was quick to remind the boys, his face set in the baleful disapproval of a monk at an orgy, "they're just a sucky team, that's all, it's not that you guys are so good, it's that they're so bad." Nary a hair. Not that night. Not to any of us. No way at all.

For Brendan Symes, it was a night of pure magic. He had heard that this might be a running game for once, instead of the usual passing extravaganza, and as first running back he was both excited and nervous about coming out on the field. "We knew they're not that good, but you know how teams can fool you." B-CC had possession first; they ran it down to the ten-yard line, and Pete White, as was typical, called in a pass play. But in the huddle, Rick turned to the running back and flashed his grin. "You want to run it in?"

"I go, yeah, man." He grabbed the ball, took off down the field, saw them gathering in closer, rushing him, then dived over everyone into the end zone, feeling like he always did when he dived, "like I was flying.

"I turn around and everyone in the crowd is going nuts, I'm going, oh God, don't let this end!

"Our senior year, to score a touchdown at homecoming!"

It was a moment he wished he could hold on to and freeze forever. Brendan already knew there was a fragility to such moments—they passed so quickly. He ached to grasp them in his hands, anchor them down somehow. His football jacket, the cleats that his mother had painted with his number, 25, these were deeply important to him. In a sense they were moments of glory made flesh.

He was aware, maybe more than most of the others, how shaky, how tenuous, was the ground on which they stood. His family, his friends, the team, the school, the night itself—this was the safe harbor. How did one bring oneself to leave? Yet leave-taking was inevitable, it was coming, you could feel it; every step they took this year brought them closer to that point.

On the field, it felt "like you can control everything." But off? "I don't want to grow up at all. I really don't want to leave anyone. It's hard. On the team, you learn to trust each other. You're risking yourself so somebody else can score. That's what makes you closer. You can never trust anyone like that the rest of your life. You can't really trust someone like that in your job." His father had plenty of college friends from Dartmouth, "but when we go back to Jamaica and he sees his high school friends, he's so happy, he hugs them. It's like family. It's hard. When we come back, we'll all have changed in our own way, it won't be the same."

He had had his fill of leave-taking in his short life. His father had worked first as a diplomat with the Jamaican embassy, then with the World Bank; the family had been uprooted several times—from Jamaica to Ethiopia, then back to Jamaica again, finally to Maryland. Maybe his need to hold on had come from that. For Brendan had the need strongly, and knew it. "I took little things, sometimes," he admitted. "A shirt, something you're not supposed to have, sometimes you've got to have it. I wanted something of Coach White's, a jacket he always wore, or a sweatshirt, I wanted to take it so bad. I know I'm gonna have kids and I have to have something to prove to them I played football."

If Brendan had a wish, it was that he could look a little bigger, a little more like an athlete; he was only five-eight. "I think all of us have the heart, but I wish you could just look at me and tell I was an athlete, like Rick. My dad says I look tough, like I can take care of myself. But I see Billy. My dad loves Billy and Toby to death—they walk in, so big and tough, with their boots and jeans. I feel so protected with them. Like older brothers." Coach White, though, had told him not to worry about size, that he was "the perfect size running back for our team." That had made him feel wonderful.

His brother was on the Jayvee this year. "He's bigger than me, faster than me," said Brendan proudly; he had taught him everything he could about football, it was almost as if he would rather see Dean succeed than himself, even. There were times this year when he had acted purposefully to protect some of the younger guys on the team. Once when Mitch started to yell at Dirkey Finley during practice about some play, he stepped between them, insisting it had been his mistake. Dirkey, he knew, would do the same thing for Dean next year, then Dean would do it for someone else.

At first, when they had moved here, his mother had "kept us isolated." Brendan and Dean had lived at the embassy and had gone to a private school in Potomac. They'd hated it, and hated living in the embassy, looking out the window, watching all the neighborhood kids sledding down the hill. "I told her I wanted to be like everyone else." She had finally relented, and sent them to the public junior high. Football was another watershed; at first, Brendan's father had to sign the release form himself. "She thought we were going to be hurt. It was pretty much a shock for her." Now, though, she went to all the games.

His father was a different story—he loved everything about the game, and spent hours hurling the ball to his sons. Coach White had encouraged Brendan early on to keep a football with him all day, going through school, so he'd learn how to hold on to it no matter what. His father came up with another idea: their home in Jamaica, where they returned every summer, was near a steep hill. Brendan's father would position him at the edge of the hill, so that when he caught the ball, he'd have to jump for it and then roll down the hill. Every day they practiced again and again. "That really helped my concentration." It was just like in a game, when you knew you were going to be hit as soon as you caught the ball, but you couldn't think about it.

"I think every kid should play. You lose and win." Either way, it was worth it.

Of course, sometimes God, for reasons of His own, decided simply to give everyone on the team a present, and homecoming night, against the feckless Walter Johnson Wildcats, showed every sign of being exactly that. From the very first whistle, the evening had that feel—a gorgeous, sparkling, beribboned offering had dropped straight down from the skies.

Brendan's touchdown was only the first golden moment; others followed swiftly on its heels. Second quarter Rick himself ran in from nine yards out for the score; then, incredibly, Brendan did it again, scored a second touchdown. It was, as Pete himself would later say, "the game of his life." Pete was glad; Brendan was one of his favorites. "A prince," he called him. Brendan was one of the politest young men he'd ever known.

Alex, who'd been so worried before kickoff that B-CC might lose, quickly realized there was no way, no way at all. His mood now, like that of everyone on the team, like all of us in the stands, was one of stunned delight. The only exceptions, of course, were WJ players, coaches, and fans; they alone did not seem to share the bucolic spirit.

At one point, Geoff, playing defense, was shocked to find himself facing an embittered WJ coach. Not that the bitterness itself came as any kind of surprise, but the guy actually articulated it! In his face! "Grossest thing I ever heard in my life. A *coach* talked trash to me."

The WJ quarterback had overthrown a pass; it was "semi-interceptable," so Geoff made a try for it and missed. "I went, ahhh, banged my helmet, I was mad I didn't catch it, and this coach I'd never seen in my life looks at me and goes, hey, Geoff—you're good but not that good.

"A coach! A coach said that!" He was almost shocked into silence, but being Geoff, not quite. "I go, I know, I thought it was close, and he's, yeah, if you're superman. The *coach* was saying that." Geoff couldn't believe it.

"We knew they sucked, but we had a field day. It was so easy," said John Han. "You didn't care about Mitch or Plante, you just had fun—tear 'em apart, go get 'em. They just weren't that strong."

"Like hitting a bunch of blind people," another boy put it. "The greatest feeling. I mean homecoming! And you're playing the saddest team in Maryland."

Even Mike Mitchem was having a wonderful time for once. "I wasn't doing what Mitch wanted, but I was being successful, it was homecoming, we were up by fourteen points, twenty points, so he didn't care, he let me do my thing." And do it he did—he grabbed a blocked WJ punt, ran it down the field for over fifty yards, and another touchdown.

Even more exciting, the punt had been blocked by Eric Knaus; his name rang out over the loudspeaker. "The best game," he said later, glowing. In the stands, we screamed, we hollered. Every new highlight whetted our appetite, and our appetite that night was unquenchable. We wanted more, more, more.

Now the cushion was thick, the outcome all but engraved in granite, there was that rare, lovely, chest-inflating surge of utter confidence which came so infrequently in any game. They can't touch us! We are truly the best men on the field! Second string, third string, everyone would have a chance to get in on this one.

Dimarlo Duvall, known as Double D, Alex's close friend, and one of the best-natured guys on the team, who never missed a practice, who cheerfully accepted his bird-dog duties without complaint, was finally finding out what it was like to play almost an entire game. Bliss, that's what it was. And the line loved having him aboard—Dimarlo could be such a cutup, always a plus in the trenches. Linemen always tried their damnedest to confuse the opposition by any means possible, hoping to entice them into going offsides with a false start, or, failing that, into simply losing track of the game and their place in it. Clouding their minds. To this end they yelled out meaningless chants: "Lemon, orange, Jell-O." They called endless huts. Rick was quick to slip in his own comments: "Fuck you, ninety-two! Fuck you, ninety-two!"

In fact, the quarterback even had a specially inscribed towel he wore stuffed in the front of his pants; a fan had made it for him in art class. The front simply showed the B-CC Barons' insignia, but the back displayed a large "FUCK YOU DEFENSE" along with a raised middle finger. Rick liked to wear the towel front side out for a quarter or so, then switch it around, hoping to elicit at least a split second of shock. Down in the trenches, every little bit helped.

But Dimarlo had his own ploy: a high, piercing *ee-ee-ee* sound only he could emit, the sound, if one had to classify it, that might be made by a chipmunk pinioned between two boulders, although actually it was his own rendition (I was assured later) of Flipper the Dolphin. Whether it worked or not was debatable, but it certainly cracked up all the B-CC players within several yards.

"I got kind of embarrassed," Dimarlo said later. "One guy just got me by my shoulder pads, took me down. I was really fat—a short, fat guy." But as the game continued, he too began to hit his stride and feel his strength; finally, playing on defensive line, in an unprecedented burst of adrenaline, he shot up the field and in front of the whole cheering crowd actually sacked the WJ quarterback. "My first sack of the season! My only sack!" he crowed.

*   *   *

It was a moment of rare, sweet success, and while he could never repeat it on a football field, it seemed to mark some sort of passage for him. Dimarlo had always been a cutup, in school as well as on the team; his noises, Flipper and others, had erupted more than once, even this year, within the classroom. "This kid could really go off," Karen Lockard said.

But the school was beginning to see a change: bit by bit, slowly but progressively, Dimarlo had started to clean up his act. First it was in history class, where he sat with his good buddy Alex; then in English as well. Slowly the changes began to add up. He was listening; he was working; his grades began to improve.

He was nominally in Mrs. Lockard's English class that first semester, but as it happened, a student teacher was the one actually handling the grading, and she went strictly by the book. His average was still one point below a B, so she gave him a C. A few days later, two football players, Shane Dempsey and Marc Gage, appeared at Karen Lockard's door, their faces serious. They had come, they said, about their friend.

"They didn't grub, but they said, is this valid? He's been working so hard, he's really trying to do it right. Is this really fair?" Neither boy had ever approached her about their own grades, and both were conscientious students. This was for their friend. Karen assured them she would review the situation, and she did: in one of those moves that made her such a rare teacher, she decided to favor justice instead of the law. The boys were right, she concluded: Dimarlo had earned his B.

"He didn't do it for me, that change. He did it for his friends. They encouraged him," she said. "And it was a real change."

"All through life I was a loner," Dimarlo mused. "Until I came back here and met Alex, and finally got friends, you know . . . and it was good." His childhood had been a tough one. His mother had left when he was three; he had never seen her again. He had heard that drugs were the cause. His father, bent on pursuing a music career, had carted him off to California for several years, where they relocated several times, then back to this area, where they moved in first with a cousin, then with Dimarlo's grandmother, who was living in a tiny apartment on a small disability pension. Shortly afterward his father left for good. "He didn't disappear, but he left. He calls once every two months.

"I have a strange family, but I'm not gonna let that stand in my way. My grandmother raised me, just about." She had done her best for him, he knew. He didn't like to ask her for anything. Since he was sixteen he had worked at a local movie theater daily, using the money to buy his own clothes. One of his dreams was to be able to save up enough to send his grandmother on a trip to California . . . somewhere warm, to help her arthritis.

Having a friend like Alex "made me more mature," he felt. "I love being with their family, the Burgesses are so smart. It's helped me to learn more, to improve my vocabulary, to be more mature." Life, he knew, was a matter of choices. "I could've easily gone down to D.C., started dealing crack, but it isn't worth it. I stay away from D.C. I try not to go down there for anything." All of his closest friends—Shane, Marc, Alex—are white, which used to disturb him somewhat, but that too, he'd realized, was a matter of choice. "It's just the way it is. I pick the friends I want to be with."

The following June, when Dimarlo crossed the stage at graduation wearing the cap and gown he had paid for himself, he would be the first person in his family to finish high school. He planned to attend community college, work hard, then transfer after a couple of years, possibly to the University of Arizona, where he could live with his friend Marc Gage. Marc, he knew, was a true student. "I know if I have a friend around who's gonna study, that's gonna make me study." He couldn't go with Alex—Alex was headed, he hoped, to The Citadel, determined to have a military future.

And although Dimarlo had no idea on homecoming night, the night of his sack, yet another major change would occur before he crossed that stage. He would have lost thirty pounds on a strict diet. His friends' pride in this accomplishment would almost surpass his own. "It's incredible," Toby told me. "Do you realize Dimarlo's actually handsome? You can see his face! He's handsome, Mom."

He could still act sillier than anyone when he wanted, still crack everyone up—like the time he found a blond wig, jammed it on, and danced his way through the locker room, leaving the entire team weak with hysterical laughter. But something was changing, that much was clear.

Who could say what cracked the chrysalis—his friends, the team, the passing years, his sense of responsibility toward his grandmother, even the minor triumph of that one sack? But the fact was it had cracked. Dimarlo had emerged, ready to take his place, a true player in the scheme of things.

The WJ game was a treat for nearly everyone, a vast, delectable smorgasbord of a treat. Ironically Rick, who was never hurt, sustained probably the worst B-CC hit of the night—a WJ tackle, who'd worked up a head of high venomous spleen, finally managed to get a bead on him and took it for all it was worth, slamming him into the ground on his tailbone. Red-faced, sputtering, in real pain, Rick waddled back to the huddle, holding his butt; his teammates guffawed unsympathetically at the sight. "When Rick gets that mad, he's so intense, it's just so funny," said Billy. It was one of those times, again, when he turned into "the devil."

WJ too incurred an injury; one player broke his arm. Later Pete, in an expansive mood, told the boys what one of their coaches had said to him. "He said that guy was so glad to get off the field, he didn't even mind!"

The homecoming parade of oddly gussied-up cars was scruffy, loud, and enthusiastic at halftime, rolling around the track. The party atmosphere had infected everyone. Inside one float, three seniors, all honor students, decided they had to mark the occasion in some special way. Surreptitiously they lit a joint and everyone took puffs. "We just realized, we have to do it on school grounds, just this once," said one.

The homecoming king was announced: Derek Milam, a popular black basketball player, one of Dave's good friends. No football players had been nominated, which was not surprising. Last year, when Billy had been named junior king, he had not appeared on the field for the honor, leaving a noticeable, embarrassing gap in the homecoming court. "He was in the locker room, of course," Toby said, exasperated. "That stuff isn't important during a game."

Down to the end the revels continued, out on the field. Geoff managed to add his usual personalized stamp to the evening with a beautiful touchdown reception of Rick's beautifully thrown pass—the score, with Eric Bachman missing only one kick out of five, was at 34–0. In the fourth quarter, mercifully, WJ finally scored, though even then, their bad luck holding firm, they managed to miss the kick.

And now the end was coming up fast. Pete, his usual poker face split wide in a huge smile, turned to face the players. Did anyone want a chance to go in on defense, anyone at all? Now was their chance, they'd never get a better one.

Toby leapt at it. He'd never played defense in an actual game. With only scant seconds left on the clock, he ran out on the field to take his position.

Then, stunning everyone, he barreled straight through the line as if he had been doing it all his life and laid the WJ quarterback out flat on his back. He turned to the crowd, arms up in amazed delight—my son, the conqueror! A sack! An utterly unnecessary overkill sack, in the last dying seconds of a totally insured win. No matter, no matter at all. The screams erupted from the stands in a tidal wave; a thrill shot through my blood.

"It was nothing like the Einstein block, nothing at all," he belittled it later. "It didn't feel at all as good. I was happy, but it was such a joke game."

And certainly that was the simple truth. But seeing him standing there, looming over the vanquished foe, tall, proud, drawing all the light in the stadium for once, his teammates running to slap and hug him, I knew that this was one of those freeze-frames I'd be carrying with me for a long, long time.

The whistle blew; the boys leapt, crowed, shook hands quickly with the luckless WJ players, then strode proudly to their just reward—the long conquering march up the stadium steps, through the packed crowd, to the locker room.

We parents gathered, twittering, at the top of the steps, joyful yet oddly tentative. These were our kids, after all. Yet there was something about the way they were mounting those steps, stopping at every rise to shake hands with teachers, parents of friends, benevolently, graciously bending their heads down from Olympia. *Were* they our kids? We felt smaller, diminished somehow, all of us. We felt, a distinctly unsettling sensation, like fans.

And the impression lingered, even when Toby emerged, when all of them emerged, to give us brief bear hugs, allow us to touch them quickly, before they moved on, huge, their faces gleaming as if they had carried some of the lights' sharp glow with them off the field. I had seen this glow on other faces before; certain famous ones seemed to hold it within them, though you were never quite sure. Did it come from them? Or were you, dazzled by their presence, merely investing them with light? Yet with some, you did know— surely with John F. Kennedy, it had been unmistakable, clearly visible, suffusing his face.

The boys had that glow tonight. Seeing it was stunning, exhilarating, yet disorienting as well. *Were* they our kids? When did they get so big? So confident? So far away?

Then they were gone, all of them, the crowd was suddenly dark, bled of color. We moved out toward the parking lot, huddling together against the sudden chill. It was not until later that I learned that Toby, at least, had gotten a small comeuppance on those steps. Climbing them slowly, proudly, he had heard someone call his name from the stands. He looked over, to see "two of the hottest girls I've ever seen in my life." Eagerly he paused, then took a closer look. In between them, arms around both, with a smile as smug as all outdoors, was his brother. No words were needed, the message was plain—having a good time, sucker?

It was the sort of incident the guys called "a good waste," and were eager to share. For whatever perverse, balancing-out reason, many of them relished such squelches almost as much, or more, than personal victories: the story you could tell on yourself. It was no accident either that Billy, one of Toby's closest friends, was the one who teased him most unmercifully about his big moment. "I told him he'd just fallen on top of Mitchem, that Mitchem had gotten there first," he said.

The weekend had started with such a bang that nearly anything else was bound to be anticlimactic. Homecoming dance had its moments—limos, party clothes, the Georgetown restaurant where many of them ate which served them octopus soup, somewhat unwisely, since the course was followed directly by a food fight, utilizing that plus a few rolls; good reggae music at the dance. And of course, for many, alcohol, often far too much. "No one in our whole limo threw up," my son announced proudly, pleasing me inordinately until another kid clarified: he could only have meant that no one actually threw up *in* the limo, he explained laconically.

The boys who went with girls they knew well had a better time than those, like Toby, who had chosen to opt for the new and exotic. But it was a good, fun time for most. Except that no dance could match the game; it was as simple as that.

And the aftereffects continued. A few days later I ran into Toby's creative-writing teacher, a woman with a gray bun and an intellectual, even professorial, mien. We talked briefly about James Joyce and the stream-of-consciousness form. Toby was doing well in the class, she said primly; at first she had thought she detected perhaps a certain ... attitude, but that had changed; he seemed quite interested now and fairly willing to work, as well. I was nodding pleasantly, noncommittally, warily—i.e., parentally, when suddenly without warning her expression underwent a total change. The professorial mien dissolved completely, her eyes blazed with fire.

"The thing is, though"—and here she grasped my arm eagerly— "did you see—that—SACK?!" She had screamed herself sick, she said. Watching her, I couldn't help remembering Pete's comment last season. Maybe when you started winning, the school stuff did get "pretty easy." It seemed that teachers, too, were not immune to the effects of the glow.

All the boys carried off a warm flush of success from the field that night; easy or not, it had been a rollicking victory, and the memory was powerfully sweet. But Brendan Symes carried off something else as well—the game football.

He had to have it. Two touchdowns on homecoming night? His senior year? No way was he letting go of that ball. He carefully propped it up on the shelf beside his bed, where he could see it first thing in the morning. And there it remained. Unmistakably real. Solid. Something a guy could hold on to.

CHAPTER TWELVE

THE BARONS were recharged. The WJ win had ignited old hopes, and with it, the team had flared into roaring, pulsating life once again. Geoff was beside himself. "We needed a blowout and that's exactly what we got," he joyfully told a local *Montgomery County Journal* reporter. Reports of their death had been highly exaggerated, the boys realized with glee. The season was still alive, and so were they. It wasn't over yet, not by a long shot. They were coming back. All bets were off.

Both Mitch and Bob were feeling certain fleeting sparks of hope themselves, though they made short shrift of the win to the boys, naturally. "You guys got a cakewalk," Bob Plante sneered at them. The quintessence of the easy win, that one had been. Well, he hoped they knew that was the last pushover team they'd face this year for damn sure. He hoped they'd enjoyed it thoroughly.

For they were in the soup now for good. Coming up right on their heels was hard-nosed Kennedy, who'd beaten them good last year. Then undefeated Whitman, who'd exploded into glory this season, followed immediately by almighty Churchill, down-and-dirty Wheaton, and finally, to top it off, mammoth, untouchable, abandon-all-hope-ye-who-walk-on-this-field Gaithersburg. Cheer up all you want, guys, the worse is definitely yet to come.

But the coach's warnings had small effect. The boys were feeling too good, and the film session only intensified their optimism. Replaying the game, delightedly watching themselves knock over WJ like so many bamboo stalks, gave everyone another boost. I was eager to hear how Toby's sack had looked on video, but he told me casually there was no way to know, the tape had run out by then. This seemed to bother him not at all, but it gnawed at me—a day later I unwisely mentioned it to a group of his friends. Immediately they were on him, jeering. "You told your *mom*? Hey, Farney told his mom his sack wasn't on the tape!" I insisted he hadn't, that I had asked, but no one was buying that. I left the room with my son staring daggers at my back. Probably when he is forty he wouldn't even remember, I assured myself, a familiar mantra I intoned whenever I had pissed off one of my sons (i.e., daily).

Despite his warnings, there was no question that Bob Plante was feeling better about the future himself. Maybe he wouldn't succeed in shaping up all his linemen, but he could see he was having a definite effect on several. Toby was developing nicely; Erik Karlson was coming along; Tae Uk was looking better than ever. He allowed himself a moment of satisfaction. No two ways about it, he knew the trick of motivating these guys. And if you could do it on a football field . . . the possibilities were endless.

"I could shave Toby's head and say, Toby, I want you to go down to that High's store with a gun right now, hold 'em up, bring me fifty bucks back. I could motivate him to do that," he said dreamily. "I could say, Toby, if you don't do that, you're not a man. He's into that, into what other guys think, into what I think." Karlson, too. "I could get him, too, I could get him . . . put him and Toby together, get them in the car, go rob some stores." His own little hit squad. Basically, two fairly level-headed kids, both of them. But with the right kind of push . . .

With some of the others, though, it was not so simple; he had to admit that to himself. John Han he found "an enigma . . . good days and bad. I can appeal to his manhood during the game, but during the week, not always." Marc Gage was another disappointment, a kid he felt was largely inaccessible to his control.

"You can motivate him when you get him in a group of people, maybe, but one on one, I couldn't shave his head and get him to go down to High's," he admitted sadly. It was perhaps a matter of clashing personalities, he thought. Actually, though, it might have been their similarities that got in the way. Marc Gage had an ironic outlook not unlike Bob's own. In the huddle, while others raged, Marc was often amused. "He tried to tackle me," he would say about an opponent, mock-offended. "That's not right. He's not supposed to do that. He's supposed to stand there and let me knock him down. I better talk to him about that."

In fact Pete, whose reading of his players' personalities was rarely off the mark, felt if any lineman was utterly unlike Bob, it was Toby. Bob was work ethic all the way; Toby viewed life from a mellower plain. It was no accident that reggae was his favorite music. "Two direct opposites," Pete adjudged them. "But luckily smart enough to take the best from each other, leave the rest alone."

Alex was also not quite as accessible as he had seemed at first, Bob felt. "He would like to be General Patton. But he's not. I'm not saying there's anything wrong with that at this point in his life, but it's a little unrealistic. He wants to be number one but doesn't want to do the work." The center continued to skip practice early in the week; many of the boys now were openly scornful about "Alex's Mondays."

Alex himself understood there was a certain split between his behavior and his stated beliefs in the importance of discipline. "I definitely have two faces," he admitted. "I can tell people to do something and they will do it, and there's a strength and power in that, and I like it. It's definitely an ego trip. I know what to say, how to do it . . . but I don't always do it myself." He hoped the rigors of military school next year would help mend this gap. He was keenly looking forward to a more rigid atmosphere, one with "respect, discipline, honor, the whole bit." Responsibility. That was one of the reasons he respected Dimarlo so—there was a guy who had been forced to take responsibility for his life, earning money so his grandmother wouldn't have to pay for things.

For himself right now, though . . . the truth was that Alex was taking it easy this year, very easy. Not just with football, with school as well. His attendance there, too, was often spotty. It really was almost as if there were two distinct sides to his personality: the inflexible, stern, no-nonsense commando who barked orders and took no guff from his linemen, and a much milder, easygoing, laid-back, almost removed kind of guy. It is hard enough when two such variant types live under the same roof; sharing space in the same body was difficult in the extreme. Especially since, given his acute intelligence, Alex was quite aware of the discrepancy between the two sides.

He enjoyed leading the line, but in some ways was finding even more satisfaction this year hanging around the Jayvee team, helping some of the young players. Not just with football—with their lives. "Just trying to help them through hurdles I had to put up with. There's an immense load of crap involved in high school." Alex could show them the ins and outs, how to get the unexcused absence changed to excused, how to get teachers on their side, how to "work their way through the system so they can get out with no problem, learn what they need to learn, move on." And they listened—that was one of the advantages of being big, especially with the younger guys. "If I have to use fear to make them listen to me, I will." Alex got a kick out of playing with people's minds sometimes. It was fun. Like with some guys—you could just go up to them and say something like "Saturday night" and walk away, and they'd be really upset. "Lots of fun."

On the team, though, Alex's lax practice attendance had finally gotten under Bob's skin, though not the same way Mike Mitchem's had with Mitch, who took such things so much more personally. But he had finally reacted. While he had not pulled him out of the game entirely, Mark Bitz, the junior second-string center, had gotten ample playing time at the WJ game.

It was a thrill, but Mark's biggest thrill came Monday, at the film session. "We were sitting in the film room and Mitch goes, hey, Burgess! Yeah, what? I'm not playing here. Why don't you watch Bitz—maybe you can learn something. Yes!" Definitely "my greatest moment," he felt.

Mark Bitz, too, Bob thought, was going to be okay as a lineman next year, as long as he was handled the right way. "A guy like that you gotta really nail a couple of times, almost browbeat him. He's gonna respond to that." Football, he felt, would have a good effect on Mark—he needed something like that to make him truly confident. "A kid who shows me his Rolex. He's just looking for a way to talk to me."

Actually, though, it was simpler. Mark Bitz was very proud of his Rolex, just as he was of his other special possessions, like the underwater camera, the sophisticated darkroom equipment. "I don't project a rich image, I don't try," he said. Yet "there are two families on the football team that everybody would describe as rich—the Loretos and the Bitzes." (Jimmy's father was a successful ophthalmologist; their house had an indoor pool.) This description did not bother him; far from it.

Alone of all the players, Mark knew exactly what he wanted most in life. "I just want to be rich. That's all I want to be. To be like my dad would be satisfying but not fulfilling. I want to be Gordon Gekko rich. That's what I desire, enough money that I can retire by age thirty. Everybody in life, all they want is security. And that's all I want. I really do believe everybody wants guarantees on something, guarantees on happiness, wealth, having a great life, something in stone. All I want from my life is a guarantee I'll never be in the poorhouse. I want it written in stone that I will have money."

In fact, he'd always had it; it was certainly not deprivation that had given birth to this yearning. His father, "regarded as one of the best project managers in the world, one of the top five," had made a great deal. "That always makes me feel safe. I'm not gonna end up moving to Summit Hills" (a large Silver Spring apartment complex mostly populated by black and Hispanic tenants, hardly a slum, but a far cry from the Bitz's lavish North Chevy Chase home).

Mark Bitz, like Toby, was Jewish, though the Bitzes were observant, temple-attending Jews, which we were not. The Rolex had been one of his bar mitzvah gifts; it had cost, he said, $1,250, which was actually a modest price for a Rolex, considering, he thought.

Both boys came from families with predominantly Eastern European roots. Mark's paternal grandfather, however, had also had a hidden past. Mark had only begun to learn the truth in recent years, after his grandfather, who had headed a newspaper dispatch chain in New York, was murdered in 1982, dropped in the New Jersey swamp, his feet wired into concrete blocks.

"It had something to do with the Mafia. I know he killed a few people. Before he died, I never knew anything. I didn't know he went to prison for tax evasion, didn't know he killed anyone. He was suspected of the murder of Jack 'Legs' Steinman.

"When he was murdered—it was in the newspapers—I answered the phone when the FBI agent called, and he thought I was my father, so that's how I found out." Mark had been ten at the time.

In recent years, his father had begun to tell him some of the truth. "This past Christmas, we were in New York and drove past a restaurant in Chinatown. There had been a shootout outside once, and my grandfather was involved; he shot a guy, who died.

"He ran into the restaurant and the owner was a friend of his, so he set a plate of half-eaten food in front of him, gave him a news-paper, and it looked like he had been eating the whole time. The owner testified he had been there the whole time. Saved his life."

Mark's own memories of his grandfather were warm and sweet. "He was a great guy." But it was only now, learning the truth, that he was able to understand certain things that had always puzzled him, like "why he always sat with his back to the wall at a restaurant." His own father had respected and loved him, but had kept his own career and life far removed from his sphere; he was a self-made man.

Oddly enough, Toby's paternal grandfather also had a hidden past, although of a very different kind. He was a German Jew, who as a young man had been imprisoned at Auschwitz with his family. Somehow his parents, desperate to save their only child, had man-aged even within those walls to bribe his way out. He had fled to America determined to round up enough money to free them in turn. One night while asleep he fell out of bed, as if hit. Only later did he learn that this had been the precise moment that his parents had perished in the gas chambers. He had no aunts, uncles, or siblings; other than a few distant cousins, he had no family left in the world. He had married, raised a son, and operated a small business in Philadelphia. Like many survivors, he had not been an observant Jew.

Toby's grandmother had told my husband the little she knew of his past; my husband's father, who died before Toby was born, had never spoken to his only child about the camps, about any of it. He kept his past sealed within him; my husband knew little about it. This had shocked me once, long ago. My husband, like myself, was a journalist; didn't journalists need to discover truth? But with the years, it shocked me less. All families, I had come to realize, even in this age of frankness, had their buried secrets. And perhaps, in the case of some, Beckett had been right—silence was the only honorable response.

Despite Mark's avowed hunger for money, guarantees, security, and toys—"I am the most materialistic bastard you ever want to meet"—his greatest love was for something that yielded none of these things: the game of football. "The rush, the adrenaline, the hitting, it's like a drug. I'm an addict."

He had not been in a street fight since eighth grade, but on the field—"Football's a violent sport and I love the violence in football." Once last year on Jayvee he had smashed into an opposing team's quarterback and heard "this scrunch. I was sitting on top of him, you're dead, motherfucker, you are dead—all my teammates were pulling me off—Mark, you're gonna get a flag! I was so psyched. His wrist was broke. I hurt that guy. It was great. I love the feeling."

He'd even had a dream once that he killed someone on a football field, "just hit 'em and they died. I was loving the dream. I sort of felt what I was doing was wrong, after it happened—but then I was loving the sympathy everyone was giving me, oh, Mark, are you okay? You must be so upset.

"And part of the dream, I was walking down the hall afterward and people were like, shit, don't fuck with Mark. He killed somebody. Interesting dream.

"In the dream, that stopped me from playing football. But nothing can stop me. I'll play it as long as I can." Mark prepared for games by "visualizing hurting people." He'd once seen an NFL interview with Dick Butkus. "He said he watched a horror movie where a baby's head was rolling down the steps, and he envisions something like that happening to people on the field, and not to him. And that's the type of vision I have when I'm on the field."

Bob's opinion that Mark needed confidence was not shared by his teammates, who felt he had more than enough and was not shy about expressing it. "He must've gotten a fortune cookie once that sicced him up or something," said one boy, a bit acidly. In fact, though, he was rarely silent on any subject. Mark was a talker.

Toriano, who loved to talk about himself, too, offered Mark a solution to what he saw as his problem. "He talks, but he doesn't talk about anything important. I told him, if you want something to talk about, I'll write down my stats for you. You can talk about them."

"I admit it, I do talk a lot," Mark said. He felt too, though, that "everybody feels they can talk to me openly. I'm not in any social group, any clique." At times he wished he was, "but I don't want to be a leech."

Sometimes he was almost shocked at the way some of the most popular guys acted, like around girls. "Some of these girls will do anything to go out with these guys, they want to be popular." And the boys knew it. He'd seen Billy and Toby once at a party, teasing a girl, making sexual suggestions, challenging her. "So, are we gonna do this? Are we gonna do that?" It had left a bad taste in his mouth, that scene, the way she had been lapping it up, just because she wanted their attention.

Yet individually, he knew these guys were actually pretty sensitive people. Once Rick had astounded him, talking about a girl— Rick, one of the cockiest of all. "He goes, she gets more and more beautiful every day." It had seemed so sweet, so romantic, so unlike Rick. That was the thing about not being in any particular group, people did feel free to talk to him that way, to reveal other, more vulnerable sides of themselves. He had actually been touched.

Of course that hadn't kept him from passing the comment on to Geoff immediately. "We ragged him for days."

He would have preferred to play fullback, but by now was fairly satisfied with this position, center. Plante, he thought, really knew how to build a line. Yeah, sure, the guy called him a bag of pus, but Mark didn't take offense—he was just trying to improve his playing. And they were improving. "Other teams might be bigger and stronger, but we're faster and smarter. I tend to think of us as analogous to David and Goliath." Like all the juniors, he was looking forward to next year the most.

The world had not stood still outside the B-CC locker room while the season was under way; events, political and other, continued to occur in that larger field, some having a direct effect on the boys inside.

The presidential campaign was nearly down to the finish line; the

second Bush-Dukakis debate was to take place this week, and most
of the boys would not have thought of missing it. As Washington-
area residents, they took a keen interest in national politics—this
was, after all, the town industry. Although unlike the rest of the
country, still basking in the fading glow of Reaganism, team, school,
and Montgomery County itself were largely Democratic; there were
few Republican strongholds at B-CC.

This year, in fact, one senior boy, Steve Pierson, a nonplayer, his
eye firmly cast on the extracurricular list on his college application
form, attempted to launch a Young Republicans Club at the school
for the first time. His friends showed up at the room, but allowed
him only a few moments of intro before they were on him, pelting
him to the ground with chalk, books, and insults. He got the point;
the Young Republicans Club was dropped. In retrospect, he
thought it had probably been a poor idea to start off with a song:
"If you're happy and Republican, clap your hands."

Oddly enough, the ongoing Republican campaign itself was making a direct impact on B-CC, though, because of one minor but
highly reported issue: George Bush's Pledge of Allegiance stand.

Officially, all Maryland students were supposed to recite the
pledge daily, but in fact, Montgomery County had dropped the
requirement in secondary schools some fifteen years back. Now
that Bush was harping on the pledge, however, school officials had
gotten uneasy. A nervous memo was sent to all high school prin-
cipals: get the pledge back in. Now. Students were not actually
required to say the words, but had to stand or sit quietly during the
recitation, the memo advised.

So for the first time in their high school careers, B-CC students
now began every school day listening to a recorded version of the
pledge ring out over the public-address system. All of them knew
exactly why this ritual had suddenly reappeared, and most were far
from pleased to find themselves pawns in Bush's game. "They
should at least wait until after the elections," said one senior, the
class vice-president. "I don't want to hear it and I don't want to say
it. It's my right to not even stand." Others blasted "Bush's ridiculous idea for gaining votes."

"It's all the Republicans' fault," said senior Jonah Davenport,
editor of the school's literary magazine. The pledge itself "seems
like servitude to your country."

Even the senior whose actual voice had been used to prerecord the pledge was unimpressed. "Just one other little annoyance in life," said Frankie Thompson. "There are better causes in the world to deal with."

"Hey, anything okay with George Bush is okay with me," cracked Matt Laessig, a basketball player. He, like everyone, was cynically aware that the Republican campaign ploy was the sole reason for the new policy.

Other fall events too served to underline cynicism. The Shroud of Turin was shown, at long last, to be a clever fake. In September Canadian Olympic track star Ben Johnson was hailed as a hero, then within days revealed as a user of anabolic steroids and stripped of his gold.

The problem of steroids was quickly brought closer to home. An October issue of *Sports Illustrated* contained a long, detailed confession by South Carolina lineman Tommy Chaikin about his own use of steroids. Chaikin was a local boy—one of the few Montgomery County students to find real success on a tough college field. Only a few years back, he had been a student at Whitman, B-CC's closest neighbor school and most intense rival.

Chaikin's admissions helped bring steroid use out of the closet. There was no question the drug was currently being used frequently by many college players; even among high school teams its use was far from unknown. Chaikin himself had never used steroids in high school, but in recent years the popularity of the drug had grown so widely, there had been a trickle-down effect.

The B-CC players didn't look or act as if they used juice, as it was called. I tended to believe their denials, in the same way (and for basically the same reason) I believed Toby when he said, "You *know* I never cheated in chem." Most, even those who had done some experimentation of their own with soft drugs, were rather horrified at the idea. "That stuff messes with the neurons in your brain," said Alex.

But everyone was sure there were players in the county who did use it. One player swore he had attended a party where he witnessed boys from another county team—a much more successful team—injecting themselves with the drug. Steroids were easily available, just like everything else was. No one doubted that for a minute.

At B-CC, many strongly suspected at least one particular boy, a nonplayer, of having done steroids. "He just got too big too fast," one boy said, and he was right; overnight the kid had turned into a tank. A few, who didn't know him well, had even muttered suspiciously about James, when he showed up at practice back in August so much bigger than before. "You better not ever say that to James," a friend warned. Those who knew him knew James did not even smoke and had come by his muscles honestly, through his efforts in the weight room. What's more, he had spent much more time developing the muscles above the waist than below, and steroids didn't work like that. With steroid use, you expanded all over, like a square.

Finally, a number of the boys were convinced Bob and Mitch had done a bit themselves. They were pretty damn big, too.

"It's very commonplace, juice," said Bob, shrugging, although he firmly exempted himself. "I can't deal with needles anyway." He did, however, know plenty of guys he worked out with at the health club who were his age, twenty-eight, and still using steroids, he said. That seemed ridiculous.

He saw a certain amount of steroid use as almost inevitable on football teams, though. "I can't fault the kid who does it. To him, at seventeen, the most important thing is winning a football game. Society puts that on kids. They say, hey, be the biggest and strongest, get all the women, all the praise . . . so why not stick a needle in your backside and get really strong? You talk about competition, looking for the edge."

The way to handle it, he was convinced, was with honesty. "You can't tell them, oh, don't do it, it's so bad for you, so terrible, your balls will shrink . . . 'cause a lot of that's bullshit.

"But you can say, go ahead, take steroids . . . but know that it will kill you. Give him the facts. It will make you stronger, you'll look bigger, you'll play for me for two years and look great and I'll look like a great coach. But then you'll be finished and you'll die, and I'll say, bye. What a dummy, stuck a needle in his butt."

Now, if it didn't hurt them . . . Bob sighed. He and Mitch had attended a high school football clinic, where a doctor had talked about steroids. "He said, out of every fifty football players, eight are on steroids. And Mitch and I just looked at each other. Eight? I wish we had three! Not eight, three!" Just a little humor, he assured me quickly.

Bob himself had taken pills while playing on his high school team, though he still wasn't sure whether they'd been speed or simply caffeine. "But we'd get pumped up as hell and rip guys' heads off." Anything for the game. These kids at B-CC, though, didn't seem to have that attitude.

What they should do, though, if they wanted to get bigger, he felt strongly, was simple—lift weights. "At this age, they've got all that natural testosterone. Now is when they can get the largest gains."

Most of the boys understood that in a college-football setting, the pressure to use steroids might be strong. Perhaps this was one more reason some of them, despite how much they loved the game, were wary of moving on to that next level. Rick, Geoff, Brendan Reed, Shane, James, and a few others among the seniors hoped to play in college, though they doubted it would be at the Division One, intensely competitive Oklahoma State level. But Dave, Toby, and Billy did not; even Alex, who hoped his football background would help get him into The Citadel, had grave misgivings about playing. College football was serious, a business, it involved money and pressure. How could it be the same? You were no longer doing it for love.

The week after WJ and homecoming went by swiftly, hurtling coaches and boys along the path toward their next contest, against Kennedy, Friday night. It was always that way, Pete thought: the losses left a dark cloud in their wake that seemed to last forever, while you hardly got a chance to enjoy the euphoria after a win before the next game was on you. Pete knew the boys had played fairly well last week. He also knew that "probably WJ played as poorly as they could play." So he was feeling at most "a little better, a little better." Nothing dramatic, mind you, just a slight tentative upward tilt.

Kennedy, too, shared some of the tough blue-collar image that adhered to Rockville, Wheaton, and Gaithersburg. Theirs was an

established program, always a plus for any team; the head coach
had been around several years. A couple of B-CC players had gone
to see them take on Blair last Saturday and emerged "really worried," said Tae Uk, especially about one oversized middle linebacker named Nigel, a markedly clear and present danger on the
field. No, this wasn't WJ, this team. There weren't gonna be any
more WJs, period.

But the guys were up for it. Psyched. That much was clear right
away to us in the stands. A lot of their early-season nervousness
had been blown out to sea forever. They'd weathered five games.
No matter what the outcome had been, they were novices no
more.

There was a breezy confidence in the way they marched out on
the home field to take on Kennedy, even—could it be?—a certain
cockiness. Possibly—face it, doubtlessly—they had no earthly right
to feel confidence. After all, what had they done but knock down
a team everyone else in the county had been stomping over?

But apparently this made no difference. Easy or not, the WJ win
had left a residue of self-assurance in its wake, like a jet stream. The
boys who ran out on the field tonight had attitude stamped all over
them, in the set of their shoulders, the roll of their gait. Joan
Wallace, Dave Bardach's mother, had noticed lately she was able to
pick out the football players in any crowd of boys. They stood
differently, moved differently; there was a dignity, a pride, even,
yes, a certain arrogance in the way they held themselves.

The Barons looked like football players tonight. And it was
quickly obvious that Kennedy, who'd happily written them off
completely, was in for something of a surprise. Last season
Kennedy had only edged out their win over B-CC in double
overtime, but that had been last season; they knew this year's
Barons were in deep trouble. Hell, everyone knew that.

Only the Barons themselves seemed blithely unaware.

The first quarter was a stalemate; neither team scored. "Why
don't they just play second halves?" Judy Burgess wanted to know.
No matter how feisty the boys looked, they always seemed to need
a certain amount of warm-up. Or something. Many of the boys
talked about the importance of the "first hit" of a game: it "fits you
to the game," one said, knocked away your nervousness; after that,
you were able to relax and play. And the odd thing, said another,

was it didn't matter at all whether you hit someone or got hit; the effect was the same.

Early in the second quarter, the entire team got its hit: Kennedy blocked a punt on the three-yard line and rammed it into the end zone for the six points. They missed the kick, but even so, that was it, the push B-CC needed. Now they were launched. Instantly, on the next B-CC drive, Dirkey Finley burst up the middle under firm offensive-line protection for the team's first touchdown. We howled our approbation.

It happened to be his own first varsity touchdown as well, and couldn't have happened at a better time. His mother, father, and six-year-old brother were in the stands. Later that night his brother Lionel, a former B-CC star player now in the service, would call and congratulate him. Only his little brother was a little confused about the excitement. "He kept saying, what's a touchdown? What's it for?" said Dirkey.

Dirkey's father, a railroad-station redcap, had played in his youth, and always encouraged his sons to play. For several years he had coached a Peewee football team in the area for his oldest son. Dirkey had been too young to play—they couldn't even get a helmet to fit him—but he'd insisted on coming to practice. Now it was his turn.

He'd taken a long time to get in shape this season—Pete would later crack that he had actually taken the full season to do it. But he had finally made it. He could fool around a lot, and did. "He's still young," Brendan Symes put it. But the boys had a lot of hopes for him; they felt once he came into his own he'd be a real force for good. "He's like a tank," Rick commented. An easygoing guy, unflappable, even-tempered, he was popular with all. "A little Milk Dud," they called him affectionately, one of the kids everyone was happy to see make it.

The kick was good, as almost all Eric's kicks were. We were up by one, and almost before we had time to even appreciate that fact, there was another explosion on the field: Geoff pulled Rick's pass neatly out of the air—an old familiar tune—for a 23-yard touchdown reception. Once again, the night was blue with our screams of pleasure. By God, WJ hadn't been a fluke! We were kicking ass again, right now! Against a real team!

Down on the field, the air was blue with something else: electrified, adrenalized, high as kites, attitude spurting out of every pore, the boys were talking trash to a fare-thee-well. Rick, whose patent intensity sometimes made even he wonder if in fact the position of quarterback really was the best place for him ("I probably should play defense"), was leading the pack.

"The middle linebacker just wanted me all game, he followed me everywhere on the field, and I kept laughing at him, I kept saying shit to him. When we'd score it'd be like, yeah, man—suck on *that.*" He knew silence was the best weapon, that nothing was more galling than when you looked up at some big guy gritting his teeth at you and just gave him "the widest grin you can muster up," right when he hit you. He knew it, but damn it, he couldn't always do it. He just got too intense, and when he did, "I talk a lot of shit."

Part of the reason Rick was so eager to rub the linebacker's face in B-CC's sudden good fortune was that the guy had gotten a really horrendous hit off on him right at the outset of the game. Rick, his butt still sore from a week ago, had found himself lifted up "by the back of my legs, shoulder and gut, and drilled right down to the ground." It hurt like crazy.

Tae Uk, feeling guilty—he had been the lineman who was supposed to handle the guy—ran up breathlessly. "Are you okay? Rick, Rick, are you okay?" Only to Rick, it sounded like "Prick, Prick." That was how it always sounded when Tae Uk said his name, and he didn't think it was an accident either, since Tae Uk usually giggled when he said it.

"Just get the fuck away," Rick growled, icy. "Chill out." In the huddle, everyone watched him warily. No one could get angrier than Rick, he could be a real lunatic. His anger, however, had soon cycled back to the Kennedy guy, where it could do some good, and stayed there.

The linebacker, though, would have the last word. At the end of the game, he tossed it out casually. "It's just a game, man, just a game," he said coolly.

"A guy who single-handedly abused me the whole game! That's the last thing I expected to hear from him. But the fact that I was coming back to him with all these comments made him think there was something wrong with me . . . I guess I was being an asshole," Rick said, reflectively.

Now, though, in this wild second quarter, was no time for reflection: they were in the heat of it. In the huddle Rick looked at each of the boys in turn; their eyes gleamed with a fire that matched his own. All of them focused, alive, completely, fully, unreservedly there. Had there ever been anything more real than this moment, right now? Tae Uk and Toby, breathless, begging: "Run the trap, run the trap. We can block this guy out." Geoff, intent: "I can get open, I can get open." All of them confident. Eager. At the top of their form, at last. This was the way it should be.

Later Toby would attempt to write down the all but inexpressible: how it felt to be on the line that night. To be *there.* "I hear the voice of my quarterback; imagine the intense expression of Coach Plante; mentally psyche myself up . . . hut, hut; almost completely without thought I pull around the right end and smack helmet to helmet with the cornerback; successful. Plante screams praise. Feel more pumped up than ever before. More intense than any feeling."

WJ had been a party, a romp, loose and crazy, a car with no brakes, a game with no real opposition. Blair had been pretty much the same. But Kennedy was starting to feel like something very different, and in the stands we looked at each other, excited, tense, almost fearful. We couldn't deny it, but almost shrank from saying it out loud. It was starting to look—could it be? could it really be?—like a true triumph.

It all depended on whether they could keep it up. The frenetic second quarter had put them up, 14–6, a nice margin but not overly comfortable by any means. More would be better. There was still another half to come. Several men, Sal Fiscina and my father among them, gave vent to these two opinions several times, darkly.

The rest of us were feeling no pain. Happy, light-headed, we felt relaxed enough to chatter merrily about less important matters. The presidential election, for instance. Had yesterday's debate pulled the plug on Dukakis for good? A lot of their friends, said Carole Stone, were voting their pocketbooks. Others nodded. I intended, I announced suddenly, to vote my uterus. It was, I realized, exactly the sort of riposte one comes up with after several glasses of wine. The game had given me a genuine buzz. We agreed quickly that Dukakis was an icicle, Bush was a wimp, the campaign a fiasco, the country in deep trouble. Thank God we at least had better things to think about. Halftime ended; we turned back eagerly to the contest we cared about, the one on the field.

The offense had shown their muscle last quarter, but it was clear now they weren't the only ones shining out there tonight. Defense—"where the men hang out," as Kong put it—was electrifying the field. Playing, as the sports announcers liked to put it, for keeps. Stopping Kennedy in its tracks.

Again and again that second half they would amaze and delight us—managing by the end to rack up no less than four turnovers. Brendan Reed grabbed two interceptions; Dave, another, in a one-handed pickoff one smitten fan described later as nothing short of spectacular. And John Han recovered a fumble.

Standing on the field, holding the ball, suddenly it all made sense to him—why he was here. At times John wondered why he even played. He truly did not like getting hit, either physically, on the field, or psychologically, by Bob or Mitch. Mitch's manner of coaching, in fact, reminded him of his sister when she tried to tutor him in chemistry. A chem whiz, now winging her way through med school, she would be a doctor like their surgeon father, and unlike him, be able to practice here; he had emigrated from Taiwan too late in life to make the change. She just couldn't understand why John couldn't get it right. It seemed so easy to her. She'd try to explain, once, twice, then finally get frustrated and walk off.

Mitch was like that with football, John thought. He saw so clearly how it should be done that he couldn't believe you didn't. That you weren't purposely thwarting him. Only Pete White knew how to explain something without making you feel terrible if you didn't catch on right away. "Coach White knows we're human."

But out on the field tonight, John knew why he hung in through all the bad times, why he kept hanging in. It was for the glory, plain and simple. "Just being out their with your pads on, like going into war, and people cheering you on and watching . . . being under the lights, with that many fans . . . it's just a feeling that's unbelievable. That's what I really love. Because it really isn't fun, varsity football, but it was a thrill being out there, to be one of the few who could do battle, and be recognized."

He was not however talking trash on the field, which made him a rare B-CC player tonight. As far as talking trash went, he couldn't see the point of it, even though God knows Mitch had urged them to often enough.

"Mitch was always telling us to go crazy. When someone tackles you, hurt him. Hurt him. That's the point to the game. Hit him so hard he can't get up and you won't have to play with him anymore. Cripple him. Cripple him for life." Talking was just another part of the process. But for John, it went against reason. "If anything, the other player's gonna get more mad, tear your head off."

Dave, too, kept his mouth shut, but for slightly different reasons. After all, he was the captain, the head of the defense; he had to set an example for these people. Sometimes the players just seemed like a bunch of little kids to him—fighting, kicking, cursing. Then he'd have to calm them down, pull them apart, yell at them to shut up—you couldn't count on the refs to handle it. Talking trash used up a lot of energy—Dave preferred to throw his into the game. Especially now, when he couldn't run like he used to be able to—the ankle injury was still slowing him down.

Christo Doyle, on the other hand, had taken to talking trash with the zeal of a convert, and was truly coming into his own tonight. "Some games you do more talking than others—Kennedy was just out of control," he said. He had come to feel, under Mitch's tutelage, that one of the best things about football was "intimidating people and saying stuff to them," and he was enjoying the operation heartily. ("Christo kills me," laughed Mike Mitchem later. "He's like a black guy. 'Whut? Whut you say? You ain't nothin'.' ")

"I was blitzing the entire game." He sacked the quarterback again and again, each time making sure the guy knew who'd done it. "I'm back again, man," he'd say, just to remind him. "And I'm gonna keep coming back every time." Then he'd push off him, stepping over him like he was dead meat—"don't come near me again, man"—maybe spitting on him, too, for emphasis. Just like Mitch said to do.

Because he had come to believe the coach was right—this was the essence of the game. You acted like that and just hoped to hell "you don't run into them later at McDonald's or something." By this game, he'd gotten pretty good at walking over opposing players, though occasionally he still slipped. At one point Jimmy Loreto saw him hold out his hand to help a guy up after a hit, then look up to the box where Mitch was sitting, stop short, and drop the kid's hand like a hot potato. Everyone knew how Mitch felt about that kind of thing.

"So much fun, so much fun," said Geoff Heintz. "A tough game, a tough team. We chased them all over the place."

"Solid, businesslike," thought Alex. He heartily approved of the way the game was going, and he felt sure that proper pregame preparation, always his chief concern, had had something to do with it. For once, he had been able to convince the linemen to isolate themselves—and stay isolated. "Everyone had been in the wrestling room, sitting, the way it should be done. And that's why we were doing so well."

Defense continued to reign. The Kennedy offense could not get a foothold, no matter how they pushed. Late in the third, B-CC offense drove down into field-goal position. Eric Bachman sent the ball flying with perfect accuracy for thirty-nine yards, putting us up 17–6. "Up" was the right word, all right—standing, screaming, arms stretched high as the sky. Oh, if only we didn't blow this one.

Then came a scare, a bad one. Jimmy Loreto, who so rarely got a crack at playing quarterback, who waited patiently game after game for his chance, was told to go in for Rick. A bit nervous, a bit off kilter—it was never easy to wait in the wings so long and then suddenly get thrown out on the field—he lobbed a pass at Brendan Reed.

The minute it left his hands he knew it was a bad throw. Fear clutched his stomach like a vise. Frozen in horror, unable to move, he watched as a Kennedy player stepped smoothly in front of Brendan, caught the ball, his body whirling toward the end zone . . .

And dropped it. Square on the ground. "I was, oh, thank God. It was the worst feeling. I realized what I did. I knew that guy was going to step in front of him . . . thank God." He was saved and so were we all. The hosannas erupted with revival-tent fervor.

And now there were no more scares. No chills, no terrors, no more quarters, no chance at all they were going to take it away. Too late! Too late for all of them! We stood cheering those last few minutes, a wall of sound, screaming down the clock, roaring it into its final seconds, as the whistle finally blew and the boys bellowed their victory to the sky.

If WJ had been cake, Kennedy was wine, pure vintage wine.

Sheer golden honey, the honey of true victory, pulsed through all our veins, throbbing, sensual, sizzling, a long, sweet jazz trumpet note held forever. "Solid. A solid win," said Mark Bitz. "We were good. We played them hard. We won against a tough opponent. Satisfying. Real satisfying, to walk off the field after that game."

It looked it. If last week they had been joyful and glowing making that march up the stadium steps, this week they were something else ... grander, more imposing, hulking, their giant shadows looming over everyone. Chieftains they were, Vikings, titans, kings of the night. Beyond us all, far beyond, way out there in space somewhere, hurtling toward distant horizons. Beyond the law.

"WE CAN DO ANYTHING." That was how they felt; that was what my own son roared at us, stalking up the steps, reaching out to tap his father on the chest, one brusque pat which very nearly collapsed him to the ground. "WE CAN DO ANYTHING."

"You get an incredible natural high after a win, and Kennedy was just ... unbelievable," said Billy.

"You can't compare it to anything else," Geoff said. "I'm eighteen and I've yet to encounter any other situation with that euphoria. Utopia! You win a game like that, it's a sense of utopia. Indescribable."

Manifestly, without reservation, they were all up there tonight. They had done it: it had worked. They were untouchable, they were invincible, they were—it had never seemed so absolutely true before—the men.

"Mothers of Bethesda," muttered one man, watching them move past, "lock up your daughters tonight."

Months later, many months later, a terrible story would appear in the news. The star high school football players in a small New Jersey town had been arrested for sexually molesting a young retarded girl. The arrests came long after the incident; the townspeople, all fans, had allegedly known and buried the story for months. Papers and news magazines were filled with commentary for weeks about the ugly forces that could erupt when adolescent impulse was fueled by arrogance—the blinding arrogance of a star athlete—and adoration, the worshipful adoration of a football-crazed community. Platitudes, perhaps simplistic, yet was there not a ring of truth to it? A true morality tale, this, and the commentators milked it for all it was worth. The dark side of being the man.

And I wanted to fight, to reject even the wisp of possibility at once, to say no, no, this could never happen with our boys, who I knew to be kind, caring, solid, incapable of such infamy.

Yet the question kept pressing in at me insistently: What if all the games had been like Kennedy? A tough game, a crushing victory, a valiant rival slain on the field; a triumphant stomp through the stadium, past hordes of cheering fans, all those eyes, wide and worshipful, all those hands reaching out humbly, just to touch. WE CAN DO ANYTHING. What if Kennedy had not been the first, but the sixth game like that this year? What then?

What effect would that kind of intoxicant—for it was an intoxicant, perhaps more powerful than any other, no way around that—have had on all of them? On Alex, Geoff, Rick, Dave, Billy, Toby, all the rest? Even Eric Knaus? How would each of them have changed, how would we all have changed, whirled up, up, up into a crescendo of golden victory, game after game, higher and higher, each a headier brew than the last?

Maybe it was just as well we'd never know.

Maybe we'd been damn lucky.

We pressed through the crowd, my husband reeling a bit from the afterglow of his son's caress. "Jesus, it still hurts," he muttered several times, to very little sympathy. I was soaring, just like the boys, far beyond the reach of middle-aged complaints. At home I posted a large note on Toby's door—"Our hero!" It would embarrass him, of course, but who cared? God knows when he'd see it anyway. Earlier this year, in a Booster membership letter, I had written that football always meant fear, to a parent—"fear when they lose, because they come home and kick the cat, dog, furniture, or family members; fear when they win because then they celebrate by going out and doing God knows what." Overly cutesy, of course—hey, it was a Booster letter—but not off base. Even as I heated up cider for my husband and my parents, so we could sit around the kitchen enjoying the win just a little longer, I knew inside: tonight was a God-knows-what night for sure.

In the locker room, though, for all the hoots, hollers, and fervent embraces, it was not the thought of celebration that riveted the boys, at least not yet. That would come later. Now it was quite another thought that swept through the narrow room, seizing each of them in turn, electrifying their souls, magnetizing their raging energy. One word. One word only. Whitman.

It leapt from player to player, throat to throat, like an electric current, zigzagging crazily, wildly, spark after spark, until every boy had joined the roar, every boy stood yelling, banging fists on the metal locker doors: Whitman! Whitman! WHITMAN! WHITMAN! WHITMAN!

We can do it! We can take them! We can smash them! Yes!

The Barons were three and three now. Gone was the hope of an undefeated season, gone the hope of state championship, disappeared in the dust, almost without a trace. It didn't matter, not at all. Not now. None of it mattered, because of what they knew this night, after their ferocious win. They were good. They had overcome. They could prevail. They could take Whitman.

Whitman, their brother school, barely three miles away. Their greatest rival down through the years. Whitman, who for the first time in its history had been undefeated on the football field all season. Smashed Churchill! Smashed Einstein! Smashed them all, in six straight wins. And were sure, sneeringly sure, lazily, contemptuously, bone-deep sure, that they were ordained to run over B-CC, leaving no more than a dull stain on the ground, the kind you saw after a small animal got in the way of one of those tractor trailers careening around the Beltway.

But the Barons were not going to let it happen. Not after tonight, not after what they'd done out there on the field, not after what they'd learned about themselves.

For they knew it now in their blood. We can get them. We can stop them. We can do it. We can beat Whitman.

WE CAN DO ANYTHING.

CHAPTER THIRTEEN

THE BOYS eventually dispersed to various parties to celebrate their win, reveling late into the night, but in a strange sense, their hearts weren't really in it. Their hearts were back in the locker room where in the flush of victory they had pledged themselves so fiercely to the battle just ahead. For the first time ever, the 1988 Barons had known the indescribable thrill of feeling, as Kong put it once, that "our destiny was in our hands." Parties were pretty small potatoes compared to that.

There followed a week of practice unlike any other yet that season. The boys had put in good weeks before, hard, determined, and steady. But nothing matched this week for intensity. Bob and Mitch were amazed. Could it be? Maybe finally these guys were beginning to catch on; maybe finally they had begun to make a real impact on the team.

From top to bottom the boys radiated energy, dedication, assurance—in a word, attitude, attitude, attitude. Daily they showed up on the field, all of them tough, determined, ready to work long hours, ready to learn, ready to practice plays again and again and again. Whatever it took. Ready at last, the coaches realized with deep satisfaction, to win.

And the coaches too were ready. Over the weekend Mitch had spent hours developing new defense maneuvers guaranteed to paralyze Whitman. He showed up Monday waving a thick stack of complicated new plays, most of them far more appropriate to college playing fields than high school. "How the hell can we learn all this by Friday night?" the guys groaned. "I mean, it's Monday morning, we have four days to prepare for Whitman, he throws in three brand-new types of defense, like what the hell is going on?" said Geoff.

But the groans were made only to each other, and they were mild ones at that. The boys wanted to win, and the man was giving them the tools to do it. They knew it. So forget the complaints. The point was to knuckle down and work. Dave as always did duty as Mitch's interpreter—"the one man," Mitch would admit, "I cannot do without." Without Dave to grasp the technicalities of these new plays, then pass them on to the other players, he knew his job would have been all but impossible. Dave shouldered the responsibility; he was proud to be the one Mitch trusted most. Yet at times it was a burden, too, handling the other guys, like an older kid forced to baby-sit younger brothers. Sometimes the strain got to him, and he snapped. "People will tell you, at times I was hell, man—I was hated," he said. "But everyone was depending on me, everyone put pressure on me." He could not allow himself to truly bond with the other players; he had to keep himself a little aloof, in order to lead them. He saw the necessity, but felt the isolation of his position, too. He had a hard job this season, as well as a bad ankle that was still giving him trouble. There wasn't much room for joy.

Bob Plante, too, had been doing paperwork: he had drawn up a fiendishly complex chart for the offense. "He'd worked hours on this offense plan, it showed the positioning, had everything down, where you go on every play, offside tackle, onside tackle. It had taken him eight hours, figuring it out," said Toby. He overheard Mitch and Pete congratulating him. "They said, how did you do that, it's amazing, there are even colleges where they don't do that."

You had to respect a guy like that. "He was never just going through the motions," said Toby. And neither were any of the boys, this week. They had earned this battle and they weren't about to screw it up.

There were, of course, one or two minor glitches on the screen. Eric Bachman, playing wide receiver, which he dearly loved— kicker was such a lonely position—had broken his hand during the Kennedy game, he discovered later, and in three separate places to boot. He had thought—hoped at least—it was just a bruise, even while it continued to swell to the point that he had to tear off his glove, to the point that his hand had become all but useless on the field, bringing Rick's ever-ready wrath down on his head. "Bachman, what the hell are you doing? Can't you hold on to anything?" ("He felt pretty bad later when he found out it was broke.")

Luckily for the team, they could do without Eric's hand. It was his foot they counted on. As long as he wore a soft cast covering his hand, he'd be able to play.

Shane Dempsey, who had already experienced his share of frustration at not getting enough play this season, also sustained an injury this week, but off the field. Way off. He had just sat down at a draft table in architecture class one morning, generally a fairly safe procedure, when a metal lever attached to the table suddenly sprang up, smashing him on the forehead. Blood gushed out of the cut; nine stitches were required to sew it up. "Can I still play this week?" Shane asked the doctor.

"Sure, if you want to rip out the stitches and maybe need plastic surgery," said the doctor, shrugging. Shane decided to opt out. Billy and Toby's doctors had issued death threats, to no avail. Someone had obviously taught Shane's doctor a thing or two about teenage boys.

Of course, Shane's injury was on the forehead, in helmet range, which made it difficult to ignore. Toby and Rick had already discovered what a massive irritant even a mere zit could be when it popped up in that area. Toby had taken to wearing an adhesive pad under a headband, to gird his forehead against the helmet's pressure. Both boys now screamed lustily whenever they donned their headgear. Oddly, neither had pimples anywhere else—only the single bull's-eye pinpoints in the center of their foreheads.

Toriano was still out with his leg in a cast, for at least two more weeks. "Without me, the two games I'd missed, we were two and oh. Felt really great," he said sarcastically. That was one stat he could have done without. James, of course, was out for good, though he stuck close, rarely even missing practice—this was still his team, after all. It felt bad, real bad, yet in a way it was interesting, too, being the observer, removed. James liked to study people—sometimes he thought he'd like to be able to put people in a little terrarium and just watch the things they did. It was fascinating. Dave, for instance, strutting around, full of himself, bellowing at everyone, now that James was off the field and he could take all the glory. Annoying—but interesting too, at the same time.

Everyone else was able-bodied—relatively, at least. Aches, pains, strains, zits, and bruises didn't count. Who didn't have them by now? Back during the Einstein game Toby had sustained a bad hit in the shoulder. After a few days of pain he allowed me to take him to a sports doctor, who told him he had a bad bruise. Bob Plante, hearing this, had been scathing. "You have a BRUISE? You have a BRUISE? Get the hell back on that field!"

The sense of single-minded purpose that had bloomed the night of the Kennedy win showed no signs of dissipating. The boys poured their energies that week into one goal and one goal only: forging themselves into a mighty missile aimed straight at Whitman's heart. Undefeated, eh? About to take it all, are you? We'll see about that.

The two Bethesda schools had been locked in rivalry nearly forever, and not just on the football field. Basketball, soccer, academic scores, even chorale groups—there was scarcely an area of student enterprise considered outside the pale of competition. And the rivalry tended to slop over from one arena to another, too. During a basketball game last year which B-CC was clearly dominating, the cheers coming from the Whitman side had suddenly taken on a new character. The cries of "DEE-fense!" had stilled; chanting loudly, pounding their feet, angry Whitman fans were now roaring for "SATs, SATs!" In the arena of scholastic scores, Whitman had been the clear champion for years; now, with their basketball team going down in defeat, seemed a good time to remind everyone of that.

Separated by only a few short miles, the two schools nonetheless differed sharply in character. B-CC, with its wildly diverse student body and city surroundings, had a scruffy urban air; Whitman, whose green lawns were nestled in a rich residential neighborhood, with not a store in sight, was predominately white, preppy, suburban, far more the sort of school people thought of when they thought of Montgomery County: the all-but-private institution.

Both were neighborhood schools, at least for the most part, though there was always a certain amount of traffic in and over county lines, with the address flim-flam game far from unknown (later in the year one B-CC boy would be caught—his family had moved into the District months earlier, but managed to hide this fact from officials). But B-CC's boundary lines extended into less affluent Silver Spring, incorporating apartment complexes, areas of modest homes, and inevitably, many more black and Hispanic families. Whitman's population was far more homogeneous, white, and upper middle class. Some county residents considered this a plus, and went to some pains to move into the Whitman school district; others, urban roots yearning, had taken similar pains to move out.

Still, different or not, the schools were close. Most B-CC kids had good friends at Whitman and vice versa; dating between the two student populations was common. So the rivalry had the familiarity and affection, as well as the to-the-death intensity, of that between siblings. Kong explained it carefully: "I don't really hate Whitman. I just want to beat them. It's a rivalry. I don't despise them, don't want to go out on the streets, see a Whitman guy and go 'I hate you.' It's . . . a tradition. I always want to beat them."

They had almost not made it the year before—only a wild last millisecond pass thrown by Rick to senior Rick Thadey, who managed to defy all laws of nature by coming down from a stupendous leap with his feet just in-bounds, had saved them. Back in the locker room, Pete had been matter-of-fact: "Well, you didn't deserve to lose last week [that had been the heartbreaking overtime loss to Kennedy] and you didn't deserve to win this week," he told them. Then the grin cracked out, ear to ear: "But we'll take it, we'll take it." It was the sort of game that convinced Billy that when it came to Whitman, at least, God was on their side.

There was nothing wrong with thinking that, this week. They needed to hold on to a few solid notions like that, now that Whitman had gone off the boards and was stomping its way into championship territory. Unbelievable, yet there was no way to avoid the facts: the Whitman Vikings, who had rarely managed to pull in more than a four-win season for years, had now gone six straight games undefeated. Last week, while the Barons had been battling Kennedy, they had rolled over B-CC's first-game nemesis, Wooten, like cream on Jell-O, a 28–0 rout.

No question, there was a different breed of Viking out there this year. Overnight the team had become top-heavy with stars, an embarrassment of riches, from quarterback Patrick Denney to running back Antoine White and receiver Ryan Kuehl—who was, incidentally, only the most notable among five quite capable receivers, as their coach was quick to point out. They had started the season flaunting a bold passing game, but as a recent *Montgomery County Journal* story had announced in screaming boldface, "Whitman can run, too!" So they could—they had run Rockville, for instance, straight off the field.

Nor were they taking this newfound glory with anything that passed even remotely for quiet pride. Flying high, their collective egos had taken off for the stratosphere. Frankly, they were full of themselves. And obviously—certainly to B-CC—they were in dire need of a pounding. It could almost, at this point, be considered an act of charity.

Conventional wisdom said that they had to fail eventually. But Whitman was having none of that. According to rumor they had already prepared enormous "Seven Games Undefeated" signs days after their sixth win, so sneeringly confident were they of their ability to wipe B-CC off the map. The game had even been arranged to coincide with Whitman's homecoming weekend—the traditional slot for the automatic easy win—yet another goad, had they needed it, to our guys. But Whitman wasn't taking off this week either. Last year's final seconds had stung hard. The Vikings were looking for blood, in shades of Baron blue.

At B-CC the intensity continued. The boys came home after long practices exhausted, almost unable to eat, completely unable to do more than glance at their schoolwork before stretching out flat— "just for a few minutes," Toby assured me, four nights running— and falling into deep, unassailable stupors. Their focus this week was total; nothing outside the field was quite real.

"Don't be intimidated by these guys," Mitch yelled at them. "They're seventeen, same as you! You can take 'em! You can do it!" And, by God, he was right, they roared back at him, feeling the truth of it to the very bottom of their souls. Yes! Yes! We can do it! All the hopes of the entire season had come down to this. We may never go to the playoffs. We may never be state champions. But we can do this. We can beat Whitman. And we will.

Friday the boys awoke to a dead gray sky, which true to the unanimous weather predictions began almost at once to emit a heavy, steady downpour. No one minded that. The boys loved playing in the rain, the muddier the better. But as the school day progressed and the rain poured on unremittingly, nervous qualms began to grow. Nearly every boy made it down to the main office at least once to check. Had the county canceled games yet? Was there any chance they would? Are you sure?

"We were so psyched," said Geoff. He and Toby shared an eighth-period art class, and spent the entire time revving each other up. "The whole period, we're like, God, I wish it were time for the game. I've never been more excited for a football game in my life.

"We were going to the office every five minutes, oh God, the game's gonna be canceled, the game's gonna be canceled . . . no, the game's not canceled."

One minute before the end of school—at 2:24 P.M.—the announcement rang over the PA system. The varsity game against Whitman had been canceled. "Postponed to a later date," said the coolly dispassionate voice.

It was a bad blow. "We were on the verge of tears," said Geoff, "me, Toby, Billy, Kong. . . ." Miserable, deflated, the boys gathered in the locker room. Paranoia was rife. Rumors of a giant plot, of cabals operating at the highest reaches of county officialdom, who had decided for reasons of their own to deny them this crucial battle, circulated freely. "They didn't need to do it," said Christo. "They knew how bad we wanted it, how ready we were, they wanted to put it off, put us off."

Bob Plante did his best to cheer them up, especially when word finally came down late in the afternoon that the game would be played Saturday night, exactly twenty-four hours later than scheduled. "It's worse for them, don't you see? Tomorrow night's their homecoming dance. They'll have their minds on their *dates*," he sneered.

That at least sounded sensible to the boys. At any rate, they were up against an immovable wall with a vengeance—there was no one to hit, no one to blame. They'd just have to handle it as well as they could.

"It's hard, we're so psyched." That was the most common statement of the day, voiced by nearly every boy at least once, and feelingly. We parents understood. How could it not be hard, to work up that kind of energy all week long, only to have to postpone it? But they handled it well, even with a certain maturity. Difficult as it was, they were not going to fall apart; they were not going to let something as minor as a twenty-four-hour postponement—no matter how frustrating—make any crucial dents in their armor. They'd worked too hard to give this one up.

Several went out for the evening with friends briefly, making it a point to be home at a decent hour—a self-imposed curfew. A few—Billy, Toby, Brendan Symes—were home at an hour even more decent than they'd intended, since the party they were at was raided at ten-fifteen. Parties in Montgomery County were nearly always raided; this was only a little earlier than most. Raids themselves were far from upsetting; actually, both parents and kids counted on them. After a certain length of time had passed, a certain amount of loud music had been played, after car after car had driven up, the cops would arrive and tell everyone to go home. This was a "raid," suburban style, though what it most resembled was the phenomenon of a parent stalking up the stairs, telling the kids to turn off the stereo and go to sleep, enough's enough.

They worked too, those raids; we parents all felt safer knowing no party could go on too long or get too out of hand. When Toby attended a St. Alban's party in D.C. some time back, he had been genuinely shocked—the cops had taken so long to show up that several fights had broken out, he said indignantly. What was the matter with D.C. cops anyway?

Tonight, all the Barons were home early. And the clean living actually did bring a reward, I discovered later. After the football guys went home, their friends continued on to another party, stopping to talk to a friend at a deli—a deli that unfortunately was under surveillance for the evening by county narcs, who hoped to spot a drug buy. As the kids pulled away, cops surrounded the car with guns. The boys were searched, and one of them was found to have a single joint in his pocket. All the boys were then charged, and one, just turned eighteen (not the one with the joint), was jailed for half the night. His mother, a good friend of mine, had been forced to lose a night's sleep getting him out. To most of us parents that seemed by far the worst part of the story.

As for the kids (excepting perhaps the one with the joint) obviously nothing much was going to come ultimately of such overzealousness, which reminded me of the Great Beer Sweep of a few years back—once again the boys had been in the wrong place at the wrong time. But I was grateful my son wasn't in the car, where he could have so easily been—football had spared us this time. At the same time it was chilling to realize the apparent ramifications of the new drug war. Were parents now responsible for checking the pants pockets of every teenager who rode in a car with one of our kids during an evening? If so, we were all dead.

Saturday arrived gray, chilly, foreboding, but mercifully dry. By noon most of the boys had already assembled at school; far too early for a 7:30 P.M. game, but their impatience overrode reason. Sitting around the house was out of the question. It was better to be together. Pete brought in a large supply of Pepperidge Farm goldfish for sustenance. Between conversation, concentration, and crackers, the boys did their best to refortify themselves, determined to work their way back to the point they'd been at just before yesterday's 2:24 announcement.

Pete's day had started poorly, with a call from player Wayne Meadows. Nominally the team punter, Meadows actually had played very little this year; over the weeks he'd reported so many illnesses and injuries that many of the boys were convinced he was purposely malingering. Now he told Pete he'd be out for this game too. While sweeping up yesterday at McDonald's, where he worked part-time, he had tripped on a curb and broken his leg. Annoyed as he was, the coach knew the kid was telling the truth. Who could make up a story like that?

Ordinarily, though Meadows was a good punter, Pete wouldn't have much minded—they'd done without him often enough. The backup punter, however, was Eric Bachman, who had a broken hand. Pete called him right away. "Can you believe our punter's broken his leg?" he said. "Can you catch the ball from the snap?"

Eric was honest. "I don't know, I can try," he said. If he couldn't, they'd have to use Billy, Pete knew. Billy was a good practice punter, but in the game, "he's such an excitable person that he's not very good at it." Eric said he'd do his best.

Pete said a silent prayer. They couldn't afford to lose anyone else. Luckily, all the boys were in the locker room early, hours before the bus left for Whitman. Even Christo, whose father was getting remarried today. Everyone. Except . . . where the hell was Dirkey? Did anyone know anything about Dirkey?

He had gone home yesterday before hearing the new time for the game, someone said; he must have thought it was rescheduled for Monday. And Dirkey's phone was out of order, so no one could call him. "Well, goddamn it, someone's gonna have to get in touch with him, then," Pete fumed. And damn it, he should've known, he should've found out . . . How about Toriano? He lived near Dirkey . . . could he find someone else in the neighborhood to get over to his house?

Somehow, someone got the word to him: Dirkey walked in minutes before the bus left for Whitman. "He wanders in like what's going on, guys?" said Pete. The coach just rolled his eyes. Up at Seneca Valley, where they had seventy guys on the team, if someone pulled that kind of stunt you could ream them out. What the hell's wrong with you! Why the hell didn't you call someone! Your ass ain't dressing tonight, no way!

But at B-CC you couldn't afford that sort of temper-tantrum relief. "Hey, we need him! So we're like . . . well, we're about to *play,* Derek, is what it is, we've got this *game,* see—get the hell dressed! Hurry up, get dressed!" No way was anyone they needed going to be sidelined tonight, especially not a tough little fullback like Dirkey. He dressed quickly, with his usual equable good nature, and boarded the bus.

The Barons were on their way. The Battle of Bethesda, Montgomery Marty had dubbed it a few years back, when the two teams had seemed evenly matched. No one was calling it that this year. None of the local sports gurus were even expecting much of a contest.

They hadn't talked to the Barons. The Battle of Bethesda was about to begin.

They had managed to recharge themselves, against all odds, against the grim onslaught of nature itself. We saw it at once, sitting up in Whitman's bleachers. The guys had actually done it, gotten back up to that pitch, that high note of readiness they had worked so hard for all week long. Watching them run out on Whitman's field in front of the jam-packed stands, with the cold wind blowing hard between the posts, it was shiningly clear: they had managed once again to whip up and wrap that fabulous scarf of confidence and belief around themselves, thicker than ever, a shield against the elements. We exchanged looks excitedly, reading the truth in each other's eyes: this was going to be a game.

"Every person on the team believed," said Jimmy simply. "Every person. In our minds, we were so positive."

Tension, yes—there was tension before every game—and before this, the most important game of all, the tension had mounted, over the week, over the long long hours of delay, to an almost unbearable level. The tension of excitement, nervousness . . . and fear, too, of course.

"We try to hide it," said Kong, whose toughness was admired by everyone. "But I think everybody's scared inside." Yet the fear was not just of pain, or injury, even crippling, life-threatening injury. No, it was simpler than that. What if I'm the one who messes up? That was the worst fear.

Toby had talked about needing to overcome his inner fear in order to go all-out . . . talked about it, in other words, after the fact. For the most part the boys avoided discussing fear in the present— past fear was easier to deal with. Rick never forgot going up against a huge black defensive lineman when he was only fourteen—the way the guy had leaned over menacingly and growled, "I want WHITE MEAT." "I'm like—Mom, waaah!" he joked, recalling. Mike Reese, Brendan Reed's stepdad, remembered "guys pissing in the huddle" out of fear back in his day. But that too was past, far past. Present fear was harder to confront. Kong was right, nearly everyone was scared inside; everyone knew it, everyone did their best to hide it.

But on this night, much of the fear had been submerged. The boys were connected by a golden chain of certainty, and the chain itself acted as a support. We can do this thing. All of us. And we will. "We believed in ourselves," said Geoff. Never before, it seemed to him, had the team been so together, so totally committed, so unified in their belief. More than brothers, more than friends; bonded in spirit.

Mitch, who had worked so hard all week on defense plays, took his men off to the side before the start for one of his patented emotional charges. "He squeezed a tear for us before almost every game," said Toriano, who was a bit of a cynic. But others, like Kong, couldn't help being swayed. The guy cared so much! Now he read them a poem—"The Man in the Mirror." If you could satisfy the man in the mirror, you could feel good about yourself. That's all any of you have to do. Be the best *you* can be.

He stared at them hard, his blue eyes like chips of steel, his voice hoarse. Now go get those bastards.

Bob, of course, eschewed poetry. "Plante? Read a poem? It would be like he showed up wearing a dress," John Han said. Bob and Pete concentrated on giving the guys the final goad, that little extra push they always believed in. Hey, maybe Whitman *had* thought postponing the game would help! Maybe that's all they thought they had to do to win. After all, this was their *homecoming,* they were expected to win, undefeated team and all that.

You gonna take that? You gonna let 'em have it? You gonna give them this one too?

Get the hell out on that field and KILL!!

And the boys charged out into the fray. For the first time all year, there was no hesitation, no shrinking back. The Barons went all-out from the first whistle. Marching out on Whitman's field, they grabbed the ball like they owned it and smashed themselves downfield for a touchdown—Rick running it in from a few yards out—before the first two minutes had elapsed. It was pure relief, to finally release some of that force that had been building up so long. We were caught by surprise, awed and exhilarated; our screams erupted almost violently. Eric's kick was good—perfect. The cast on his hand was no problem.

Our shock at this explosive start was nothing compared to that of Whitman's, players and fans alike. Like a giant beast they howled in pain, furious at the unexpected wound—what the hell was this?—and fought back hard. Before the first quarter was out, they too had scored, their amazing rb, Antoine White, rushing fifty-five yards for the touchdown. No, these guys were no paper tigers. No one had expected they would be.

But their kick failed, and the score stood at 7–6, B-CC's favor. Now the battle began to rage in earnest. The Vikings would not again be caught dozing at the wheel, as in the first vital seconds— and as for us, that early wild burst of success had had an almost mystical aura. How could the boys ever achieve the absolute brilliance of that one perfect moment again—when every single player had been filled with the same exalted purpose? It had been magic, and magic—motivation, as Pete called it—all the emotion in the world, could only take you the first ten plays. Maybe the first quarter. After that it came down to skill.

So the game became a clash of defensive skills, the ball going first to one team, then the other. Eric had worried about punting with his bad hand; the guys had assured him confidently they'd make sure the punting was kept at a minimum. Some minimum. Down the field, punt; down the field, punt. Eric had never seen a game with more punts in his life.

The giant psyche—"It's like an orgasm, the psyche," Mike Mitchem had said, "it's great, but then it's over"—had popped early on, but the boys were finding their rhythm; they were not folding, they were not bailing out. They were relying on skills, but they had spent a long hard week honing those skills, and now, in the brink, they were not being found remiss. Whitman's fury and rage were all too obvious. They had not expected this sort of fight—hey, they were 6 and 0, goddamn it! They struck back hard, hard and not terribly clean. When a number of what seemed like glaring Whitman penalties to us had gone by uncalled, Sal Fiscina, sitting low in the stands for once, shook his head, his hound-dog face drooping lower than usual. "They're giving it to them, the refs are going to give them the game," he muttered, disgusted. "Homecoming."

But the referees were finally galvanized into action when a knot of ferociously hyped-up Whitman players on the sidelines roared toward Geoff as he careened out of bounds for a pass, lifted him up, and before our stunned eyes, literally upended him over the chain-link fence.

To us watching in the stands, in horror, it was only Geoff's incredible coordination that allowed him to twist in midair and avoid smashing down on his head; only his amazing control that allowed him to jump back onto the field, hands held out, palms up—cool it, you guys, let's just take the penalty—managing just barely to halt the surge of angry buddies, Tae Uk, Toby, Brendan Symes, Dimarlo, all of them moving in menacingly, glowering, protective, for the kill, only split seconds away from a free-for-all slugfest.

"Hey, I wanted to help. I'm not gonna stand around, let my friend get thrown over the fence, you know?" said Dimarlo.

"I thought it was going to be a big fight," admitted Brendan Symes. "I ran up to this guy. I was about to hit him. Toby was right behind me. We were just gonna kill him."

Luckily, on the field Geoff's control prevailed—the boys swallowed their rage and took the 15-yard penalty reward. In the stands we had no such limits to restrain us. Leaping to our feet, we screamed for retribution, screaming now directly at the Whitman crowd. I thought briefly of the two-minute hate scene in Orwell's *1984*—the sense of blood lust in the air had never been thicker. "Little rich kids school," Brendan had called Whitman; spoiled-rotten elitists. Tossing our man over the fence—assault! Flat-out assault. We hated them all. We deserved to smash them. This wasn't just a game anymore—it was a crusade! Against evil!

Behind me, Lana Smith sat immobile, breathing hard. She, at least, had had experience with control—at one point, on the long walk to Switzerland and freedom, during the war, she had hit a few trees with her walking stick. She was only four years old, after all, bored and tired. But the soldier's response had been immediate and hard. "Don't do that, little girl," he hissed at her sternly. "The Germans . . ." and he cocked his finger at her head to illustrate.

Yet even she had her breaking point. Minutes later, Geoff again came down near the sidelines from a leap, and there was once again a threatening gesture from a Whitman player. And this time Lana had had enough. She stood suddenly, her small body stiff; in a clear cutting soprano that had the ring of absolute truth, she screamed: "If you lay a hand on my child again, I will kill you."

The rage had been there, inside us, from the start of the game— for we too shared the boys' rivalry against Whitman, we too dearly longed to see them brought down hard. The fence incident had only underlined it, poured kerosene on the smoldering flames, so that they were now flaring, leaping, all but out of control. The rage had been there already; it was quite real.

But now it had been activated. Now we were all in its grip in the stands, ablaze with an almost political fanaticism, which like all fanaticism held no room in it for any cool voice of reason. Only Judy Burgess continued, between her screams, to knit steadily on a large project intended for a newborn niece. "Put that down!" I roared at her. "This game is too exciting for knitting." Breathless, apologetically, she explained: she would love to stop, but the only game she had not knitted through had been the game when Alex . . . she looked at me, helplessly, unable to finish the sentence. The nightmare game, of course; Alex stretched out on the bench, un- seeing. I nodded, understanding. Breezy, practical Judy Burgess. A singer, true, but also an accountant, an MBA, who even dreamed of numbers. As superstitious as all of us now. Driven into magic, by the sheer force of the game.

And the battle raged on. At halftime the score was still 7–6. The Barons ran off the field cheering wildly, as the Vikings glowered in high dudgeon, slinking to their lockers, eyes on the ground. It was not over, not by a long shot, but the Barons had unequivocally ruined Whitman's halftime homecoming festivities, and this alone seemed a notable feat, worthy of hearty self-congratulation; in the stands we giggled nastily in the general direction of the Whitman fans. We were giddy, drunk, all of us parents, not that we'd had anything to eat or drink, since none of us wanted to contribute to Whitman's fund-raising via its concession stand. It had come down to that. Suburban warfare, a clash of PTAs.

Never had we enjoyed a halftime more; the very floats and pom- pom girls seemed bedraggled, the Viking streamers swept by winds of loss. Our sense of satisfaction was bone deep; we pulsed with the current of the boys' assurance. For once, there were no dire com- ments from any of the men about the tiny lead, about the full half still to come. Destiny—we knew it, just like the boys did—was on our side.

Whitman, who'd obviously spent the break pawing the locker-room floor, and unquestionably being horribly reamed out by their coach, burst out on the field like wild men. Now the game toughened up even more, became harsher, coldly serious. Whitman, we sensed, was not going to give up an inch. Our offense suddenly seemed unable to do a thing. Tae Uk, reeling, dizzy, sensed in a vague way that he was losing out; that hit he'd gotten a while back had really affected him. He felt removed, sleepy, almost feverish. Others on the line sensed it too. "What's my name?" Marc Gage kept demanding, poking him. "Tae Uk, what's my name?"

Brendan Symes was still hanging tough. He'd gotten a deep cut on his face in one pileup; the blood was flowing, but that only intensified his determination. "Look what you did to me!" he yelled, joyous. "Look at that! And I'm still coming at you!"

Alex, though, was not happy. Intensity and passion were never his favorite métier. He had the sense events were sweeping all of them along, like a cork on the high seas; he felt the lack of control sorely. "I wanted to kill them more than I wanted to beat them. We were so excited, I was, that I lost my thinking." An offensive line without a steady hand at the helm was like a rudderless boat; Alex sniffed chaos and anarchy in the air and it bothered him profoundly.

Yet the defense was still holding up proudly. Brendan Reed, Corey Dade, Geoff, Billy, Dave . . . all of them. Dave was masterful, directing his men, "making up for everybody's mistakes," as he saw it. But his injured ankle was obviously bothering him. At one point he was limping so badly it seemed impossible to the coaches that a referee wouldn't spot it and send him out. Hoarsely, guiltily, they yelled at him: "Don't limp, Dave! For God's sake, don't limp!" They needed him out there so much! Dave did his best.

But at last there was a tear, a crucial rip—the Whitman quarterback managed to pull away for a long pass to the star wide receiver, who swept it over the line for the score. Whitman's kick was good; the score stood at 13–7. Now the chips were down with a vengeance. Had it all been a fluke? Would it all now begin to crumble? Were our boys really capable, after all, of smashing this team? We held our breath, we clutched hands, believing, believing, actively fighting our disbelief, pushing it off as if it were a solid object.

And the boys came back. Incredibly, wildly, in the one way they knew how to do it best—with a 55-yard touchdown reception, Rick to Geoff, a pass out of legend, they had made it, they had come back, the score was 14–13, and now everyone in the stands was on their feet. No socializing anymore, no talking, no smiles—just wild roaring. The Whitman crowd was murderous, ugly—there was no question these people were fully capable of reprisal should their team go down for good. We knew it. But we were fearless, our violence more than a match for theirs. The boys' adrenaline had spilled over all of us—the air was electric, manic, with the feel of a sixties rock concert, one of the big ones, but even more danger-ous, aggressive, out of control. Closer to a sixties riot, in fact. It would not be surprising, right now, to see a bottle thrown—to hear an explosion—to see a sudden cracking spurt of flame. I actually *wanted* a chance to take them on, I realized; I was hoping for it. And I wasn't the only one. Other mothers, too—demure Lana Smith, Carole Stone, my own mother, even—were standing, bodies tense, faces contorted. Ready to fight.

It had come down to the last two minutes, finally. Whitman had the ball far down in B-CC territory, holding on to it with grim, steely-eyed resolution. We roared, roared, our belief still strong—the cold wind was in their faces, destiny itself was in their faces. Our defense, still gritty, stopped them. Once, twice, they were within inches of missing their first down. A second more of play, a crunch of men, a hand—one of our hands, a Baron hand—went up from the field, holding the ball. Had we recaptured it? But the whistle had blown. The referees carefully counted the inches, as we held our breath. Whitman had made the down. The ball was returned to Whitman—they threw themselves brutally against our battered line one last time—and made it through the goal. Our groans filled the night.

Suddenly another mother, Nancy Dahl, was with us in the stands, talking fast, furiously, in her high voice. The whistle blew after, not before; we had it, we had it, she insisted. I was there! I saw! My father disagreed quietly, his voice like death. The ball had been down on the ground, he told me, we had not regained possession. On the field, Whitman made the kick.

And now only seconds were left in the game—tiny drops of time. But seconds were enough! They had to be! To come so close, to do so much, they had to be enough. Swiftly the boys lined up. This was one of those plays they had worked on over the week. A trick play. Jimmy would go in as quarterback, throwing them off. He would toss the ball back to Rick, as Brendan Symes and Geoff took off, running for their lives. Rick would hurl it with all his strength far, far downfield. It would work—it had to.

Jimmy crouched, waiting for the snap, fighting his fear, his hands shaking slightly from the cold. It was a funny thing—Alex was the veteran center, the starter, the one who always snapped the ball. Yet Jimmy himself, who went in as quarterback so rarely, was used to Mark Bitz, the backup. On the Jayvee team last year, Mark had always been the center who snapped back to him. He felt comfortable when Mark was the one snapping. He knew where to put his hands, where the ball would come. With Alex, he was never sure.

The thoughts rushed into his mind unbidden, unwanted, in the final quick beats before the snap, even while he knew he was letting himself do the unforgivable—he was thinking! Thinking!—yet unable to stop himself. "Right before the snap I was like oh my God, it's Alex, I had that feeling, that hesitation, that second before the ball got there, I knew . . ." The snap came back—Jimmy froze, clutched, fumbled—a Whitman player leapt on the ball, howling like a demon from hell. Stunned in horror we stood, mouths agape. . . .

And it was over! Over! All of it! The whistle blew, the Vikings leapt to the air screaming, screaming; it was over. The boys stood frozen, mute. Geoff fell to his knees on the field; Rick, standing over him, lay a hand on his shoulder. They remained that way, utterly still, for a long moment; a statue of defeat. Over! Good God, how could it be! It was wrong, wrong, all of it! Lana, behind me, clutched her purse to her chest in tension, breathing in whimpers. Her oldest son pleaded quietly, "Don't go down, Mom. He's with his buddies. That's where he wants to be now."

We didn't go down. We lingered in the stands, as the crowd

cleared out, as the Whitman team whooped its way gloriously off to the lockers. No handshakes this time; a rarity, but the hypocrisy would be too much. The boys slowly gathered in a corner of the field, shoulders sloping, faces translucent, wiped clean of anything but defeat.

Once last year, after a beautifully played close one, a game they should have won—was it Kennedy? Wheaton?—Pete did something very simple. He stood in the locker room and shook hands with each boy as he came in. Not out of pity; there is no room for pity on a football team. Not because they had lost. Because, he said, they deserved it, for the way they had played. And because of Pete's calm manner, his blessedly even temper, the boys believed him.

What would he do now? God, they looked bad, all of them. I watched Toby pass a hand over his face. Sal Fiscina and Jack Burgess climbed down the bleachers to the field, their own faces emotionless, the faces of veterans—football and war—faces the boys would not mind seeing right now. The rest of us walked to the cars slowly, slowly. We said nothing to each other, any of us. There was nothing to say.

The boys slowly moved off the field. Nearly all were crying. Billy and Geoff, who had both played offense and defense and been on the field nearly every minute of the game, were still on the ground, sobbing. Pete stood over them, trying to get them moving, awkward as ever in the face of their sorrow. Come on, you guys, don't worry about it, let's go.

"I was just physically, morally devastated," said Geoff. "We couldn't move. I could've dug my own grave right there, I would have gotten in and said throw on the dirt. I was ready to hide forever."

Finally Mitch came up to them, got down on his knees, tears in his own eyes. "You guys did good. You did the best you could," he told them. "We lost, but we lost together." Once again, like after the Einstein game, he told them to let it out, not to try to bury the pain. "I want you to know I am here for you."

The two boys stumbled to the bus, helping each other, their arms wrapped around each other, "we were both heaving, crying so hard." When they got there Billy suddenly whirled and smashed his helmet into the side of the bus as hard as he could. Pete, hovering nervously, tried to calm him. "That's enough, Billy, Geoff, come on, get on the bus."

"Maybe I shouldn't have displayed such emotions on the field, not shown them . . . but I couldn't hold them in," said Geoff. "We were so sure—we were *convinced* of winning. Breaking them. We were convinced. It was a given. A given we were going to win. And we didn't. It was . . . like having a guarantee fall through."

"We played so hard that game," said Billy. "And after, I just looked up, saw all those jocks from Whitman, oh God, I felt so sad. I wanted to beat them so bad. I hate Whitman so much. I cried, I cried."

"It hurt like crazy," said John Han. "Everybody was hurt bad. You played your heart out and you lost. Everybody was just crying. Even Mitch. A coach crying! And when you saw him you felt so bad that you had brought this pain to him."

Each boy grappled with his own sorrow. They had given their all; it had not been enough. Later that night, at home, Brendan Symes played the videotape his father had made of the game. He had kept the camera focused tightly on the field down to the end, while Brendan's mother, who had hated football so, who had tried to keep her son from playing at all, stood beside him, sobbing like a baby. Again and again Brendan rewound the tape and played it over. Maybe if he watched it enough a pleat would open in time, a tiny line of reality would swerve, God would relent—and the outcome would change.

"I kept watching the play where Jimmy dropped the ball. Kept watching. I kept saying to myself, I could've picked it up! The ball was right there! I could've picked it up and run around the end or something. We could've, we could've, 'cause we did so much," he said.

"Coulda," said Kong mournfully. He sighed deeply. "Coulda, woulda, shoulda."

No one blamed Jimmy. "We had chances, we had plenty of chances, it wasn't his fault," said Billy. "He came off the bench cold," said Dirkey. "I might have done the same thing if I came off nervous, knowing the game depended on me." Mike Mitchem was disgusted, but more at the coaches. "So stupid. On the play we needed to win, you give it to Jimmy? You give it to him in the clutch?"

"I was so positive in that game, that I was going to go in there, we were going to win," said Jimmy. "I went in—it was freezing—the ball hit my hand. It was like having no hands, it was so cold. I saw it in front of me. Some guy was holding my leg. I could see the ball, a foot in front of me. Like knowing you could get that, and you can't . . . the worst frustration. I was mad about myself, I was mad about the game."

Endlessly, endlessly, on this night and down through the year, they would wrestle with the questions of why and how. It had been so close, they had been so sure—how could it have happened? "If we'd played Friday night," said Christo sadly, echoing many.

Some took a cosmic view. "I had a bad feeling that night . . . something about the weather," said Geoff Heintz. "I get bad feelings about weather. I don't like stormy weather."

For Alex, though, in the end it had all come down to the line. His control had slipped. He had not done his job as captain, as coolheaded leader. "It's a captain's job to make sure people are calm, ready mentally, psyched but not too psyched, that they still have their mind on the job. Or you can't get the job done," he said quietly.

"I didn't calm down the line, and without an offensive line, the team loses. Rick can be a superstar, Geoff too—it's nothing without an offensive line. And there was none that game. A nightmare."

But to Geoff, it was even simpler: "I think what it was . . . we believed in ourselves, that's why we won the first half. But I think in the halftime, such a long halftime, too long, people started to think. I think they began to think too much. I did my best to go around telling everybody, dudes, come on, we can do this, we can win, we're killing them. But I knew people were going to phase out, and they did."

At home that night I too mourned; we all mourned. It was very quiet in our house in fact, for a couple of days. Toby could not be spoken to. "I don't want to talk about it," he said firmly. "The offense played like shit." And later, "I hate football. I wish I could quit," for the first time ever. He lay on his favorite sofa, staring at the ceiling, morose, unapproachable. "The greatest game in the world," he had said long ago. "When you win."

And I wanted to fight, how I wanted to fight! To get in there, to punch, to flail away at *something,* to change reality, adjust it a few inches one way or the other—change the tape! Change the ending! Why should any of them have to feel this pain? And yet I knew, not only that I could change nothing, but also, somehow, in with the hurt, like a solid nugget of truth, that it might be a good thing I could not.

Maybe something about the immutability of life was being learned here, and hard as it was, that didn't make it a bad lesson. My son, all the boys, were getting a bruising glimpse of the nature of reality, and if they could stick it out . . .

But on the other hand, I almost couldn't believe what I seemed to be buying into. It almost felt as if I were being pulled away, torn from my true self—my compassion, empathy, caretaking, my willingness to bend the rules—my very nature! My father, when I was very young, had never let me win when we played chess, his favorite game. I remembered the sick feeling I'd had inside each time we played—the impossibility of ever overcoming that opponent, ever overturning that reality, the dismal acceptance, after a while, of sure defeat. Remembered it so well that when my boys were little, I had always made sure they won at the games we played. They would never have that feeling! Always, they would know they could win, that there were second chances, that anything was possible, that they could succeed. Later, yes, they would get other lessons, out there in the world, I knew that. I didn't care. My responsibility was to ensure that with me, as children, they faced the future with unlimited hope.

A fairy-tale reality! That was what I had wanted to give them. A fine thing at age four, perhaps, but had it stopped there, really? Had I not actually continued, however subtly, to bend reality, ever so slightly, to make it easier on them? And had I—I could not believe I was asking myself this, but I was—had I, after all, just possibly been wrong?

I was, I realized in shock, changing, almost against my will. Becoming initiated into a more implacable world. A world where rules didn't bend, compassion changed nothing, a world of honor, fierceness, courage, stoic acceptance, and bleak, eternal unfairness. You tried your best, with every inch of your being, and sometimes it wasn't enough. You failed—and you could do nothing to change that. A sour world—yet was it maybe, just maybe, the real one? A world where only the final outcome mattered, the world my son had moved into. The world of all our sons.

And yet there was something I did not know at all that night, did not come to understand until long after, until I had spoken finally to each of the boys. It was this: that for all the pain, for all the devastation, it was the experience of the Whitman game they remembered, and honored, and loved beyond all others, and would never forget. "The intensity of it! The intensity! The emotion!" one boy after another said to me, their eyes shining. "My favorite game," said Brendan. "I cried so hard."

"A heartbreaker," said Billy. "But then after, you just remember how good a game it was, how emotional it was. The most emotional game."

But Geoff was able to express it best. "To see Kong after that game, all dirty and scraped up, crying, because he'd tried so hard— Brendan Reed, Corey, Billy—we'd fought so hard. And Toby. I'd thought Toby was just a party-monger once, I loved the guy but that's what I thought. But my outlook was completely wrong. I saw he cared, he really, really cared. I hadn't known that before. It was such a good feeling, to know he really cared. Even months later, sometimes, we'd look at each other in art class . . . ah, Whitman. It was that. And seeing the whole team, so wracked. The most intense feeling . . ."

He leaned forward, deeply serious. "And I want my mom, my dad, my brother, I want Doug, I want Tony, I WANT YOU—to understand that feeling. It's such a feeling, God, if you can feel it too. I want you guys to feel that. If you can, if you only can . . . if you can get half of what I get out of it . . . just by seeing it.

"Because it was the best time, the highlight of the season, that game. Such a sense . . . that intensity. Even though we lost. Even though. There's no other feeling in the world that can touch it. And I will never ever forget it."

Some thirty years ago, I attended a football game at my own high school, one of my first. Like Whitman, this, too, was a highly awaited game; our team, too, was playing their fiercest rival, a contest they always approached with a great deal of spirit though they had not, in plain truth, been able to best them even once over the past ten years.

This time was to be different. After a full game's worth of tense, gritty effort, with neither team able to break away and score, our boys managed to place themselves in quasi-field-goal position seconds before the clock ran out. We were still a full forty-four yards from the goal, no sure thing at all, but options at this point were nil. We held our breath as the kicker swung his leg, the ball lifted, flew straight as a die, hit the top of the bar, the whistle blew—and, incredibly, the ball dropped over the goal and into the annals of Washington-Lee mythology.

The hysteria, the euphoria, I remembered well. But there was something else I remembered too. The following week, the story was being whispered through the halls; whispered, because the tale was so shocking. Someone's mother had told someone else's mother, who had told her daughter, who unable to resist had passed it on through the school. The kicker had been so overcome by emotion that when he got home that day—he had actually cried.

And I knew in my heart that thirty years later, many things in the world had changed for the worse, especially for young people. That we had new scourges, drugs, and plagues, and fearful economic woes, that we had lost some of our idealism forever, mislaid it for good, and no longer felt, as we had back then, in the dawn of civil rights, of the New Frontier, that the answers to our problems were simple, or graspable, or even perhaps existed at all.

But I also knew despite everything that a world in which boys could cry in front of each other and not be ashamed, a world in which they could be proud of their capacity to feel strongly, could prize their emotions, was a world which had changed, in one small way at least, made one tiny barely discernible shift—how hard for an aging pessimist to admit, yet it was true—for the better.

But emotional realizations were not the only legacy of the Whitman game. There was a final ironic coda that I would not discover until long after the season was over. It concerned the most dramatic one-shot frame of the entire evening, arguably of the entire season—the vision of B-CC's star receiver hurtling over the fence like a blue meteorite, tossed there callously by the forces of evil. It was a scene we in the stands had reacted to with righteous horror at the time. Yet it had not been, apparently, quite what it seemed.

No one doubted its reality that night—not coaches, referees, players, or parents. Few doubted it even later on. Rick, Geoff's closest friend, was the only one to even mention an alternative explanation, shocking me profoundly.

"That's so Geoff," he said, amused. "I think he was running, he got nudged, he saw the fence coming, there were no potentially hazardous cutting edges or anything, boom, flying, his legs flew up, he went over." And his hands described an arc in the air.

Still, I refused to believe. But Geoff, when asked directly, was silent for a full count of three, in itself odd enough to warrant suspicion. Finally he lifted his eyes to meet mine, grinning.

"Look, I won't say I did," he said. "The guy hit me, I knew the fence was there, I went over it—maybe I'm saying to myself, look, we're gonna get fifteen extra yards, I'm gonna be able to talk to someone in the stands, and it's gonna look good. Gonna look good.

"I'll do anything to steal a spotlight, I'll admit that. He pushed me. Maybe I didn't have to go over." Again he grinned impishly.

So much for pure evil, I realized sourly. We had been conned, all of us, by a bit of expert showmanship, from the team's number-one showman. Now along with my various reactions to the Whitman game, I had yet another one to deal with: I felt like a prize chump.

CHAPTER FOURTEEN

FOR MANY REASONS Whitman had been memorable for everyone, and the boys, every one of them, would come in time to cherish that memory.

In time. Not right away, though. Not by a long shot. It was a sullen, irritable group of young men who straggled in Monday afternoon to view the videotape of their grand misfortune, an experience everyone could have done without. Depression takes many odd forms; in adolescent boys, for instance, it can emerge as the keen desire to inflict damage. A glance around the room was sufficient proof that at least today, that was the predominant mode, all right. To a man, the boys looked ready to punch someone out.

Mitch for once held his fire, keeping the cracks down to a minimum. The defense had performed well; it wasn't *their* fault they hadn't won. He was proud of the boys, proud of himself, and feeling magnanimously, smugly compassionate toward almost everyone, especially his best friend.

Because Bob, for once, had lost his cool almost completely. He'd had a few seizures during the game, too, at one point throwing a chair out of the top box where the two coaches had been forced to confine themselves ever since they'd been ordered off the field, following Mitch's penalty-inducing freak-out at Einstein, three games back. Theoretically they could still have some connection to the action even up there by way of speaker phones, but in fact, it was all too easy for the boys to ignore instructions squawked at them long distance. As the game continued, again and again Bob had seized the phones, demanded to be connected to one of his linemen, then let go: "Tae Uk, WHAT THE GODDAMN HELL ARE YOU—" But he was aware he was having small effect. Hence the chair.

Now, though, with the videotape running quietly, no one could pretend not to hear him, and Bob's rage waxed supreme. With icy fervor he blasted the offense line up one end and down the other. To a man they were worthless, pitiful, useless, and dumb; certifiable bags of pus. Pussies, all of them! Major card-carrying pussies! Worst in the county! The state! The universe!

Hearing this, Tae Uk watched the screen nervously; he had a nearly photographic memory for the sequence of plays, and he knew what was coming up—the guy he was up against, a short little guy, was going to pick him up and throw him into the dust. Any minute, any minute . . .

"That's it! That's it!" roared Bob, as the sorry tableau unfolded all too vividly across the screen. "I can't take it! I've had it! That's it!" And he stormed out.

"On my play," said Tae Uk unhappily.

The offensive line had been on the rack before, certainly, but never like this; slumped in their chairs, wordless, watching Bob Plante slam out of the room, they looked guilty, demoralized, and beaten. It was like experiencing the loss all over again, only even worse. This time their own coach had flattened them to the ground. "Of course, a lot of that was theatrics," Bob explained later, airily. The point was to wake them up, get them mad, prod them toward future improvement. But no one looked particularly electrified at the moment. They looked like a bunch of kids who'd just been told they weren't much good. Maybe later on this would have a motivating effect; right now, they just looked sick. The other guys eyed them helplessly, embarrassed for their discomfort.

Toby had actually gotten one or two decent comments from Bob, amazingly—instead of bearing the brunt as in the past, he had even received a few passing pats on the head. It helped some, but the line's poor showing as a whole weighed heavily on him. Alex, though not demoralized—Alex never got demoralized, his capacity for detachment serving him well in this area—couldn't help agreeing with Bob and feeling somewhat personally responsible. If he had just been cooler . . .

There wasn't much comfort for anyone that day. Lunkhead, Toby's friend, was one of the few to achieve a tiny personal victory of sorts. Skinny, gangly Lunkhead was rarely able to hold a block for long, but at one point during the game he had—he'd fastened the guy securely and brought him to the ground. Unfortunately, the ref had immediately thrown a flag and called him for holding. Pete confronted him on the field at once: "Were you holding?" No way, Coach, he swore earnestly; that was a good, clean block.

Now, as the tape played on, he waited nervously to see how much the camera had picked up. It had been a decent block, pretty much, but truth to tell he *had* been hanging on to a large handful of the guy's jersey, he just hadn't thought it propitious to bring it up right then. The play came on the screen, and the block, thank God, looked clean as a whistle: you couldn't see the hand that was holding the jersey. "See, see, that was a perfectly good block, nothing wrong with that block," said Mitch. Lunkhead smiled modestly, sighing with relief.

Geoff, of course, managed to cull a few ego boosts out of the session; Geoff, as everyone knew, could get an ego boost out of almost any game videotape. Jimmy, sitting next to him, could have killed Mitch. The tape had almost rolled to the bitter end, the point just before Whitman's final score. Geoff had gone for a safety blitz—which proved in retrospect to have been a bad mistake.

"Well, here we are," said Mitch, with heavy sarcasm. "We had our best player on a blitz, and he didn't tackle the guy, and we lost the game."

Geoff, the eternal optimist, took in only one part of the comment. "You catch that? Huh?" He nudged Jimmy. "You hear what he said about 'best player'?"

"He didn't understand that Mitch had said he screwed up, he missed the tackle," said Jimmy, sardonically amused—he was used to Geoff. Sometimes he wondered just what heights Geoff would go to, in his cockiness; the better he played in a game, the more Jimmy would wonder, God, what's he going to be like after *this*?

Yet at the same time, there was something endearing about it, hard to resent. "Geoff never cuts on you. If I do something well, Geoff will like, yeah, you did. Rick will like, you stink. Rick, he has the most stories about girls and his life and how great he is you can possibly imagine. You can't win with him. Anything you say, he has something better." Jimmy enjoyed watching them both, though he did think Rick must be a little insecure. Geoff, now—he'd never had an insecure moment in his life. Sometimes Jimmy would almost play a game with him, telling him how great he was, just to see how much praise Geoff could take. So far he hadn't found any limits; he was beginning to think quite seriously there might not be any at all.

As if the Whitman disappointment hadn't been humbling enough, the next game the Barons faced was against Churchill. No other down-county team had Churchill's reputation; these were tough, hard-bitten, and seasoned guys, "huge, steroid-inflicted studs," as Alex put it, grimacing. A winning team; a longtime winning program. With a parent Booster Club so dedicated, enthusiastic, and well fixed it was rumored the team received catered breakfasts before every game, with huge steak dinners for afters.

Churchill blew all Mitch and Bob's favorite stereotypes out to sea. This was no blue-collar, farm-boy school like Seneca Valley or Gaithersburg, no way; this was staunchly upper-middle-class country. The school drew its population mainly from the ranks of ultra-swanky Potomac with just a pinch of less affluent Rockville for ballast. Potomac itself had grown by vast leaps in the last few years, townhouse developments springing up on fields like clumps of black-eyed Susans, but its traditional horsey estate ambience was far from dead. Polo was still a weekly tradition out here, played against a carefully crafted backdrop of strawberries, chilled champagne, foreign diplomats, and baroque music.

This was Churchill's native soil, and by all rights, according to Mitch and Bob's best theories, should have given birth to a thoroughly wimpy team, even worse than B-CC. Instead, the Churchill Bulldogs were, and had always been, a real piece of work. Large, full-bodied players, ninety a season, turned out to play at Churchill;

they were the essence of the cookie-cutter team, a group who would not have looked out of place on an Oklahoma field with an oil rig or two in the background. Their quarterback fit the pattern perfectly: he was blond, handsome Jim Kemp, son of Congressman (and ex–football player) Jack Kemp. His older brother was already playing pro.

"One of those schools where you think all the players are the same guy," Rick described it. He lowered his voice to a manly rumble: "Hi, I'm Jim Kemp, quarterback for Churchill, my dad's a congressman." Whereas at B-CC, of course, "we're all queers, we're all really weird," he said proudly.

"Fred Shepherd (Churchill's coach) gets the players because every male in Churchill comes out for football," Bob explained. "If we got every male at B-CC, we'd have a dynasty too. Some of those basketball players . . .

"But he gets 'em, and they know they're supposed to win. That's the key. They know in every game they play. So when it's fourteen–oh at halftime, they're saying, well, how're we gonna win this game? 'Cause we're supposed to win. It's an attitude. Shepherd's instilled that over a period of time, fifteen, sixteen years. I think he's resting on his laurels, he's not very innovative—but he's got the studs, he doesn't have to be."

Beating Churchill last year—and on their homecoming night, as well—had been a triumph beyond any the boys could have dreamed. "Probably the biggest night for B-CC ever," Pete called it. "We'd never beat Churchill. An unbelievably glorious night." The fact that it was that precise game which had kept Churchill out of the playoffs had been the gilt on the lily. But did this mean they could start viewing Churchill as a regular rival, someone they had a good chance to beat on a continuing basis? Forget it. Everyone knew last year had been a fluke to some degree, just like everyone knew it was a fluke when Whitman had beaten Churchill this year in the first game of the season. These things did happen, but it wasn't the way the bets lay.

The Churchill game this year was the last home game of the season for the Barons, the last time any of the seniors would play on B-CC's field. In honor of this, Pete had declared Friday night Senior Night. Each senior would have his name called over the loudspeaker as he ran out. In addition, fried chicken would be served in the stands to all the parents. Gratis. Churchill wasn't the only one who could come up with perks, even if we hadn't gotten up to the level of weekly steak dinners quite yet, he figured.

Unquestionably, Whitman had left a certain undertow of apathy in its wake. Along with everything else, the game had snuffed out for all time the last tiny flicker of hope that they might yet by some act of God make it to the state playoffs. It was one thing to realize, reasonably, that such a thing was probably not in the cards; quite another to know it beyond a doubt. They were down to playing for pride, and a pretty squashed pride it was, at the moment.

James was finding it all extremely hard to take. He had cut off his cast himself this week and had even told Pete he might be able to play, though he knew his knee needed more healing time, and that his mother, had she known, would have locked him up in his room for a month. But it was hard, hard. The team was down, they needed him! Especially on the defense line. And no one wanted a crack at mighty Churchill more than he.

The fact that he was sidelined hadn't broken James's spirit; he was still able to use his mouth. "Mr. Arrogant himself," Dave called him. Finally, tired of listening to his tales of former prowess, Dave corraled Christo to act as judge. "I said, all joking aside, Christo, who's the best linebacker? He looked at both of us and said, Dave.

"James said, but I run faster. I'm like, James, I have a broken ankle, what do you want me to do?"

Dave was satisfied with the interchange. "I don't like to talk about myself. I lost a girlfriend in tenth grade from that, so I don't do it anymore. I let other people do it. Christo, tell the man."

James knew he'd had only four games to prove himself; he desperately wanted another chance on the field. But was it a good idea? That's what he couldn't decide. "I just don't know if I should or not," he told Geoff Heintz.

His friend was adamant. "You're looking for a college career. Don't even worry about high school, it isn't that important," he said. "If you come back, you've got a chance of really hurting yourself.

"I think he already knew that, but he wanted to hear it from somebody else," he mused later. "He listened to me." Resigned, James told Pete he had decided not to take the risk. He would let his brain overrule his heart, for once, and stay off the field.

The team's apathy lifted as the week progressed. After a few days of silence, Toby's mood improved at home. He, at least, had not performed badly, Bob had said, and this knowledge allowed him to retain some sense of pride in himself. Geoff and Billy, who'd weathered many more disappointments in their long football careers, bounced back even faster. You let it go, you kept moving forward; that was the only way to handle it, they knew. It wasn't turning into the season they had dreamed it would be, certainly, but there was nothing for it but to accept the reality and move on. What other choice did they have?

I myself was battling a kind of low-key grief this week. If it wasn't whether you won or lost but how you played the game, then why was I feeling so bad, I wondered. Because, of course, in football, winning *was* all—especially to those in the stands. I remembered Toby's unhappiness last year, when he'd spent every game standing next to the bench, rarely getting out on the field. After a loss, he would come home inconsolable, darkly brooding. Once, I had left him to his misery, gone to the library, and been shocked to see several first-string players there, tackling their homework loudly, looking none the worse for wear. I was confused: they had been on the field, not him. Shouldn't they be feeling worse?

It didn't work like that; now I understood. Nothing was worse than the frustration of seeing things go bad and not being able to help, to get in there and unleash your own energy. It was true for a sidelined player—and maybe even more true for someone in the stands. "When your friends are in trouble, you gotta do something," the boys had told me, talking about their off-field rumbles. Maybe that was it—I, too, wanted to do something and could not. Something had been happening to me over the past weeks, I realized uneasily—the boundary lines between myself and the team were blurring almost into dust. I had felt the Whitman loss right in my gut, and not just as a mother of a player, either. What was going on?

The boys who had actually been there, out on the field, were handling their disappointment better than I was. "It would have been nice," Rick said wistfully, "to win all ten games, to be the football men of the school." This was not to be. And yet, and yet . . . still, it was football.

Pete was glad to see the guys come around, shake off some of their lethargy, quit moaning, and get back to work. This was one of those times a coach had to be thankful for the natural resilience of adolescence, all those life-affirming hormones roiling around. Even with the Whitman loss behind them, even with Churchill looming up in front of them, an all but guaranteed fiasco—Pete had seen a few tapes of the team in action, that line was *huge*—the boys were optimistic. That's what he meant by having no sense of reality at that age, and a good thing it was, too. He wasn't about to destroy it, either.

"You never let them know . . . because football is the most psychological of any game in a lot of ways. We might have sat and looked at the Churchill film, and, oh God, I can't believe it, how good they are—but you think, we might be able to attack them here, attack them there—you go out with a good face.

"The kids know in their minds how tough the game is gonna be, and they steady up under the situation."

Actually, there was almost a relief in facing a team as good as Churchill. The Barons were so clearly the underdogs that no one expected anything at all; losing would hardly be a humiliation. On the other hand, whatever they did do against Churchill would look damn good. In one way, it was a no-loss situation.

But there was another reason why by Friday, every boy was feeling good again. Whatever happened, whatever was in store, they were about to go out on their field and play four quarters of the best game in the world. No one could take that away.

The Churchill players loomed against the darkening sky, every bit as huge as promised. As the Barons went through their warm-ups, studiously avoiding glancing across the field, Churchill broke into a loud, raucous chant aimed at disrupting their cadence. The bastards couldn't even wait for the whistle.

"They're pissing me off," Bob spat at his men. "Damn, they're pissing me off. I don't like 'em. Tae Uk, Toby, you got to start a fight. I don't like 'em."

"Sure, no problem, Coach," said Tae Uk.

"I don't like 'em, start a fight," he said to each lineman. He surveyed his boys, eyes bright, lips curled. "Tae Uk!" he bawled. "How much you weigh?"

"Ummm, two hundred, Coach?"

"No way! You weigh two-twenty!" He stalked off. Seconds later Mitch, eyes blazing, marched down the line, taking in the troops.

"Tae Uk!" he growled at the little lineman. "How much you weigh?"

Tae Uk sighed. "Two-twenty?"

"NO WAY," Mitch yelled. "Tonight, you weigh two-fifty!"

The senior players were announced one by one; each ran out, forming a line in front of the stands. We applauded them as they stood, serious, earnest, unmoving, a little uncomfortable. There had been moments over the past weeks when they had seemed to hover far above us, titans, lords of battle. Why was it that now, standing there, they all looked so damn young? Three more games, I told myself, as the sudden familiar chill pierced my heart. Three more games, and he's safe.

The Churchill Bulldogs, as many observers duly noted, were on a mission tonight. This was no mere win they were after; they were out for revenge, pure and simple. They needed a giant payback to make up for last year's blistering defeat, and a giant payback was what they intended to get.

Their determination was like a palpable force; what's more, they had the men to handle the job. Most of the first half was a mortifying rout, as Churchill's players rolled over the Barons, scattering them like marbles, pushing through our defense like so much tissue paper, scoring once, twice. . . . "Boys against men," said Kong heavily.

"NO!" screamed Bob Plante at halftime, bellowing directly at the offensive line. "This is NOT the way it's gonna be!" They had failed miserably at Whitman last week, they had not hung tough, they had not shown courage—and goddamn it, this time, against this team, they were NOT going to fold. He didn't care what happened, he didn't care what the outcome was, he didn't care WHO won—they were not going down like this! He wouldn't have it! All that training, all the time he had spent on them—goddamn it, they were not giving up! No! NO! NO! NO!

And out there again on that field, after halftime, against one of the toughest teams in the county, incredibly, a miracle began to occur. The offensive line—Bob Plante's men—began to come into their own. Began to show muscle. Began finally, at long last, all of them, to do the job.

"We broke so many expectations," said Toby. "We came out and kicked ass completely. And it was great. Nothing better in the world."

James, standing tensely on the edge of the field, saw it at once. Up to then the game had been upsetting him terribly. "The guys on defense were saying, I'm not going back in there, they're overpowering us. I *never* had that attitude, even if it was so. But Brendan Reed, Mitchem, they had been coming out, saying, forget it. I was like, these are my boys, they're not supposed to be like this, it was hurting me so bad."

"I was getting killed," Mike admitted. "Physically outdone."

So James made a conscious shift in allegiance. "I went to the offense. I said, Toby, go kill 'em, man. And Toby said, you got it. This guy was like six-nine. Toby was blocking him.

"What I did—I kind of went into Toby's body. It was like— Toby, do what I would do out there." Standing on the sidelines, he kept his eyes glued to Toby. Every block Toby threw, James felt; when Toby overcame his opponent, James felt the surge of victory in his own body. Injured, sidelined, but undaunted, he had found the one way he could still be on the field.

The Barons were on the board at last—the offensive line was giving Rick a chance to maneuver finally, and he had managed to run one into the end zone. The entire offense was utterly wired, drunk on the sudden realization of their own capabilities. He was right, Coach Plante had been right all the time. They *could* do it. Who cared what happened? They were kicking almighty Churchill's ass, and it felt fine.

"I was so psyched," said Tae Uk. Some Churchill player got a cheap shot on Geoff and started yelling at him, "and I was really mad, so I grabbed Geoff, pulling him behind me and got in the guy's face for Geoff." He hadn't known quite how big the kid was until then—also, by this time, Tae Uk had almost come to feel he *did* weigh 250. He had to throw his head back so far to glare at the guy that his neck almost cracked. "I wasn't even scared, Coach Plante had made me so psyched." Luckily another Churchill player pulled the guy back.

Down in the pit, nearly everyone was talking trash on both sides of the line nonstop. Whenever Dimarlo came in, he added a full complement of chipmunk noises to the fray. One Churchill player started mouthing off at Rick, always a mistake. Anything was fair grist for comment now, and unfortunately the most distinguishing characteristic about this player was his nose. "Don't hit me with that nose!" Rick taunted him. "Better get that nose out of the way, you'll miss the ball."

"Nothing too creative," said Billy. "Just . . . nose jokes."

Geoff too, of course, was always an eager participant in the war of words. "Coach White had told me before the game they'd over-heard some of the coaches saying, Christ, B-CC? All we gotta do is hurt Smith." Nothing like hearing that just before you went on the field.

"Early on, the first pass play, I was running to catch the ball and the biggest ape, running full steam, hit me with his shoulder pad and flipped me. Complete flip. And he goes, that's what it's gonna be like all night, Smith. You ain't gonna catch nothing."

As far as Geoff was concerned, that was a clear challenge. "So every time I caught a ball, I'd go, that's one. That's two. After every pass play.

"They were all dicks during that game, the biggest assholes. Smith, you're a fuckhead! Come in my zone, I'll kill you!" Finally even Geoff had had enough of it. He walked over to quarterback Jim Kemp. "Hey, Jimmy, look," he said. "You get your boys to stop talking trash, I'll get mine to shut up. Let's just play some football, okay? We can't go on, this is fucking ridiculous. I mean, the refs were threatening to call the game off, we were talking so much." The Churchill quarterback promised he'd do his best.

Rick was able to connect with Geoff with a long pass for a second touchdown. We yelled strenuously, not that we expected it to do much good. The minutes were dribbling away, the score was

30–13, no one in the stands or on the field had much hope of anything spectacular; this game, we all knew, had been pretty much nailed down from the first. Yet out on the field the offensive line continued to show force. Not for glory, not for victory—only for the pure, sweet pleasure of the thing.

"It was our best performance ever," said junior lineman Erik Karlson, who was getting more playing time this game than ever before. "Tae Uk and I had this little fat porker in front of us. We were controlling him right and left, laughing at him, hey, you want to take him this time or do I get to cream him?"

Toby, knocking his large opponent off again and again, was on fire, blazing with the realization of his own ability. Had anything ever felt this good? The team was losing, but he was winning. All the hard work had come down to this point of true success, at last—fighting Churchill, in the last home game of the season, Toby was reaping his reward.

It was intoxicating, without question. Close to the end, "Toby was like, hey, why don't we start a fight?" said Tae Uk. "And I'm like, yeah, man, let's go. Alex was like, I'm not backing you guys up, don't do it. But me and Toby were like, let's go, let's go."

The little lineman was hoping for a crack at the big-nosed guy. "Hey, why don't you come my way?" he taunted him. So the next play, Tae Uk let his guy, the one he was supposed to block, go by him, Nose came at him—and tripped, landing right on his face. "Yeah!" Tae yelled, grinning. "Like that!"

The guy Mark Bitz was up against when he went in for Alex had really been annoying him. "I'm gonna kill you," he kept promising. Finally Toby, playing next to Mark on the line, decided to give him a hand. "I'll set him up, you hit him—let's knock the shit out of him." It went off like a charm. "Boom, the guy was on the ground. Fantastic," said Mark.

But the offensive line's fierce battle could not stay the inevitable forever. The whistle blew, the last home game was over. The Churchill men hooted their success, a collective megaphone blaring the message to the skies. Billy, lying flat out on the field yet again—another game, same position—looked up to see "one of the hottest girls" from Churchill looming over him. "Ha-ha, you guys lost," she sang. Growling, he spit several choice words up at her.

The Churchill players swiftly bundled her off. "They didn't get mad at me, though." He felt they understood.

Geoff stood facing the opponents who'd been "such dicks" throughout the game. A large linebacker walked over to him, pulling his shirt over his head. "Geoff, I'm new here," he said. "I used to go to school down in Texas, and we have an old custom. The defensive captain always takes the shirt off his back and gives it to the player who played best on offense.

"I want you to have this." And he handed it to Geoff.

"It meant so much," said Geoff, who for once was shocked wordless. He cradled the shirt, "the most scummy, sweat-filled shirt," like it was a prize trophy. Which in a way, he knew, it was.

The Bulldogs ran off the field; our boys strode up the stadium steps through the stands, the last such march any of the seniors— Rick, Geoff, Billy, Toby, Dave, Kong, Brendan Symes, Brendan Reed, John Han—would ever make. They kept their eyes straight ahead, as always after a loss; but the offensive linemen had a glint in theirs. Too bad they had lost, yes, too bad. But Lord, for a while there, hadn't it been fine?

Back in the locker room, Mitch was furious. He stomped up and down, hurling clipboards, chalk, anything solid he could lay his hands on. They had let him down, the entire defense; for two cents he would bench the lot of them. You guys are shit! They were going to see a few changes in the lineup for next week, they could count on it. Bunch of worthless, scummy bastards—and he seized a green trash can and threw it against the wall so violently it smashed in two.

But Bob—stern, emotionless, tightly controlled Bob Plante— was almost beside himself with joy. He could not stop grinning. He bubbled over with pride. "You did it," he told his linemen, his voice hoarse. "You really did it. You kicked ass! Good job, good job. Oh, what a great job you did!"

"He was so happy," said Tae Uk, "jumping up and down. We did do good. We did really well. All of us. Marc Gage, me, Toby . . . after that game, Toby was just . . . the man."

And that was exactly how he felt. Ever since Einstein, Toby had felt good about his playing. He knew Bob Plante was happy with his development; he felt the deep personal pride of someone who has managed to reach a goal he set for himself. He had been determined to become a real football player, and he had made it. Even with the disappointment of Whitman last week, he had known—Plante had made sure he knew—that he himself had not fallen down on the job.

Tonight, with Churchill, however, had boosted that pride almost over the top. The toughest team he had ever faced, and he had taken them on like a pro. Fearlessly. The team might have lost, but he himself had been unvanquished. He had felt proud before on a field, happy, joyful, but this feeling was different. Tonight, what he was feeling—reveling in—was power, his own power, coursing through his veins. A stable, level-headed kid, Bob had called him. Not tonight, though. Tonight Toby felt ready to take on the world.

The boys cleared out slowly that night, more slowly than usual. Many of the seniors were reluctant to leave. They had played the last game they would ever play on this field. The season was drawing to a close; an era in their lives was coming to an end. There would be other eras, lots of them; they were ready and eager to push off into that unknown sea. But it is never easy to leave something you love, not when you're young, not ever.

One by one, though, each boy finally managed to pull himself up and go. Until there were only two left. Rick and Geoff.

Without even discussing it, they found themselves back out on the field. It was dark, all the lights were out, the crowd long since dispersed; they had the field to themselves, just the two of them out there alone in the night. They began to pass the ball back and forth to each other in long, arcing loops, hurling it far up into the sky.

And suddenly they were yelling crazily. "All right—third and eight, down by eighteen, against Einstein! Geoff Smith fades back—he fades—Rick Fiscina throws the ball—he lets it go—it's up, up—Geoff's going for it—he's in the air—he's got it! He's got it! Touchdown! Touchdown B-CC!" Screaming wildly, laughing, hugging each other, pumping the night air with their fists.

Because they knew finally how close they were to the end.

Long after most of the boys had left, Bob made a last cursory sweep of the locker room before locking up. About to go, he heard a sound and turned to investigate. Sitting on a bench in the corner, alone, still in his football pants, his head bent down, crying, was one of the second-string players, John Everett.

John, a senior, rarely got much chance to get on the field. His father, Dick, gave enormous amounts of time to the team, taking pictures, helping run the concession stand, even rearranging his business hours so as to be available when needed. A deeply involved parent, he was a widower, raising three children by himself. John was the oldest. His mother had died when he was six.

No boy on the team was more intense, more hardworking than John. "If intensity made the player," Pete once said about him. Unfortunately, it did not. Try as he might, he had never attained a starting position. Tonight he had barely gotten in to play at all.

"I try so hard," he explained, as Bob crouched down next to him on the bench. "I try so hard. All I ever wanted to do was just play."

The sight of this boy, miserable and suffering, cut through Bob's macho armor like a laser. "Jesus, I was Jell-O," he said later. Quietly, almost gently, he talked to him. "Right now, the most important thing in the world is to play high school football," he said. "But you know what you're going to learn from this, working so hard? Someday the Ricks and the Geoffs, the great athletes, they're going to work for you. You're going to make the money, because you know what it takes to get there. You'll be pulling down three hundred G's and they'll be making fifty thousand dollars and they'll be going, hello, Mr. Everett, how are you? It's true."

"He told me he was like me when he was a kid," said John. "He said, you got guts. Like, not everyone can be like Mitch, all-county, or Rick—you have more guts than they do. Stuff like that."

Later that night, still shaken, Bob told Mitch about the incident. "We both got a little teary-eyed," Mitch said. The picture of John sitting there in the locker room, with everyone gone, his head down, the lights dim, moved him deeply. "It was like something you'd see in a movie.

"He'd said, Coach, I try so hard and work so hard and I just can't get it done. He was realizing . . . he got away from blaming others about his problem, and had come to the realization that he just wasn't that good. That's hard for a young kid to accept. Kids, there's nothing they can't do. But he had looked it in the face.

"That kid—he showed up every single day for practice and he never complained and he worked his ass off. People don't realize—it's *easy* to be Rick Fiscina. But those kids who don't play, who come to practice and then get no reward, like getting in the game—they're the kids who have real character."

Toward the end of the season, Dick Everett talked to Mitch. He said, "I know my son is not a very good athlete." And Mitch said, "You're missing the whole point. You've got to be so proud of your son. Because he has character. When I look at him—I hope my son has that. I don't care if he's a great athlete. He knows what hard work is all about."

It was the difference between him and Bob, Mitch felt. "Bob was never a great athlete. He had to work hard. And me, it put me behind. Because everything came so easy. That's the great thing about sports. It's not just fun—it does turn into actual life."

But because both Bob and Mitch knew a young boy could have a hard time handling all that character building, and because they knew that no matter what they told him, or how true it was, he was just a kid and he was hurting, they made a mutual pact: John would get a chance to start in next week's game.

That weekend a small group of players went on a fishing trip in upper Maryland: Toriano, John Han, Tae Uk, James, and another friend, Matt, who was not on the team.

Toriano had just pulled his cast off, too, like James—though, unlike James, he had no intention of sitting out the last two games of the season. After all, it had only been a hairline fracture—how bad could it be? The doctor had said he didn't think it was such a hot idea, it might be better to wait til next year, his senior year, but Toriano had done all the waiting he wanted to do for quite a while, thanks. It was time, past time, to put his money where his mouth had been all season. He knew most of the guys who'd been listening to him brag probably felt the same way.

Toriano did not like getting hit. Speed was his thing. He had the moves, had always had them, developed them when he was small. The youngest of four kids who doesn't like getting hit had sure as hell better develop a few moves early on.

He was fast; everyone knew it. Last summer, while he was hanging out with a bunch of his friends down in D.C., a man had suddenly come up to him, talking crazy, waving a gun in his face. Crack junkie, Toriano was sure. He hadn't waited. He'd taken off, running like the wind, down back alleys, throwing himself under a parked car where he waited for nearly an hour. His friends couldn't believe it when he finally climbed out. "You're alive!" they screeched. It was at times like that you really appreciated speed. Also when he took a cab down to visit his grandmother in D.C. and realized he didn't have the money to pay for the ride, he'd be out of that car and up an alley before the driver even got a good look at him.

"The speed-and-grace king," Mark Bitz called him. "The most dangerous man in an open field in Montgomery County," Mitch had said once. Toriano appreciated such comments, but saw no reason to wait for them. He was fully capable of reeling off his attributes all by himself, and often did. He presented a girl in one of his classes with his autograph, grandly, because one of these days she'd be so glad to have it, he assured her. He referred to Geoff, the hands-down flashiest guy on the team, as "Mr. Excitement, the best player on the team, ah, I mean, the second-best player."

Disgusted, his girlfriend had finally told him one day, "When you get back from your trip, let me know."

"I was like, what trip? And she said, you know, that ego trip you're on." Toriano grinned. Kong, he said, simply held up his hands whenever he saw Toriano walking toward him. " 'I know, I know, fifty yards a catch, two hundred-some yards.' He knows my stats better than I do!"

Actually, one time even Coach White had told him he talked about himself too much. "He said he was tired of hearing it, that it was a team sport. And everybody was saying, yeah, laughing."

But Toriano didn't mind. "I like everybody on the team. We're a bunch of individuals playing this team sport. The Chinese connection, Jamaican. Dirkey, Corey, and I call ourselves the jamming juniors." Sometimes he and Tae Uk squared off. "Chink!" "Spook!" "Chink!" "Spook!" It cracked them both up.

Toriano was one of the guys Bob was referring to when he said Mitch knew how to motivate black kids. You couldn't tell a guy like Toriano he was a bag of pus, Bob felt; it wouldn't work, he'd just blow you off. But Mitch could go up to him and tell him he was a vicious dude, and that would have an effect. Of course, it wasn't just acting—Mitch really *did* think Toriano was special; he was one of his favorites.

Toriano knew he ran his mouth a lot. "Everybody tell you how much I talk about myself?" he asked when we first met. But talking too was a talent he was proud of. He was a top-notch player in the eternal ragging contest that went on between the boys, a version of the ancient black street game, playing the dozens, "joning on each other's mothers." He was especially proud of one recent, though hardly original, riposte: "Why don't we get off mothers for once? I know I just got off yours." Why was it always, always mothers, I asked tiredly. I had wanted to ask someone for years. Toriano was matter-of-fact: "Just . . . what offends you most, I guess," he said.

His own mother, who ran her own beauty shop, had always backed him up, whatever sport he wanted to play; she came to all his games. "She liked me playing sports because I kept my grades up." Also, Toriano felt sports helped you handle things. When one of his brothers had been killed in an accident years before, "I stopped doing everything for a year. Then after that I got into sports, and it kept me going in a way."

But football was the best. "Football—football makes you famous." Though he was one of the few who felt the game did not necessarily help you get girls, at least not immediately: "We stink after football games."

Determined to get his leg back into shape fast, Toriano was glad of the fishing trip, it would give him a chance to do a little hiking. After driving about an hour into the country, the boys parked their cars near a small rural store, took their gear down to the banks of the river, and spent a full day fishing, "talking about everything." ("Toriano didn't know from fishing," James cracked. "He just wanted to go so he could talk about himself, which he did, *all* the way up, *all* the way back.") It was almost dark by the time they climbed back up to the cars.

Matt, they discovered, had locked his keys in his trunk, while getting out his gear. He hated the idea of going all the way home and returning with a spare set; maybe they should call Triple A, who would get the car started for him.

James and Tae Uk went to the store to use the phone. It was growing darker. The store, they saw, became a bar at night, and the bar was full. There were a number of trucks parked nearby, trucks laden with gun racks, hunting equipment. One even had a deer carcass hanging off the back. The drivers were standing in and around the store-bar, full-bellied, tough-looking customers, quintessential country types. They eyed the boys—one black, one Korean—coolly, contemplatively.

"All of us are minorities, except Matt," said James. "And we're thinking these guys are hicks—in class we'd seen some of those news clips from the sixties, and our minds . . . we're getting worried, worked up."

James and Tae Uk made two trips to the store, trying to get the AAA on the phone. By now it was almost completely dark. Nervously the two boys tried to kid each other out of their fears. "Hey, we're not scared! We're starters for the football team, man! If anyone comes, we'll just tell them how good we are in football!"

By the last trip back to the car, the truck drivers had begun to throw a few hooting noises in their direction. The boys piled into John's car to wait for the AAA rep to come. It was now completely dark, but John didn't want to turn on the lights and drain the battery. "We got to get out of here, man," the boys urged each other, scared. "It's too dangerous. We ought to go now."

Parked straight across from John's car was a battered van. As the boys waited, suddenly a match lit up in the front seat. "From the light you could see this raspy beard—our minds pictured this big man with dark glasses and hat and this little knife, sitting there, waiting," said James.

The cigarette—they could see the lit tip—burned slowly down. "It didn't move, it didn't move." Another truck, this one filled with men laughing raucously, pulled up behind them. They were now trapped between the two vehicles. Within a split second, the boys had veered over into full, total panic.

"It was like—they're gonna kill us! We really believed our lives were threatened," said James. He and Toriano were the loudest. "We're gonna die, we're gonna die!"

"We're thinking, they're gonna hang us to trees," said Toriano. "I could just see a fishing pole sticking out of the window of the van but I swear to God, it looked like a hatchet. We were just, oh my God, here they come—"

James hit the light switch. Now the guy had gotten out of the van, he was standing there in front of them, just like they'd pictured him, big, bearded, straight out of the Mississippi delta. . . .

There was a bang on the window of the car. By now John was in Toriano's lap, while Toriano himself was doing his best to climb under the steering wheel. They knew it had to be Matt at the window, he was the only one still outside, still trying to get into the trunk of his car. "But it might be this other guy." Who knew? James locked the door. "I was gonna save number one, I locked it."

The sheriff guy got back in his truck and drove off. The people in the truck behind them pulled out. The boys sat huddled in the dark, shaking, sweating, nauseous.

"It was so scary," said James. "We went from macho football players to six-year-olds—crazy. Ridiculous. The rural atmosphere, these hicks with guns. Scaredest I've ever been in my life."

"John Han!" yelled Toriano, the first to get his breath back. "That's the first time I've ever seen your whole eye!"

John came right back: "Well, I didn't know anyone else was even here. All I could see were eyes and teeth."

The boys drove back home in John's car, making the hourlong trip in about twenty minutes. They got Matt's spare keys, a few heavy sticks for ammunition, and drove back out. No one was around. By now their stomachs were sore from laughing at themselves. Big men! Football players! Yeah, they'd shown those guys, all right.

"Why didn't we get out and tear him up?" James wondered. "I was mad at myself. What if I'm in a situation where I have to defend myself and I lose my wits like that? I don't want to die like that. The uncertainty—I couldn't control it. I didn't know what was going on. We became so juvenile.

"But it was so funny. . . ." After they finally got home for good, James got out of the car, then turned and announced with his usual calm decisiveness, "I know where I'm sleeping tonight. I'm sleeping in my mother's bed." Everyone laughed, but in sympathy, not contempt. Any other time it would have sounded ludicrous. At the moment, it didn't seem like such a bad idea.

CHAPTER FIFTEEN

THE TEAM began the next week of practice in good spirits—not euphoric, naturally, but a far cry from the slough that had followed the Whitman rout. At 30–13 the game against Churchill had at least been respectable; in spite of Mitch's ranting, everyone on the team felt fairly good about it, even the defense. I knew this loss hadn't stung like Whitman had, but even I was shocked at how cheerful Toby was coming home the night of the game—he had never been this up after any defeat. The offensive line, he told me, had been terrific—the exact opposite of last week. This time the loss wasn't *their* fault, he felt. He said nothing about his own personal success. For Toby, bragging was as unappealing as whining about bad treatment; neither fit his idea of being a man. But it was obvious he was pleased as punch about something.

The next day something happened that made everyone feel even better. Springbrook, Mitch's own down-and-dirty up-county alma mater, smashed Whitman to a pulp, in a humiliating 45–3 debacle. "Showed them where they belong," as several of the Barons put it, happily.

Logically, one might think that after their own loss to Whitman the team would not have minded seeing them go right to the top, proving no one could best them. But logic had nothing to do with gut emotions. All they wanted after last week was to see Whitman get creamed. No, they hadn't managed to pull it off, but someone else had. In an important sense it was the thought that counted.

Only two games remained—Wheaton and Gaithersburg—and neither looked particularly hopeful for B-CC. But the guys had gotten a second wind, or was it a third or fourth? No matter. At any rate, they were prepared to relish the rest of the season, whatever the odds.

At least most of them were. The defense, especially Mike Mitchem and Rene, the first-string linemen, were feeling sullen. Mitch's announcement that he intended to let some of the second-string players, like John Everett, start the next game, had infuriated them. It was a vintage Mitch decision, just another example of what Mike called his "'rigidity—he thought he was the mind, he would mastermind schemes and he'd want them done." But to start fooling around with the lineup at this late date was a real insult, he and Rene thought.

Both boys were feeling embittered, close to quitting. Finally even Mitch saw the need for compromise. He would let the second string play first quarter, the first string play second quarter, and whoever did best could play out the rest. Okay?

He knew the boys were mad, but he was philosophical. "You gotta remember in this job, not every kid's gonna love you. You can't please everybody, there's no one perfect method. What you gotta do is be as fair as possible." The Churchill game had gotten under his skin. He felt the defense had let him down, and he didn't mind kicking a little butt. Not to mention the fact that he had never warmed up to Mitchem after their early blowout. Plus he was determined to give John Everett a chance to play.

"Those are the kids you get the most reward from. Teaching Geoff to play free safety, I love the kid, but when he intercepts the ball you expect it. How hard is it to coach great kids? The challenge is to coach the others."

Wheaton was a day game, and away, two strikes against it right there, but the football deities had decided to give the boys one big break to compensate—the weather. Saturday, November 5, 1988, was full of the Barons' all-time favorite football-playing weather: rain, lots of it. Not just a few discreet drizzles—steady, solid sheets of the stuff. Every now and then it would shut off, like a faucet, only to resume pelting moments later with renewed vigor. It was almost as bad as the rain that had caused the cancellation of Whitman two weeks before, but since it had had the decency to start late Saturday morning, none of the games had been called off.

Even before the game the Wheaton field had been reduced to dank, gloppy swill, and not a boy on the team was unmoved by the sight. Mud! Mountains of mud! What could be better? It was something you tended to forget when talking to them, these articulate young men, many of them busy applying to college, planning their futures—how much every one of them still loved playing in the mud.

"Maybe it goes back to my little-kid years. I always like to play with mud and water," said Csaba Hadas, the Hungarian-born defensive lineman.

"When it rains, every little kid gets dressed and goes out and plays mud football," said Geoff. "They don't stay in and watch TV. But you grow out of that. Wheaton was a throwback to being a little kid. Organized football in the mud. What's better than that?" A legitimate, even honorable, excuse to get out there and wallow in the muck.

The Barons were thrilled. Waiting in the locker room, they feared only one thing. Not that Wheaton would win. Not that they would go down in disgrace. Only that the rain might stop before they all had a chance to burrow into the field's oozing goo.

"We were all just, God, I hope this rain continues," said Geoff. "We wanted to be dirty."

The fan turnout that day was exceptionally slim. For the parents in the stands, perched uncomfortably on wet bleachers, sharing umbrellas, the gap between adolescence and middle age loomed wide. We were years beyond the point of enjoying being out in this sort of weather, associated in our minds with unpleasant things like laundry and bronchitis. The boys might have been pumped; we were just wet. Nor were we feeling terribly optimistic, after the last two games. We watched the field dourly.

Bob Plante stalked up and down before his troops with a commander's swagger. One of Wheaton's coaches was an old friend of his, which had set his competitive juices flowing even thicker than usual. "For this game, don't do it for your mother. Don't do it for yourself. Don't do it for your father, your grandmother—do it for me!" he demanded. The boys laughed.

"I'm serious! I know the guy. After the game, when we blow him out, I'll say, hey, you—good game."

Wheaton, tough and scrappy, had already had a winning season and was anxiously primed to make short shrift of the Barons. They rolled out onto the field, grabbed the ball with gusto, and pushed it downfield through the glop for a touchdown within a few short beats. They roared; we groaned. It was apparent Wheaton, too, enjoyed playing in the mud.

But not like our boys. Instead of being thrown off by this immediate seven-point handicap handed them so early in the game, the Barons seemed visibly to square their shoulders. The gauntlet had been thrown; very well, they accepted the challenge. This was, after all, the exact reverse of the first few moments of the Whitman game—and everyone on the team knew how that had turned out. Yeah, sure, they'd scored once. Now try doing it again, sucker.

And to Wheaton's clear irritation, it quickly became apparent that doing it again was not going to be easy. The grimier the B-CC boys got, the more soaked, the more mud-encrusted, the harder they played. The mess on the field had exceeded everyone's fondest hopes—it was a mud bowl, a mud fest, an extravaganza of slime. The sheer abundance of the stuff seemed to unleash a primal force in all of them.

Billy, however, had gone over the top. "It was—like cocaine in my body, I was so crazy, out of my mind," he said. "I was so pumped up. It made me have more energy, the rain. I was crazy that game."

At one point a Wheaton player fell in a pile on top of Dirkey, and Billy, galvanized, ran up and kicked him as hard as he could, just as the play was ending. Slowly, dramatically, the player pulled himself up to his full height. It was impressive. "I suddenly saw he was bigger than me. Damn, he was ugly. I had to act tough, so I sort of shoved him—but inside, I was like, man, he's probably killed a few people."

Billy's flair for the dramatic saved him. As the guy stalked toward him, flexing ominously, "I'm going, yeah, whatever, moving back to the huddle like I don't have time for this stuff." Feigning disdain for all he was worth, backpedaling swiftly, Billy managed to make his escape.

One of the best players on the Wheaton team was running back Eric Reid. Before the game B-CC had been quite pleased— delighted, actually—to hear the rumor that he would not be joining them today, forced out by a torn ligament in the knee. In truth, however, only Eric's jersey, number 20, had been sidelined; Eric himself was on field and fully operable in jersey number 21. A not infrequent ploy.

Billy had taken the unknown 21 on as his personal target. "I talked so much shit to him, I was like, slow little scrub, wow." It wasn't until much later that he realized who he had been bad-mouthing; it gave him a distinct chill. "I didn't know he was the stud. I never would have done it if I'd known he was stud man Reid."

In fact, it had been Eric Reid who had gotten the score for Wheaton—but still, none of the Barons had caught on to his true identity. Visibility was not at a premium today. "We just figured this was a new running back, some kid, they weren't going to give him the ball. Then we were shocked to find out he scored," said Alex. Not until halftime would the Barons realize who they were dealing with. "Somebody recognized him with his helmet off."

The entire team was aware Billy was out of control. At one point, when he was given a penalty, Steven Efantis, the part-time wide-receiver coach, yelled at him to get in shape. "Fuck you!" hollered Billy wildly, running back on the field. No one could touch him today. Covered with mud, his eyes blazing, he was a maniac. "I was so crazy the coaches were scared. My teammates were grabbing me and shit, I was so wired. Just because we were playing in the rain."

Even Rick couldn't handle him. "Rick wanted Billy to get in between the zone, to drift on the pass plays, and Billy was doing something he thought was better," said Sal Fiscina. Finally Rick went to Pete. "Coach, you gotta tell Billy to do it," he begged. "He doesn't believe me." Pete cracked up, but did pass the word on.

"Then, the next play, Rick threw a horrible pass that didn't even come close—if I had been Billy, I would have gone back in the huddle and beaten him up," said Sal.

Just before he sent him in, Mitch, on the sidelines, glanced over at John Everett. The kid was flushed beet red, panting, close to tears. Christ, he'd overpsyched himself. Mitch threw an arm around him and started talking to him quietly, trying to bring him down. Both he and Bob were pretty psyched themselves, too, actually. Because of the rain, the small turnout, Pete had told them they could stay on the field this time. No freak-outs, though, no matter what.

Toby was one player who was in no danger of overpsyching himself; he had been brought down to size early on. Since last week, when he had tossed around his outsized opponent like a Dixie cup, Toby had been feeling considerably larger than life. He had taken it rather easy at practice this week, in fact. Why knock yourself out? Obviously he had muscle to spare, no problem. Wheaton wasn't known for humongous players anyway.

He strode out on Wheaton's field a bit coolly, assumed his stance almost nonchalantly, casually eying their line. Nothing much here. This was going to be a breeze for a Churchill slayer. But on the first play, the guy up against him—a perfectly normal-sized kid—smashed into him like a torpedo, helmet to helmet, and knocked him flat in the mire. This was bad enough. But standing over him, the guy plunged the dagger home: "Fucking pussy," he muttered down at him disgustedly.

Toby's Churchill assurance went up in smoke. "He stuck me good; it was awful." He slumped back to the huddle, utterly dejected, his mind filled with only one thought—maybe, maybe, if there really was a God, it wouldn't be on the tape.

He wasn't the only offensive lineman having problems today. Both Marc Gage and Alex had spent the morning taking College Board tests, the three-hour ordeal every senior underwent at least once. Making the switch from multiple-choice answer sheets to on-line blocking was difficult; neither was handling it well.

Marc was acting so out of it he looked dazed. "What's my name? Hey, Marc, what's my name?" Tae Uk kept insisting, poking him, eagerly returning the favor Marc had done for him at the Whitman game.

"Leave me alone, it's the SATs, not a concussion," said Marc, annoyed. Alex, too, was so stolid, so uncharged, so atypically silent that a couple of the boys even wondered whether he was stoned.

"He's such a commando type usually," said Billy. He wasn't; the SATs had just taken their toll.

Unsurprisingly, given these weak spots, the line was not shining out there at first; Rick was finding it difficult to maneuver in the terrain; the game was stuck for most of the first half in a three-downs-and-punt limbo, back and forth between the teams. In the stands our irritability level grew, fueled by the wetness as well as the general lackluster tail-end mood of the season itself. Toby was right, I thought moodily—the greatest game in the world. When you win. The last two losses had managed to put a dent in everyone's enthusiasm. We sat in the stands, water dripping off our coats, spirits dampened, expectations limp. Occasionally the sun split between the clouds and we all put down our umbrellas; seconds later we had them up again.

The rain was not the only thing falling thick and fast on the field. Penalty flags were dropping like flies all over the lot. One, against Wheaton—an illegal receiver downfield—was contested at such length the game all but ground to a halt. Finally something had happened on the field to rouse us into response—a low rumble of anger began to grow in the stands. We were incensed at their coach's lack of sportsmanship. What sort of example was that for the boys, we asked each other righteously, didn't he know a ref was never wrong in a game? Couldn't he take his medicine like a man and let them get on with it? He was obviously wrong, couldn't he see it?

Pete stood silent during the fracas; the boys glowered and grumbled; Mitch and Bob bit their tongues, avoiding the nearly irresistible urge to join in for fear of banishment. Undaunted, we yelled down a few choice catcalls of our own, feeling like pillars of moral rectitude. The image of Senator Ribicoff staring down Mayor Daley at the '68 Chicago convention popped to mind. "Yes, how hard it is to hear the truth." We, like the refs, were utterly, indisputably, exquisitely right on this one.

We weren't at all, of course, and neither were the refs, as every B-CC player on the field at the time cheerfully assured me later on. Actually the Wheaton coach was completely correct, the call had been totally unfair. Blissfully unaware, we roared out our displeasure in tones of high ethical fervor. "Get this down!" we howled at

Jon Wexler, the reporter for the B-CC *Tatler*. "Tell the people the truth!"

The game pressed on, in between penalty calls; our sense of moral outrage ebbed and flowed accordingly—at least we were reacting to something—then suddenly engulfed us completely yet again. Finally, finally, Rick threw one of his long, jewel-like precision lobs down to Geoff, who leapt heroically to meet it, bringing it down safely into the end zone. Our first touchdown! At long last! We screamed with joy, then seconds later even louder, with horror—another flag had fallen! Two flags! My God, they were taking it back, charging us with not one but two penalties! Good Lord, these were the worst refs in the world! How could they do something like that?

They were the same refs we had been applauding fiercely only minutes ago for their brave decision to penalize Wheaton, but that bothered none of us. This time, they were dead wrong.

And of course, this time they weren't.

In a way it was the Geoff-over-the-fence business all over again. Things were always more complicated, fuzzier, than they seemed. The closer you got to the field, the less football resembled TV (good and bad, black and white, a neat solution tying up the ends just before the credit crawl), the more it resembled the irony, mess, and impossible-to-disentangle muck of life itself—a place where no one's hands were entirely clean. What was amazing was how much we, the grown-ups, still yearned for the fairy tale, with its heroes and villains and tidy resolutions. How much easier it was for the kids to face the real.

Now, for instance, instead of throwing themselves down on the ground in fits at the lost touchdown—an option some of us parents were seriously considering—the boys seemed to toughen up even more. The defense was blazing. Mitch had let the first-string line take over for second half—the contest was over. Dave was hitting on all cylinders. So often this year Dave had felt his responsibilities as defense captain weighing him down—he had had to relay the plays in from Mitch; direct the action; and, on top of that, the guys counted on him for motivation. "Get me up, Dave!" they'd yell at him. "Get me up!" Wanting him to smack their helmets, roar them into life like some kind of athletic Frankenstein.

Late at night he'd lie in bed, going over the plays in his head, trying to be prepared for anything. No question, the job could be a burden—at times he got so furious he'd give the entire defense huddle a huge push, knocking them all down at once. Goddamn it, you guys!

But this game was actually starting to be fun. He'd gotten a crack at Eric Reid, too, tackling him as he ran out full speed, a collision that left both boys lying flat out on the sodden turf. The next play, Eric had looked over at him and winked, acknowledging the hit—a great feeling. The rain, the mud, all of it was contributing to his enjoyment. For once, his sense of responsibility was not wearing him down; for once this season, Dave was having a good time.

Bob Plante had given his offense a blistering going-over during halftime yet again, and that, plus the lost touchdown, was spurring them on to better play. "It wasn't that easy to move in that stuff," Tae Uk noted plaintively, but by second half, the offensive linemen had found their rhythm again. Rick was moving well, both on the ground and in the air, with nice, smooth spurts, until Dirkey plowed through for the score. It was even at last, 7–7. The clock was ticking hard, but the boys were up, manic, riotous, gloriously filthy. They had a chance. We, too, had a chance—that was how we felt. Rain forgotten, past defeats forgotten, we howled lustily, back in the fray once again.

Toriano, finally back on the field after four weeks off, had spent the entire pregame period assuring everyone they could expect to see some real fireworks today. Typical Toriano—talk, talk, talk. "I hope you do something, you haven't done nothing all year," said Bob irritably.

"Sure, I'll do something—I'm gonna score for you," Toriano promised brightly.

Bob had had it. "Score?" he sneered. "I bet you fifty dollars you don't score."

They were well into the fourth quarter, and so far Bob's fifty dollars was safe. Toriano was frustrated. How could you score if Rick never threw you the ball? Him and Geoff, him and Geoff . . . sometimes it seemed like it was true what Mike said, those two had formed a pact to make each other famous. "Don't let that white boy show you up!" the receiver coach yelled at him. Well, sure, but what was he supposed to do?

He had to do something, so he did. Unfortunately, it was the wrong thing—the offense was moving again, nice and steady, and Toriano clipped a Wheaton player. "Why don't you do something right?" yelled Pete; he, too, was disgusted.

Time was running out. Now he had to do something colossal that would grab everyone's attention, redeem him in their eyes fast. On the next play, supposedly blocking for Geoff, he made a grab and missed his man, tumbling splat down in the mud. Wheaton, overjoyed, managed to grab the ball. Toriano had done something spectacular, all right. He'd handed the ball back to Wheaton with less than two minutes on the clock, with the score tied at 7–7.

The Barons, all of them, glared witheringly at him as they ran off the field. Big man, big talk. Thanks a lot, fellow, you might have just lost us the whole match.

But the mud gods were smiling on B-CC today, smiling on all of us. The defense refused to give up. Dave, playing harder and with more fierce enjoyment than he had all year, refused to give up. With Wheaton pressing hard, practically at the goal line, the boys did what they hadn't been able to do two weeks ago at Whitman, the all but impossible: forced a fumble at the goal line. And now we were all standing, screaming, pleading, umbrellas forgotten, past disappointments wiped away. Hope had risen like a phoenix on that sloppy field, pulling all of us up in its wings.

The Barons offense was back on the field—seconds, seconds remaining on the clock. Last chance. The only thing was hurry-hurry, offense—no huddle, just get out there, everyone take off down the field as fast as possible, and Rick hurl it to—whoever.

And Toriano knew it was his. It had to be. He'd had a rotten game, he was the goat of the team at the moment, this was the absolute last chance to prove himself. Only, being Toriano, he had no doubts, not even now, not even after back-to-back embarrassments that might have squelched a lesser ego. Hey, wasn't he the greatest? Last year there had been a kid they called the Legend. Toriano liked to tell people, with great seriousness, "The Legend is no more. The Myth has arrived." Usually they groaned. Well, this was his chance, his only one, to make good.

With less than twenty seconds on the clock, he took off down the field, flying, and cut over the middle. Rick bombed it at him straight as an arrow. Toriano pulled it down at the 25-yard line and ran like a shooting star—for his life, for his reputation—all the way down into the end zone for the touchdown and the victory.

"We were just trying to get into field-goal range," said Erik Karlson. "And the next thing you knew, Toriano just took it all the way. After I saw that, I was like, oh my God, Tae Uk, let's go. We just started running down the field, looking for people to hit."

"The speed-and-grace king" Mark Bitz had called him. "Raw talent," Toby said. Well, he'd actually done it, finally, it was worth it, even though every boy on the team knew inside, even as they rushed to him, yelling, knew that, as one said, "Toriano will be talking about this forever."

Geoff was the first to reach him. "You did it, you did it! I'm so proud of you!" he howled, flinging his arms around him. "I told you you could. Now, next time, block for me, okay?"

"It made me feel good, to hear him say he was proud of me," said Toriano. He took no umbrage at the blocking comment—Geoff was perfectly right about that, he knew. Crowing, the boys surrounded him, hugging, pounding, congratulating. He had done it, done it at last—come up from the ashes, exploded like a comet, brought home the win in a final blazing note of molten glory. Just like he had dreamed.

"It was incredible, incredible," said Mark Bitz. "Another win against a good team."

Never had a game ended so spectacularly. The whistle blew and all of us, mud and rain be damned, ran out on the field. We had not done it at Kennedy, or at Walter Johnson or Blair, but we did it now. We hugged who we could, in passing, getting smears of dirt on our coats, arms, faces.

We had come out today chastened and low key, expecting nothing, and we had been handed a tight, well-fought, down-to-the-wire, delicious win. We wanted to share the glory, share the pride. We wanted—yes! middle-aged and flu-prone as we wer!e—to share the mud. Boys who had played very little, like Jimmy, also ran out on the field to throw themselves face down in the glop, to remove the curse of a clean uniform.

Bob Plante was jubilant. The Churchill fight had been a good one, but this was a win—and against a coach he knew. "Fantastic game," he told them ecstatically. "You came back—you did what you had to—you took it all." Toriano basked in his glee—it was almost as good as getting that fifty dollars, which he had a strong feeling he'd never see. The linemen glowed. They had come a long way, Bob Plante's line, from those early days. Damn, if only the season were just starting now—they could show some of those teams like Wooten or Rockville a thing or two. But still, they had come through for him today. They had done their coach proud.

"Pinnacle of the season," Bob would call it, later. "Kennedy was a good ball game, but Wheaton was the pinnacle. Losing at half-time and then we came back and really won. The offensive line came back and did what they had to do to win."

"A good win," Pete agreed. "Maybe not a major upset, but a good win. To beat Wheaton is always big." Then, too, there was the extra fillip that came from the knowledge that Wheaton had downed B-CC last year—revenge was always sweet.

"Everyone was so happy," said Erik Karlson. "Coach Plante was overwhelmed. That bus ride home. There was mud everywhere. We were so loud, sitting in the parking lot, the bus was rocking back and forth, all the Wheaton fans were yelling at us. The bus driver said, you guys better shut up."

The win meant nothing, as far as the big picture went, of course—it was much too late. Too late for the playoffs, too late for any dreams of bringing home a championship, too late even for the modest goal of topping last year's 5–5 record. After all, what had it been but a good, solid, unexpected win in the twilight of the season?

So it meant nothing—except personally, to every kid. And to every one of us parents. To see them, joyous, mud-slaked, euphoric, was to know the truth—that the personal was all that really mattered, now or ever.

And standing on the field with them, mud-stained, my heart pounding, it hit me for the first time with staggering force: why, I had never wanted to be a cheerleader, like my husband had accused—never at all, even thirty years ago. Or a pom-pom girl or a fan or even a girlfriend of a hero. What I wanted—what I had always wanted—was to be out there on the field myself. This was why I had responded so strongly to Toby's athletic exploits right from the beginning, why I'd felt he'd opened the gate to a world that had been closed to me. To me, not to him. Why, I had felt just like James had during the Churchill game all this time, without the insight to understand it—for hadn't I, too, been standing on the edge, unable to play, forced out to the sidelines forever? My eyes glued to my son, longing. Toby—do what I would do out there! Do it for me, my son!

I was the one, all along, who wanted to be there. To feel that joy, that sense of mastery—even the hits! Even the pain! Even the losses! Experience all of it, denied me by my body, my generation, my gender. Feel it, revel in it, all that I had missed. Like the poet Whitman, another eternal observer who had also stood on the sidelines, longing to be able to say in reality, "I am the man. I suffered. I was there."

That had been it; that had always been it. How silly, not to have known. I stood in the mud and let the truth flow through my veins. The boys moved past me, huge, hulking, mud and exhilaration stamped on their faces, taking deep gulps of the victory-charged air. I gulped the same air, I matched them breath for breath.

CHAPTER SIXTEEN

IN A FAIR and equitable universe, Wheaton would have been the end. To have gone out on Wheaton, the mud bowl, would have meant going out in a blaze of glory, despite the lack of statistical consequence, despite Whitman, despite Churchill, despite everything.

But of course, Wheaton was not the end. There was still one more game to play, against Gaithersburg. And as with Churchill—if anything, more than with Churchill—no single member of the Barons, boys and coaching staff alike, held any real hope deep down that they stood much of a chance against them.

A graph of the season so far would have looked as erratic and bumpy as the Barons' offensive line—the Wooten plunge, the sudden upswing at Blair, a crash down to Rockville, the lowest point of all, up, up, up with Einstein, WJ, and Kennedy, moving higher and higher, then down a dip with Whitman, further down with Churchill, the blessed final surge at Wheaton. Yet, uneven as it was, the graph held a certain honorable symmetry. There was no shame to it. You could look at it and feel okay, especially if you'd been there and knew.

But Gaithersburg was the toughest team on the schedule—far enough up-county to have that dangerous aura of farm boy about it. Townhouse developments were proliferating in the area; there was a gigantic mall; but much of the area was still rural. Teens out here still engaged in the sport of cow-tipping, in which a group of boys ran full speed at a dozing upright cow and knocked her flat; also mailbox polo—driving down a country road, seeing how many mailboxes you could decapitate with a stick. No, Gaithersburg was still country, all right. More than one Baron had the uneasy feeling that Gaithersburg would be, in the gloomy words of Kong, "like stabbing a person that's already dead."

So in some ways, without actually admitting it, many of the boys did consider Wheaton the end, at least in their hearts. Practice the following week was almost perfunctory. "Kong and I were pissed all week," said Alex; they were the two who most prized military readiness. "No one was doing anything, everyone coming in late for practice." Of course, Alex himself had been late to practice many times throughout the season. His own playing had faded in and out. At Wheaton, he had hardly been a real presence on the field. But this did not matter. He knew how it *should* be done, whether he himself did it that way or not—and it bothered him greatly when the other boys flouted the rules. As a leader, Alex could not get over feeling he was entitled to bend a few rules himself—not, actually, an entirely unusual way for a leader to feel.

The boys' lackadaisical attitude this week drove Mitch up the wall—laid-back B-CC, shrugging their shoulders at the inevitable instead of holding on till the last possible second. Where was the hunger? The will?

Yet even his screams and insults had a mellower sound. The truth was, Mitch could no longer play nasty, rotten bully to quite the same full-scale effect. His cover had been blown for good—too many of the boys had seen his softer side. They knew he cared and that Bob cared too, by now—cared about *them,* not just the game— and that a lot of the meanness had been a big act all along. And they knew, finally, that the coaches were not that much older than they were.

The fall was ending, the season was ending; there was a true wintry chill in the air the night of the Gaithersburg game. Already, many of the boys had moved on, in their minds, to other fields. The will to strive for that all-important sense of focus, that keen concentration on the moment, had faded in many of them. Some actually dozed off in the bus on the long ride out to the school.

"Something about it . . . we just didn't care," said one.

"We wanted to win and play well, but we had to be realistic . . . it was Gaithersburg," said Kong. "So I just wanted to play well."

Mitch, of course, was as up as ever. "Great football weather! This kind of weather always gives me a hard-on!" he announced happily. In the locker room, he pulled all the defense guys over to one side for the last pre-battle charge.

"You guys don't understand how much you mean to me," he told them, his voice throbbing. "You're the first high school defense I've ever coached alone. I feel like I've succeeded because we're like a family.

"I just want you to go out there and have fun tonight. Regardless . . . regardless of what happens." Dave, Geoff, Kong—in fact most of the defense players were deeply touched. Not all, of course. Mike and Rene had been at loggerheads with the young coach too long to be swayed; his insistence on sidelining them during the first quarter of Wheaton still stung.

And Billy had never been won over. Yes, Mitch had mellowed, he had cried with them and reached out to them in the past weeks. But Mitch's manner and methods had gotten under Billy's skin from the start; he did not like being manipulated, and he despised what he considered to be Mitch's posing. A lot of the other guys, it seemed to him, had forgotten by now how upset they'd been with Mitch back at the beginning, how hard they'd had to work to try and recoup their morale as a team. They were ready to hail him as a great guy. Billy hadn't forgotten and didn't intend to. They were the ones who had made this season work, not Mitch; it was important to remember that.

Yet all the boys, however they felt about the coach, knew that the win-fixated Mitch was offering them the most generous gift he could tonight: telling them to just enjoy themselves no matter what.

Because from the looks of it, there were going to be few surprises out there. The farm-boy reputation had been no lie—the Gaithersburg players were solid as steers, bursting with the kind of muscles that only came from prodigious daily plowing of the back forty. They stood on the field watching the Barons file out with delighted smirks on their faces, as if a singularly appetizing treat had just been set before them. They're our age, they're our age, several B-CC players reminded themselves. There was no escaping the fact, though, that they certainly *looked* older.

The whistle blew and the farm boys chowed down with a will. Bellowing lustily, they covered the field, exploding through lines, tossing the Barons over their shoulders like hapless calves. No doubt about it, these guys could play.

"Don't get in my way," they cooed luridly. " 'Cause I'd just hate to have to hurt you."

"Jesus, WJ lost to you guys? I can't believe it," they hooted.

"They'd just come up to the line like they were going to blitz, and just stand there, just stand, not even a football stance, like— I'm gonna blitz. Right in your face," said Rick. "And you'd be— great, you know?" Incensed, Rick turned to the weapon that never failed him—his mouth. "Fuck you, ninety-two, fuck you, ninety-two," he howled out the cadence; right in their fat faces.

Not that it bothered them. "They were talking like crazy," said Tae Uk. "They were psyched." God knows they were good. At one point, he'd looked up, seen the middle linebacker running at him, turned to block him—"I'm supposed to be a fast person"—and the guy ran him over and slammed into Brendan Symes with full force. It was almost surreal, Tae Uk thought, getting up, dazed. How did the guy get from here to there? How can he do that?

Yet maybe just because of how good they were, they did not take even small defeats kindly. One guy Tae Uk was blocking with fair success suddenly wigged out completely after the little linemen stopped him for the third time—grabbing his jersey for leverage, he kneed Tae Uk right in the balls.

"I couldn't believe he did that! It hurt like crazy. To do that, especially when they were killing us . . . it pissed me off so bad. I was like, I WANT YOU!" He would have given anything to just go at the guy right there, the hell with the penalty, but Pete, on the sidelines, noting the dangerous glint in the little lineman's eye, pulled him over as soon as he could. You start a fight, you take off your jersey and get on the bus. Right now. Got that? Tae Uk nodded and managed with difficulty to rein in the impulse.

The points were piling up, all on one side—18–0 by the end of the first quarter, 31–0 by the end of the second. The score didn't hurt so much—they'd expected it—but "that they were talking to us while they were beating us!" said Toriano. "That got to us.

"When Geoff would catch the ball they'd tackle him and say, I know you don't want to get up, 'cause I'm gonna hurt you. It was like putting salt in the wounds. And when they'd get off you, they'd put all their weight on you and push off. You had to smack their hands away."

At one point, Toriano yelped when one guy landed on his just healed leg. "Hey, watch it, that's my broken leg!" he squealed, then watched with unease as an evil smile broke out on the player's face, and knew he had made a bad mistake: now the guy would be aiming for his leg every time.

"Their coach was even talking! When Rick was trying to run the ball, he'd say, you're not gonna light up the scoreboard like that, son, you better throw the ball."

The scoreboard: it loomed over the end of the field like a bad report card blown up to giant size for all the world to see. It was too much for one B-CC senior, Zeke Gundy, a onetime player who was close to many of the boys. Zeke took his responsibilities as a fan seriously, often going to strange lengths to entertain the team. On several occasions during the past weeks he had urged everyone before practice to be on the lookout for "4:30 Nerdy" or "5 o'clock Charlie." Sure enough, at the appointed hour, Zeke would appear, pedaling a green bicycle around the field, occasionally blowing a small party horn with élan, cracking everyone up.

Tonight, though, called for a somewhat grander gesture. The boys were being crushed; the scoreboard was beaming the horrible truth out for all to see. Maybe the Barons couldn't get up there. But someone else could. Shinnying up the pole, Zeke unplugged the neon sign, as a final end-of-season present for everyone, including himself. "It was just too embarrassing," he told Pete, who showed up at the police station later that night to free him. "Something had to be done."

The point was well taken—certainly nothing was happening on the field. At halftime Mitch pulled all the defensive players over to the side once again. A certain amount of warmth had gone out of his face now, but his voice, when he began to speak, was carefully calm. He had told them he wasn't going to yell at them tonight, and he had meant it, he said quietly. It was the end of the season, they were all family, that was the important thing. He knew they were doing their best . . . but . . . but . . . BUT GODDAMN IT, YOU GUYS, WHAT THE FUCK IS GOING ON HERE? WHAT ARE YOU TRYING TO PULL? I'VE NEVER SEEN SUCH SLOPPY, CRAPPY PLAYING IN ALL MY—"

"And he was off," said Geoff fondly. The boys exchanged grins. Bad-mouthing Mitch, back in the saddle again. Completely losing any semblance of serenity, Mitch even unleashed a few blasts at his most cherished, dependable knight, Dave, for the first time all season. Dave had never been the brunt of Mitch's temper before, and it felt crummy. Sure, he hadn't been knocking himself out on the field—who had? But after all this time, after all his work over the season, to be dressed down in public like some lowly scrub . . . Dave smoldered. For the first time, he understood what some of the other players had gone through with Mitch. It made you mad all right, but not at the other team—the one it made you want to kill was Mitch himself. The other guys looked on, awed, yet not entirely unpleased to see Dave himself get dressed down, for once.

They weren't going to win, that much was sure. But a wave of defiance swept through the ranks of the team as halftime ended. What the hell, what the hell—they might as well get out there and enjoy it. "Geoff, man, this is just you and me," Rick told his buddy. "We're calling our own plays out there." Bob and Mitch had taken Rick aside several weeks ago and given him a few pointers about reading the defense. It was the subtle stuff you had to look for, how far one guy was leaning on which foot, things like that. A quick study, Rick had picked up fast. Since then, he had been ignoring many of Pete's directives in favor of his own. After all, he was the one out there, not Coach White.

The wind was blowing hard up in the stands; we sat up there, chilled, disgruntled, waiting for the massacre to continue. We were not surprised at any of this; we all knew Gaithersburg's reputation and had geared our hopes down accordingly. But still. Too bad it had to end like this, on this cold rural field, instead of in last week's mud; the boys would be mournful, upset, filled with a sense of loss.

But within minutes of the second half we realized they were going to be none of these things; they had made up their minds to go out with bravado, spirits high. There was no mistaking the looks on their faces. Outmanned, outskilled, out of luck—"outspeeded, outgraced, outsmarted," as one boy put it—they weren't going down whimpering. It didn't matter, nothing mattered, except that they were playing the game they loved.

And this realization released sudden energy, pulling the boys into the game for the first time. Almost as a byproduct, their play tightened, toughened up. No, they couldn't score—but amazingly, neither could Gaithersburg suddenly. And it was clear, very clear, who was having the better time.

Christo, who had built up a full head of steam—"I was really pissed off because they kept running all over us"—finally managed to release it where it could do some good, slamming their quarter-back into the ground. "I just flattened him, the guy was like in the air."

On the sidelines, Mitch, who never praised anyone during a game, grabbed him. "Jesus Christ, that hit was so amazing I have a hard-on!" he blurted. No matter that changes of weather, too, could prompt this condition. Christo knew he'd been given a compliment he could prize forever.

Kong, who had known from the start they would never win this one, concentrated on personal victories, racking up tackle after tackle, for a grand total of twelve. However bad the game, at least this he could feel good about.

Toriano seemed determined to stick to last week's pattern. He caught a long pass, headed off with his usual speed, zipping around players adeptly, only to be cut down without warning—"I didn't even see the guy"—the ball popping out of his hands like a greased pig. "You can brag now," James teased him, back on the bench, and even a girl he knew came down to the sidelines to taunt him. "Everyone's talking about you big-time . . . how come you can't hold on to the ball?" But disgrace never flattened Toriano. "I was like, throw me the ball again, throw me the ball again."

In the last quarter, Rick did—and this time, the speed king came through, running it all the way down to the end zone, just like he had at Wheaton. Touchdown against Gaithersburg! Whatever else, they wouldn't have a shutout! We howled as if they had taken it all.

(And as far as Toriano went, it might as well have been true.

Later he would have the pleasure of running into a bunch of Gaithersburg players who started ragging him at once about his team. "Yeah, but, uh . . . wasn't that a fifty-five-yard touchdown I scored against you guys?" he asked softly. They shut up at once— they'd picked the wrong player to brag to.)

Geoff, too, was having a wonderful time. As always. For Geoff, the fun of football overrode everything. It had when he was a little kid, and it did now. Yeah, winning was wonderful, greatest thing in the world. So was being in the spotlight, grabbing the ball out of the air at the last possible second while the crowd went crazy, all that stuff.

But it wasn't everything, never had been. The locker room, the guys, being out on the field . . . just being out on that goddamn field . . . that was the real magic. And it could never fade, no matter how bad you were losing. Nothing—*nothing*—could take away that joy. "The second half of that game was the funniest, I think, for almost everyone," he said. "It was a good way to end the year. We had no chance of winning, it wouldn't have mattered if we had won, we wouldn't have gone to any playoffs, so we were all just having a good time."

Billy, too, felt satisfied. Against all the odds, in the face of almost certain crushing defeat, the team had managed, on their own, to wrest some good out of the night. They had refused to knuckle under to despair, were insisting defiantly on enjoying themselves no matter what. All of them together. It was like the meeting, he thought. Then, too, there had been certain givens they could not change or control. What was important was to discover the things they could change—and to do it.

"It would have been really depressing, losing that bad, after the season, so people tried to make it like fun," said Tae Uk. "The O-line was like, why don't we pick on 40? Jump on him? Doing stuff like that.

"People didn't want to take it seriously, so we were like making fun. Telling jokes, on the line. Rick and Geoff were telling stories in the huddle, dumb jokes. Having fun. We knew we were out-manned."

He, of course, hadn't completely lost his fighting spirit. Spotting one big Gaithersburg player mouthing off, Tae Uk challenged him loudly from the sidelines."I hope you're a junior! Man, I sure hope you are! I want your ass next year!"

"Uh, he *is* a junior," someone muttered warningly.

Tae Uk gulped. "I'm like, damn. Damn."

The end of the season was minutes away; each senior, facing that end, reacted differently. On the sidelines Rick was walking up and down the ranks, shaking hands, grinning, cool, confident, collected. Alex, as usual, was feeling somewhat detached. Well, it was almost over, all of it. Silly sport, actually, when you thought about it. His father wasn't entirely wrong. Well, it would help get him into The Citadel, certainly. It had been good for that, at least.

Dave strove for balance. His anger at Mitch had faded already; he was already feeling a certain sense of loss, despite the onus of the season, but he struggled to keep it in perspective. "You have to love the sport while you're playing, but you have to be able to leave it, so if it's that time, over, you're mentally prepared." He felt he was. It had been a hard season, with his ankle, with all the demands Mitch had made on him. At least he had come through, he felt. He had done his job, he had not faltered.

Toby felt only "a kind of relief" at the moment, especially considering the sort of game this last one had been. Purposefully, deliberately, he pushed aside all thoughts of finality; he would deal with that another time, after tonight. "The sadness came later."

Kong was mournful, yet oddly lightheaded. Much as he loved it, there had always been pressure involved in playing football, always worry. Now, suddenly, he knew that in a matter of minutes that pressure would be lifted off his back for all time. He had always hoped to go on playing, maybe in college, he had always hoped he'd grow a little more, yet he sensed that very probably this was it, the end, that football was over for him forever. It was hard—yet there was something almost refreshing about it, in a funny way.

But Brendan Symes felt only a yawning sorrow. "Is this it? Football? Oh my God, is this it? The glamour, the lights, going in the locker room . . . is it really over?" The end; he was facing the end and knew it and knew there was nothing he could do to stop it from happening.

And as the whistle blew, ending the last game for the 1988 B-CC Barons, the boys' various emotions swept up into the stands, engulfing all of us for the last time. We snorted in cheerful disgust, because it had been such a silly game; we swallowed hard, a little tearful, because it was the end—for me, the closest I would ever get to being on a field myself, I knew. But we breathed in a long sigh of total relief too because we were parents, after all, and it was over now, over for good, at last, and the boys on the field—hugging each other, shaking hands, rubbing heads, laughing like maniacs—had survived.

As if by mutual consent, the boys avoided any soppy emotional scenes that night; the ride back to B-CC was a merry one. "No one was crying, everybody was rocking on the bus," said John Han. "Slapping high fives . . . we were all happy. You'd think people'd be down after a loss like that, but they'd beaten us so bad we didn't take it seriously."

One reason for the good spirits, he felt sure, was that "we knew we'd never see the film. Maybe Plante and Mitch will see it twenty-five times, but what the hell, we'll never see it. They'll never yell at us again."

The seniors were in the process of divesting themselves of their armor. "Anybody wanna buy a neck roll?" "Who needs shoulder pads?" The juniors grabbed the prizes eagerly, if a bit nervously; the old guard was changing in front of their eyes.

"It's just like . . . it was over. End of an era," said Mark Bitz thoughtfully. "Rick and Geoff . . . the end of an era."

"All my life, something's been hanging over me . . . my sister, all her friends, Rick, Geoff . . . and to know next year I'll be quarterback, with no one above me . . . it's a weird feeling," said Jimmy.

So many of the juniors had spent the year feeling like that. Corey, Dirkey, Toriano. Always there was someone—Rick, Geoff, Alex, Dave, Brendan—hanging over them, casting shadows. And now those shadows were moving on, leaving the field. The idea would take some getting used to. But for now, at least, they were all still together, on the bus, in uniform, teasing, loving, feeling like family, calling out the usual taunts. "Hey, Christo, that last tackle of yours, I had him, you didn't have to knock yourself out," Jimmy razzed.

It was enough. There was a feeling of satisfaction, even peace in the air. They had made it through.

"I can remember when I played football in high school . . . there

was a feeling sometimes that you had really gone through something, passed over, crossed through," said Sal Fiscina. "Somehow
you felt you had accomplished something. Advanced somewhat, in
terms of growing up." It was a feeling he had found nowhere else.

"Football is a lot of work. And these kids aren't accustomed to
working. Any kid who's grown up in B-CC is not accustomed to
hard work—not compared to a generation ago. They've had a time
or relative tranquillity, of affluence." Yet they had chosen to place
themselves, each of them, purposely, in a situation "where they had
to deal . . . show courage, strength of character . . . go through
work, effort, regimentation, repetition." Defer gratification, accept
responsibility, deal with consequences.

"And where else at that age are you going to get that?" he
demanded. "Walking around the mall?"

The season was over—ended on a sour note, supposedly. Yet for
some reason the boys did not feel sour, not at all. They had not let
the game, the coaches, the dismal situation, any of it, bleed them of
the joy that was rightfully theirs. Instead they had turned the tables
on everyone and gone out laughing and unashamed. Geoff summed
it up simply. "On the bus ride home, we were . . ." He paused for
a moment to find the right word. "We were content."

CHAPTER SEVENTEEN

THE FOOTBALL BANQUET— the grand finale of the season—was scheduled for six days after the Gaithersburg game; a gala, by-invitation-only affair. The banquet took planning—flowers, food, engraved invitations, trophies—but it was worth it, if only to see the boys in formal dress. Most of them still chafed at ritual in their daily lives; getting them into suits for family celebrations or religious holidays could be a formidable task. But the banquet was different. This was their ceremony, not one of ours, and they were prepared to relish it to the hilt.

The setting this year struck some of us as exceedingly appropriate—the large upstairs hall of the Bethesda–Chevy Chase Rescue Squad. The boys, discreetly tailored, achingly handsome, sat together at round tables in the center of the hall. Parents gravitated naturally to tables on the side.

The large room shone with light, quivered with emotion. This was the beginning of the end for the parents of seniors, we knew. Tonight our sons left football. Within months, they would be leaving school, leaving home, leaving—there was no avoiding it—our lives. We were well aware of this progression, had often enough, it seemed, fervently longed for it. Yet tonight it made our throats hurt. I could already hear the Processional in the air clearly, and inside knew I was echoing the universal plaint made in the face of all loss: damn it, I'm not ready for this.

None of us were. But none of us let on. We chatted brightly, chomped our way through the buffet, giggled, flirted, spouted suburban banter, glanced over at the boys, exchanged smiles, and avoided each others' eyes. The boys may have been bound to each other by football, but we were bound by parenthood, an even more ancient union. The cords of empathy running between us stretched tight. Nothing needed to be said. We knew how we felt.

The boys, of course, were far removed from all this emotionally, as they would soon be physically. The concept of weltschmerz was completely foreign to them, anyway—had they been informed of it, they would have hooted in disbelief. Poignancy and regret were for pussies: it would take many years, and probably the experience of fatherhood, before they could understand what we were feeling. They, on the other hand, were high as kites. They had emerged from the crucible and were ready to mark the passage with a bang-up finale. Sitting together, cordoned off from the rest of the room by invisible ropes, they were a self-sustaining energy zone of adolescent enthusiasm, emitting raucous, foot-stomping hilarity and beaming self-congratulation. They applauded each other loudly, laughed uproariously at the most minor cracks. Despite our proximity, the sense of different levels remained acute. We were still in the stands, they were still on the field.

The Jayvee coaches led off the ceremonies. B-CC's Jayvee had weathered a dismal one-and-eight season "but these fellows stuck it out, they came out, worked hard, gave 100 percent," said Coach Matt Noble valiantly. He called out each player's name and in conclusion, presented an award to Alex, who had given a good deal of time to the junior team during the season, helping out with coaching, serving in his favorite role as leader.

Then Pete took over for the varsity, and it was obvious Pete was the man of the night. There had been times during the season when his authority had seemed to dim, when the force of Bob and Mitch had seemed almost to overpower him. But tonight it was Pete at the helm, without question, expertly piloting the season into the end zone with his own brand of dry wit, and impersonal yet comforting warmth.

Calmly he announced each boy's name, handing out pins and letters, spoke a bit about each, zeroing in on every boy's finest moment with his amazingly sharp memory for detail. Corey's Einstein touchdown, Dirkey's Wheaton catch, Toriano's twin touchdowns in the twilight of the season. With Lunkhead, he singled out Gaithersburg. "I know it was not a pretty sight, that game," he said, pausing to let the guffaws run their course, "but he made three terrific catches there."

His teasing, of course, threaded throughout. "Mark's limping," he announced as Lunkhead hobbled up to get his letter. "What's new, huh?" Mark Bitz, he advised us, was "a center . . . a guard . . . a talker." Wayne Meadows, the erstwhile punter who had broken his leg just before Whitman "had more things happen to him than Carter's got little liver pills." Mike Mitchem, he announced—to whoops of appreciation—was "our number-one mean man."

But invariably, too, he gave each boy something solid to hold on to, words they could remember. Tae Uk: "You can't tell a player's heart by how much they weigh. If they were all like Tae Uk we wouldn't have any problems." Dirkey was "the most improved player over the last half of the season." Christo: "Good people . . . we're looking for big things out of Christo next year." With consummate skill, he pulled off the trick that had eluded so many parents, teachers, and coaches down through the years. He made every kid feel good—and he made it look easy.

Toby, Billy, and Toriano—the three who had returned to the lineup strictly against medical advice—each got an extra pat on the back. Billy "was determined he was going to be out there for the team and the rest of us." Toriano was told not to play "and he says, nah, I'll play. We're certainly glad he did." Toby was "injured, but he didn't let that hold him back." Several of us in the audience winced at the reminders, breathing a quick thanks that nothing worse had happened. The boys had been—we had been—very lucky.

But not always, and not all of us. "Life is not always as fair as it should be," said Pete somberly, announcing James's name. But "he has a long life ahead of him and James is going to be playing someplace; he's not going to be sitting home next year, he's going to be out there playing," he added staunchly. Calmly and with dignity, James came to the front to receive his letter.

"We're gonna miss them, we're gonna miss them," said Pete, as each of the seniors came up. "But time moves on, seasons move on." It was a thought directed solely at the adults in the audience. Maybe later it would hit the boys; for now, it seemed, they had recovered that football-honed Zen state of theirs—they were entirely focused on and utterly enjoying the moment. No looking back, no looking forward: now. Maybe you had to be a 17-year-old kid to reach that state; either that or a Buddhist monk. It was doubtful any of us middle-aged suburbanites would be getting there anytime soon.

"Well, if I was counting right we have seven trophies . . . and we have seven names left to call," Pete drawled. The air tensed with excitement. The trophies stood tall, silver, luminous. Moving briskly, with his usual aversion to emotional moments, Pete reeled off the winners. Dimarlo Duvall was the outstanding member of the scout team. The kid who had once disrupted classes had been rewarded for his dogged discipline. Kong, who worked harder than anyone, received the coaches' award. The boys cheered fiercely.

"I'm bringing up Bob here and he's gonna present the outstanding lineman award to Toby Oppenheimer," Pete said. My heart clutched; I had not expected this. Bob mumbled quickly. "We don't have a big offensive line. Even Toby . . . he's what, one-fifty, one seventy-five?" He paused, then blurted suddenly, "But he plays like he weighs three hundred." Toby strode up to his reward. "I knew I could do it," he had said. "I was *destined* to do it right."

"It was so cute, Toby was so nervous, waiting," said Geoff later. "I said, Toby, you know you're going to get it, not Alex—you know you are."

He had made it. "How did it feel, standing up there?" his father asked him later. Toby let out a huge sigh of happiness. "Like the biggest orgasm in the world."

Brendan Reed—the player's player, the guy "who should be everybody's favorite," as Corey Dade said, took the Outstanding Back award. "Stand up, Brendan, you're a hell of a man!" said Pete ringingly. Mitch then took the mike to give the Outstanding Defense award to Dave "the gentleman who helped me out . . . I could never have done it without him . . . this gentleman here, the key to the defense." Dave stood proudly, accepting the tribute he had earned. On his way back to his seat, James leaned over to congratulate him, smiling ironically. "Dave knew, too," he said. "He knew, if it hadn't been for my knee—it could have been me up there."

Rick got the Most Valuable Player award. Despite the rocky start, he had "fought his way back to being the number-two passer in the county," Pete said. Rick was a guy who "gets a lot from his family," Pete added, glancing down at Sal and JoAnn. "And he gives a lot back. He's gonna move on. We're gonna miss him."

And Geoff—to no one's surprise, least of all his, of course—received the 1988 Outstanding Player award; he swaggered up with his usual bouncy gait. "His stats," said Pete, "will stand a long time at B-CC." In a few weeks, we would get the news—Geoff had made the prestigious honorable mention all-Met list, as well as first string, all-County. Both Rick and Billy were named second string all-County.

The boys stood before us, serious-faced, holding their trophies, for one long beat, while we clapped. "Fourteen weeks," said Pete, over the applause. "If you'da smelled that locker room you'd know it was fourteen weeks. We sweated it out together, yelled at each other, called each other a couple of names sometimes, but when it was over, we could all shake hands and enjoy ourselves together."

Geoff, Rick, and Dave took the rostrum to hand out plaques to the coaches. "They're out there not only because they love the game but because they love us," said Geoff, as always able to express emotional truths directly. "We'd like to show them right now a return of our love."

We all rose, cheering, for the last time; stayed on our feet, tears blurring our view. It was over. "Oh," said Carole Stone mournfully, in her low voice, her eyes on Billy, her youngest. "Why didn't I have more?"

Jo-Ann Fiscina, Judy Burgess, and I stood silently, watching Rick, Alex, and Toby, all three of whom had been playing together . . . moments ago . . . in nursery school. "Well," said Jack Burgess jovially, noticing our faces, "and what are you girls going to do now?" All of us had been working women for years; maybe some other time this would have hit us as a stridently chauvinistic remark.

Not now. Tonight, it mirrored our own thoughts too clearly.

Our boys—in each case the youngest in the family—were leaving. We had held on tenaciously, squeezed all the juice we could out of this football season. But it was over; we were finally being forced to admit it. The season was gone, the year was passing, the most important part of our lives was ending forever. What were we going to do now?

Frankly, we didn't have the slightest idea. I comforted myself, once home, by attempting to arrange Toby's jersey, letter, and trophy into a properly impressive tableau on top of his shelves, fiddling with the display so often over the next few days that finally he lost patience. "It's not a shrine, Mom," he said firmly. And he was right. It had been his season, not mine, after all; they were his mementos; it was his room. His life, too, if it came to that. As Bob Plante had bellowed to his line, again and again, it was time to show a little courage. I would never be a football player, but I figured I could follow that one directive—at least this once. I grinned bravely, squared my shoulders, and cleared out.

The 1988 season of the B-CC Barons was complete. It had not been a winning season, nor even a break-even season; it had had its full share of pain, humiliation, compromise, injury. There had been moments of shame as well as pride; petty, selfish spasms, arrogance, cheap shots, cruelty—along with joy, compassion, kindness, even sacrifice. The boys on the team had experienced potent thrills, high emotion, brotherly bonding, loud humor, occasional flashes of self-knowledge, innumerable large and small shifts in the way they perceived the world. An average high school football season, no more. No less.

Time would soften the edges around some of their memories. But not all. Many moments of this season the boys would be able to recall with perfect clarity the rest of their lives. The adolescent lens is a powerful one; pictures taken then have a tendency to remain stamped on the brain. The boys would take their memories of this season with them into a new century; in some ways, impossible to foretell, they would undoubtedly affect the paths they took.

The experience had changed them for better and worse. They had learned something about courage and hard work, about facing fears, about putting themselves on the line. But along with that, inevitably, in the manner of soldiers everywhere, they had come to feel distanced, in a certain sense, from those who had not been there, from the civilians, parents, friends, siblings, who made up the rest of the world. They had been there, we had not, and there was a certain barrier between us just because of that. It would take some time before that barrier would crumble.

They had struggled for three long months to achieve a proper mind-set—that supreme state of grace in which you truly believed you were, in Bob's phrase, "the toughest SOB coming down Rockville Pike," the mark of the real football player. Fucking attitude! Get it up, they had urged each other in the trenches. Well, they had, they had. Only now that football was over, now that they were off the field, what now? A mind-set wasn't something you could peel off and toss in a hamper like a set of shoulder pads. Like returning vets from every war ever waged, some of the boys had trouble initially fitting back in the world.

A handful attempted to ease the transition by plunging immediately into the rigors of wrestling . . . Alex, Rick, and Geoff among them. Alex loved wrestling—much more than he did football, to tell the truth. The sort of guy who was drawn to wrestling was more the sort Alex respected—someone who knew the importance of discipline, for instance. Like he did himself. Geoff, on the other hand, hated it. He just thought it was a bad idea to spend a season without a sport of some kind. He knew himself; God knows what would happen.

Toby too briefly considered wrestling, until the coach made a tactical error by trying to persuade him with what he thought was the perfect prod: "You a man or a woman?" he sneered. Unfortunately this was reminiscent of one of Toby's favorite movie scenes, in *The Parallax View,* in which a barroom bully challenges Warren Beatty. "You some kind of a girl?" "Yeah, I'm a girl," he answers coolly. Toby decided not to wrestle. The end of the season left him feeling a bit depleted, time somewhat heavy on his hands. The sport had claimed so much of his attention, it wasn't easy to reassume a football-free life. For a time, nothing off that field had seemed quite real . . . certainly nothing off the field was important.

Yet within a few short months, Toby had fallen in love with a beautiful little blonde who had scarcely even bothered to attend a game during the season. Football just didn't interest her much, her tastes ran more to poetry and art. "I can't believe you're writing a whole book about it," she told me honestly. And my son—who had spent fourteen weeks consumed with the sport—just beamed at her. The football aura, I noted, had begun to fade . . . there were, after all, other things in life.

Each player handled reentry in his own way. For some, there was an increase in the use of adolescent opiates—drinking, pot smoking. Seniors, especially, were susceptible—it was considered almost an obligation to run at least a little amok in senior year. Parties escalated sharply. "For a while there, weekends became a blur," admitted one player. Finally he was concerned enough to discuss his pot intake with another player, who made a wise suggestion: Why not just try to do without it for one weekend? Because he trusted his teammate, he did—and found that it worked. He didn't need it to have fun after all.

Others were less wise, and an occasional parent rebelled. In the spring, one player's mother, returning home from a brief trip to a horribly disheveled house that had obviously been partied in, retaliated that evening at the family's traditional candlelit Mother's Day dinner. Seizing her son's card, she stuck it into the candle flame, then threw a suitcase at him and ordered him out of the house. The banishment was a brief one, lasting only a few hours, but it left him noticeably chastened—and most of the rest of us mothers struck with considerable admiration when we heard the tale.

More than one boy found himself in a minor skirmish with school authorities at some point over the following months, some for the first time in their lives; a handful received their first suspensions. They were more likely to run their mouths, to challenge others in and out of the classroom, to push matters to a confrontation. To act, quite simply, as if they had an attitude.

But how could they not? This was what they had worked fiercely for months to attain; what their coaches had pleaded, urged, begged, demanded they develop. Now suddenly, back at school, back in the world, it was being seen as an attitude *problem,* no longer something to be encouraged. Even mature adults have trouble facing 180-degree turns; for the boys, it was terribly confusing. With time the problem would recede, as the boys became reaccustomed to the strictures of high school once again. But not for a while, and perhaps never completely.

And it was not entirely true, in fact, that attitude had no place in the ordinary world. Late in the year, B-CC faced an odd, disturbing threat: a man had been wandering around the area, it was reported, knocking down women on the street, hitting them over the head, then running off. Principal Nancy Powell made an announcement one morning, warning everyone to be on the lookout.

Karen Lockard, the English teacher, went down to the main office soon afterward. To her surprise, a group of boys had gathered there, a large number of them football players. They had come to offer their protection, they said; they were ready to do whatever was needed.

"The attitude was, this man's after our women. We'll get him. It was like a vigilante group. They can't do that to *our* women." On that day, at least, no one did much complaining about attitude. The looks on the faces of women teachers and staffers said it all. Our heroes!

Football had been responsible in part for their reaction, as football was responsible for many things. To a greater or lesser extent, football had changed them all.

As it had changed us parents as well. A number of us, too, had problems adjusting ourselves to an off-season existence. Missing the excitement of games, missing, in fact, each other—for we too had shared something out there, up in those stands, screaming, groaning, clutching each other in emotion—we found ourselves gathering together often, wanting to spend time in each other's company. In a funny way, football had revived the adolescent in all of us—or perhaps just dissolved the fake armor of middle age to reveal the teenager still throbbing below. We rarely spent our time together in superficial chatter, either; often, in fact, our discussions bore an odd similarity to the late-night talk sessions of my college days, when words like love, death, existentialism pierced the night . . . talk bent on figuring out one's life. In some magical way, football had opened us up to each other; revealed our true faces. Because of it, we were able to connect in a way rare for people our age. New Year's Eve found us all together, at Judy Burgess's cozy home, laughing, talking, commiserating, exchanging stories about our lives. Why had we taken the routes we had taken? How had we arrived at this point?

The boys were pleased. "Mom, I always told you you'd really like Mrs. Stone," said Toby. And so he had, years before—but it took football to make us friends. The boys sensed they were somehow responsible for bringing this into our lives, that this too was a lingering legacy of the season. And they were right.

The season, with all its joys and discontents, had ended at last. Had it been worth it? Would they do it again if they could? Would they want their sons to play? The answers were unanimously positive. "I'm not going to push my kids into sports," said one boy (many players were adamant about never pushing a child). "But I will definitely ask them, 'Would you think about playing sports? Because it will really change the way you think about yourself.' "

Football, many boys felt, was an especially good way to get out some emotions, like anger. "When I was really angry, I'd use football as my little scapegoat," said one player. "Some things you get built up inside you can't release any other way. I don't like blowing steam off at people. My mom and dad would explain stuff and I'd say, I understand—but then I'd be carrying this around. But then football would come—just this object, this object you can totally destroy if you want to."

"It's cliché-ish, but mind and body . . . If I didn't have a sport, if it was just academics . . . you can become depressed," said Mike Mitchem. For him, too, football was a perfect venue for "venting my anger. You mess up on a test, you're ready to kill someone, go out on the football field."

"It gets out your aggression," said another. "And it feels real good. It shouldn't feel good, but it does, especially when you hurt someone. It should feel bad but it feels good. You got a lot of inside aggression you want to get out . . . but when football season is over, you can't anymore. You gotta control it."

"It gives you an identity, football, and I need that," said Geoff, with his usual frankness. "I'd be afraid to go to school and not play football.

"I was lucky. I got to experience B-CC football in such a way that only a handful of guys got to do. You don't have to be the best athlete to enjoy it. I feel sorry for these people who had the opportunity in front of them and didn't take it." For Geoff, win or lose, the season had been—as always—a joyful one. Though nothing had topped Whitman. In a way, that had been the most memorable game of his life, he felt.

Regrets? Sure, they had a few.

"I was glad to see us come together as a team, but I was disappointed, too, because we didn't make that step up," said Dave. He'd hoped they would best last season's record. "I felt I'd kind of let my friends down, from last year. I had the responsibility of carrying on what they'd left off, at least get a five–five season, maybe one better."

"I guess when the season was over, I was kind of relieved," said Kong. "It was like a bad dream in a way. It had some good moments, but . . . you know how always the bad feelings stay with you longer than the good feelings."

Yet "people might say, why do you play, you always lose . . . but you don't really want to go to a team that always wins. You want to go where you hope to win and you're doing something about it. You help turn it around."

"It would've been great to win the whole season, but it was fun anyway," said Rick. "Whether we were playing a crowd of five thousand at home, or to two people standing in the rain at Wheaton—always fun.

"It's always been a part of my life, it's great fun, but . . . it's football. It's in the fall. After that, it's gone. There's so much more to life. You come out, it's like . . . well, season's over. It's a memory for me." Yet on the other hand, Rick fully intended to play at Georgetown next year. "I'm not ready to stop playing football at all."

And Geoff would be waiting in the wings at James Madison University, where unfortunately they were somewhat overloaded with wide receivers at the moment. His optimism, however, was untrammeled. The minute his time came, he would get the coveted gold ring—a free ride. This would mean that his talent, his prowess, would be directly responsible for saving his parents a great deal of money, which more than anything made him feel very good.

Brendan Reed, too, intended to play, at Western Maryland. Alex was using his football background to help him get into The Citadel (though once there, he would eventually assume a position as manager, not player—a position better suited to his leadership aspirations). James still had hopes of playing at nearby Montgomery College. But Dave, Billy, and Toby, along with most of the other seniors, were not planning to play in college. All three had received one or two tentative recruiting calls from coaches at nearby small colleges, which was flattering, but they were not really interested. It would not be the same, they knew. They felt they had been given a chance to play the game the way it should be played—for love.

"Every guy should play football," said Brendan Symes adamantly. "It's the all-American thing to do. You have to play." Once during a game he had looked up to the stands "and I saw a really old guy, with an old varsity jacket on. I was like, that's gonna be me one day. Coming back to see a game. I can just see myself. I know I'll bring my kids."

"A lot of people I know, they're like, why do you play, man?" said John Han. "It's crazy, so crazy. You bang heads—I remember going home every day, taking aspirin.

"I said, shoot . . . you can't beat the feeling. Walking out at night under the lights, hundreds of people in the stands. Like a natural high." He shook his head, his dark eyes bright. "It was glorious. Glorious."

Late in the year, Karen Lockard found herself faced with the grim prospect of teaching a poetry segment to a senior class overloaded with football players—Toby, Rick, Kong, Brendan Symes, Shane, Dimarlo. Her heart sank. "I thought, I'm never going to be able to sell this to these guys. Even though I knew they liked me. I was really hesitant." Many of them had already declared themselves completely repelled by the genre. ("I hate all poetry," was the way Toby had put it to me some months back. None of my attempts to change his mind, grabbing books feverishly off the shelves, sticking various verses under his chin, had made the slightest dent.)

Still, she was willing to give it her best shot, and after a determined search, managed to unearth a poem called "Adrenaline," which she hoped might appeal to them.

"It was a man reflecting on the news . . . three people who climbed Mount Everest and fell to their deaths . . . someone jumping without a parachute . . . all these examples of people taking it to the edge, for the rush, the thrill, and then losing.

"Then it flips back to where he's sitting in his garden, thinking about cutting the roses. The whole idea of, why go for that rush when it's easier to stay in your garden?"

The poem did more than appeal to the boys; it had an electrifying effect. Suddenly every one of them was sitting up, fully awake, intense, charged, clamoring to be heard. No one had to explain this to them; this was something they knew all about.

"They said . . . it's just like football, Mrs. Lockard. And there's nothing like it, nothing. You're out there on the line . . . you get hurt! It hurts! You hit so hard it hurts! But you don't care. There's nothing like that feeling.

"You're turned on, you're pumped. Those were the terms they kept using—we're pumped, Mrs. Lockard. We're high. There's nothing like it, it feels so good. And the afterward . . . the roller coaster, the emotional crash when you lose.

"They said, it's better than sex. And these guys had agreed sex was everything. They told me once, you gotta understand, we're pumping hormones, all we think about is sex.

"Football was the analogy . . . and they all agreed. It's so great, they said. They just went nuts."

After that, something changed in their attitude toward poetry, too; by the time they were required to start writing their own, they were not only enthusiastic, they were openly competitive. "Poetry wars," said Karen Lockard. "Whose was better? Who got to read theirs first?

"It was a real eye-opener. They really got into it." They weren't just jocks, any of them, she realized. There were other sides to them, and they were getting to the point where they could let those sides out—use their minds, reason, even write poetry.

Obviously they were growing up. She had known the seniors four years. It struck her suddenly they would be gone very soon. She would miss them. Every class had its own personality, but these guys . . . there was something special about them.

"When I first got to B-CC, it was like drug dealers were the coolest people . . . those kind of troublemaker guys," said Billy.

"They were the most well known, I guess the most popular people. Athletes weren't.

"What our class did, black and white, was show how cool it was to actually not be into that scene. The coolest black and white people in our school are the ones that play sports. The cool thing became playing sports. I can't believe I got that far in football. That's what I always wanted to be. Coach White just brought out the best in me."

The season had not been spectacular, by any standard. Yet Billy felt a deep satisfaction, looking back at it. The way they had worked together to get over that hump, early on—and had been successful. And he had played a part in that; he knew it, and it made him proud.

"Football makes you the man. Look at the Super Bowl, look at our society . . . it makes you respect football players when you're young. And when you finally start to live that dream"— his eyes were far away, focused on some interior landscape—"it can go to your head. It really can."

Mitch and Bob had their own difficulties facing the end of the season.

"It was hard for me to let the kids go," Mitch admitted. "I got very upset at the banquet. My girlfriend said, what's wrong? Everyone was leaving.

"They're all good kids. At the banquet, Bobby and I said, that's what it's all about, it makes it all worthwhile, all the fatigue, the complaining, it all worked out." After the ceremony, Christo's mother told Mitch how much she hoped he'd be at B-CC coaching next year, for her son.

"I yelled at that kid! I demoralized that kid in front of everybody. There's no kid on the team I yelled at more, ridiculed more, screamed at more . . . and still."

He shook his head. B-CC kids were different from the guys he had grown up with, it had taken some adjustment to deal with them. "Football is just a small step in the evolution of their lives. A very small step. Whereas for a lot of guys at Springbrook, it's their last gasp. They don't have the connections. A lot of them will be blue-collar workers, this is their last moment of glory."

Yet there had been something about this team, the Barons, the kids, all those different types, that had affected him very strongly. "Black, white, all those barriers, all those stereotypes, it's all garbage. At the end of a game you'd see a Hungarian guy, a black guy, a Chinese guy and they were all crying—they care so much." Just like him. "I genuinely love all those kids."

Late in the spring, practically at the end of the year, Bob came by the school to see Pete. A number of the boys were hanging around the weight room, some of them working out, like Kong—he just couldn't break the habit, even if his football days were over—others goofing off. As Bob walked in, there was a stunned silence. Then everyone reacted at once, hooting, moaning, squeezing their eyes shut, waving him away with their arms, bellowing in mock agony.

"Ah yes, gentlemen," said Bob. "I can feel it—I can feel the love in the room, gentlemen, I can feel it coming out."

And the funny thing was, of course, he was right.

EPILOGUE

Months later, Mitch and I sat at a deli. I sipped iced tea; he ate a turkey sandwich. Calmly we discussed the season. Between bites, Mitch ruminated about his coaching philosophy—the necessity of turning boys into brutes, the need to unleash the buried animal that lies dormant in us all.

"Well?" I interrupted suddenly. "And did you? Were you able to do that?"

At once his eyes, those odd, blue-ice eyes, softened behind his glasses. "Didn't even come close," he said to me reassuringly, meeting my eyes directly. "These are nice kids."

And I relaxed. But in a sudden rush, their faces streamed past me, an internal gallery, each coming briefly into focus. I heard their voices, saw their earnest expressions:

- I owe him. He's taught me. I just want to kill somebody now, to go out there and hurt somebody, make them stay on the ground.
- I'm the kind of player . . . I really like to cause the other player pain.
- You don't want to hurt anyone . . . well, you do, really. You want to hurt somebody . . . it's true.
- It feels so great.

- Nothing better in the world.
- Nothing ever felt so real.

I heard, too, like a drumroll, the words of the young boy quoted in the paper after the Central Park wilding horror: "What happens is—your heart gets cold but you don't know it."

And my reassurance fled, leaving in its place a chill. I knew these were good kids, our kids, decent, loving, sensitive. And I knew, too, that football had done good things for them—swelled Toby's confidence in his ability to take on new challenges, to master new worlds, however difficult; shown Billy he has the power within himself to change situations; given James a lesson in accepting the unalterable with true dignity; helped Dave and Alex develop as leaders. Were these not wonderful experiences, of the kind we devoutly wish for all our sons? And more: football had given them, given all of us, joy—the kind of joy Geoff expressed so well. Opened us up in different ways, helped us discover new truths about ourselves. All of this was real, I knew, all of it valid.

Yet the chill remained, and I knew it, too, was real, was undeniable, and would not fade with time; a part of the picture, a part of the truth, a part of the legacy.

I drop by the practice field at B-CC in August to check out the start up of the 1989 season; stand for a time watching the boys go through their paces. "How do you feel?" "JUST GREAT!" Their faces are eager, straining, attentive; their movements crisp, synchronized. Mitch and Bob are gone this year, coaching a team at the far end of the Washington Beltway, in Alexandria, Virginia. It was hard to leave B-CC, but they were promised official positions and couldn't turn that down. Without his young assistants Pete seems happier and more sharply in control than ever, introducing plays, directing drills. Jimmy Loreto shows up with a red bandanna that could have come straight out of Rick's locker. "He looks like Rick, he walks like Rick," jibes another kid; Jimmy just throws him a white-toothed quarterback grin.

Amazingly the August weather is almost pleasant this time around, nothing like last year's humid hell. "We're gonna let you run down a hill on a cool day; pretty tough, eh?" yells Pete. His cracks are just as snappy. "Jose, you bring in that green card or we're gonna deport you!" "Tae Uk, don't you be eating at your parents' restaurant and then breathing that garlic on us."

By the end of the practice, almost despite myself, I am flushed, excited, pulled back into the maelstrom once again. I come home energized, manic, talking a mile a minute. "Erik Karlson got so much bigger, my God, he looks like Alex," I tell Toby, who is leaving for college in a few days. "Jimmy's arm looks real good. And Corey and Dirkey—they're so fast! Dirkey is really in shape this year. Toriano seems so much more mature, ready to work. They're looking great, all of them. Just great."

Toby looks at me, amused, almost paternal, already far away. "Well, of course, Mom," he says casually.

"This year, they're the men."